MONOPSONY IN LABOR MARKETS

The economics of monopsony power results in lower wages and other forms of compensation, as well as reduced employment. Wealth is transferred from workers to their employers. In addition, the employer's output is reduced, which leads to increased prices for consumers. *Monopsony in Labor Markets* demonstrates that elements of monopsony are pervasive and explores the available antitrust policy options. It presents the economic and empirical foundations for antitrust concerns and sets out the relevant antitrust policy. Building on this foundation, it examines collusion on compensation, collusive no-poaching agreements, and the inclusion of noncompete agreements in employment contracts. It also addresses the influence of labor unions, labor's antitrust exemption, which permits the exercise of countervailing power, and the consequences of mergers to monopsony. Offering a thorough explanation of antitrust policy, this book identifies the basic economic problems with monopsony in labor markets and explains the remedies currently available.

Brianna L. Alderman is a Theodore H. Ashford Fellow and a Ph.D. student in the Department of Economics at Harvard University. She holds bachelor's degrees in economics, mathematics, and statistics from the University of Florida. Her current field interests include industrial organization, labor economics, and antitrust economics.

Roger D. Blair is a professor of economics at the University of Florida. His research and teaching centers around antitrust economics. He has coauthored *Monopsony in Law and Economics*, *Antitrust Policy in Health Care Markets*, *Antitrust Economics*, and *The Economics of Franchising*. He has published over 200 articles in economics journals and law reviews.

T0371545

Monopsony in Labor Markets

Theory, Evidence, and Public Policy

BRIANNA L. ALDERMAN

Harvard University

ROGER D. BLAIR

University of Florida

Shaftesbury Road, Cambridge CB2 8EA, United Kingdom

One Liberty Plaza, 20th Floor, New York, NY 10006, USA

477 Williamstown Road, Port Melbourne, VIC 3207, Australia

314–321, 3rd Floor, Plot 3, Splendor Forum, Jasola District Centre,
New Delhi – 110025, India

103 Penang Road, #05–06/07, Visioncrest Commercial, Singapore 238467

Cambridge University Press is part of Cambridge University Press & Assessment,
a department of the University of Cambridge.

We share the University's mission to contribute to society through the pursuit of
education, learning and research at the highest international levels of excellence.

www.cambridge.org
Information on this title: www.cambridge.org/9781009465229

DOI: 10.1017/9781009465212

First published 2024

A catalogue record for this publication is available from the British Library

*A Cataloging-in-Publication data record for this book is available from the
Library of Congress*

ISBN 978-1-009-46522-9 Hardback
ISBN 978-1-009-46525-0 Paperback

Cambridge University Press & Assessment has no responsibility for the persistence
or accuracy of URLs for external or third-party internet websites referred to in this
publication and does not guarantee that any content on such websites is, or will
remain, accurate or appropriate.

*To my coauthor, for providing me with the courage
and countless opportunities to follow my dreams.*

BRIANNA L. ALDERMAN

*In memory of my parents, Duncan and Eleanor,
who would have been proud of their little boy.*

ROGER D. BLAIR

Contents

Figures

Tables

Preface

British economists A. C. Pigou, J. R. Hicks, and Joan Robinson recognized that powerful employers could underpay their employees by paying wages that were below labor's contribution to the employer's profit. Robinson termed this gap between labor's value of the marginal product and the wage paid *monopsonistic exploitation*. For decades, monopsony in the labor market was treated as a theoretical curiosity that lacked much – if any – empirical relevance. Recently, however, imperfect competition in the labor market has attracted much-needed attention. Theoretical developments and mounting empirical evidence have resulted in policy concerns by the White House and in Congress.

Much of this interest can be traced to wage stagnation, reduction in labor's share of gross national product, and abusive practices such as collusion on compensation, no-poaching agreements, and noncompete agreements in employment contracts. Policy proposals and antitrust enforcement efforts are ongoing on a continuing basis. The result is that some of what follows may become outdated. But this is the nature of research in dynamic areas. We are confident that the basic principles we have presented will stand the test of time. You, the reader, will have to be the judge.

In this book, we begin with the economic theory of monopsony. We follow the theory with a survey of the empirical evidence. We also provide policy analysis involving antitrust enforcement and some labor law. In the chapters that follow, we address the law and economics of wage-fixing agreements, no-poaching agreements, noncompete terms in labor contracts, unions and collective bargaining, mergers that affect labor markets, and wage discrimination.

Acknowledgments

We owe much to many people and several programs. For past collaboration, we must thank the following scholars: Tirza Angerhofer, Kelsey Clemmons, Christine Durrance, Jeffrey Harrison, Jessica Haynes, John Lopatka, Richard Romano, Perihan Saygin, and Wenche Wang. All these scholars have contributed to our understanding of monopsony and its influence in the labor market.

We have received incredibly generous advice from Richard Romano, Paul Oyer, Lawrence Khan, Herbert Hovenkamp, and David Sappington.

It is simply impossible to overstate the importance of the help provided to us by Professor Sara Bensley. Her assistance with legal research was always delivered with enthusiasm and good cheer. Thanks, Sara.

We also thank our friends Ms. Savannah James and Ms. Isabella Acosta for helping us with manuscript preparation and cover design, respectively.

Our work on this project has received generous financial support from Dr. Patricia Pacey, the Robert F. Lanzillotti Public Policy Research Center, the University of Florida McNair Scholars Program, the University of Florida Social and Behavioral Sciences Graduate School Ph.D. Preparatory Program, and the Department of Economics at the University of Florida.

Acknowledgments

1

Monopsony in the Labor Market

1.1 Introduction

Monopsony is the label that Joan Robinson attached to a market in which a single employer faces a competitively structured supply of labor.[1] If that supply function is positively sloped, the monopsonist can depress the wage that it pays below the competitive level by reducing the quantity of labor that it employs.[2]

Intuition suggests that reduced wages will lead to lower cost and lower output prices that will benefit consumers, but our intuition fails us in this instance. Profit maximization by the monopsonist leads to undesirable economic consequences: lower wages and salaries, reduced employment, and social welfare losses. Moreover, there are no consumer benefits. In fact, the monopsonist's reduced employment leads to a reduction in output, which will increase, rather than decrease, output prices. In *The Wealth of Nations*, Adam Smith observed that:

What are the common wages of labor, depends everywhere upon the contract usually made between [employers and employees], whose interests are by no means the same. The workmen desire to get as much, the masters to give as little as possible. The former are disposed to combine in order to raise, the latter in order to lower the wages of labor. It is not, however, difficult to foresee which of the two parties must, upon all ordinary occasions, have the advantage in the dispute, and force the other into a compliance with their terms. The masters, being fewer in number, can combine much more easily…. Masters are always and everywhere in a sort of tacit, but constant and uniform, combination, not to raise the wages of labor above their actual rate.[3]

---

[1] Joan Robinson, *The Economics of Imperfect Competition* (1933) at 293, 295.
[2] In Chapter 2, we spell out the technical details of monopsony.
[3] Adam Smith, *The Wealth of Nations* (1776).

1

As with many things, Smith was very perceptive. Over time, employers grew along with their power in the labor market.

One hundred years later, Senator John Sherman pointed out that labor markets needed antitrust protection, arguing that a trust "commands the price of labor ... for in its field it allows no competitors."[4] For some reason, these early insights, along with the work of A. C. Piguo,[5] J. R. Hicks,[6] and Joan Robinson,[7] did not gain much traction. Recently, however, economists and policymakers have recognized the ill effects of monopsony and have offered some actions aimed at mitigating – if not eliminating – the monopsony problem.[8]

In our view, vigorous enforcement – both public and private – of the antitrust laws can play a large role in reducing the ill effects of monopsony power in the labor market.[9]

1.2 Pervasiveness of Monopsony in the Labor Market

Historically, economists believed that labor markets were perfect, that is, that labor supply functions were perfectly elastic. All employers – large and small – could hire as much or as little as they chose without any impact on the wage rate. British economists Piguo and Hicks recognized the possibility of imperfect labor markets but did not appear to believe that this had much empirical relevance.[10]

Robinson,[11] however, provided a fairly complete theoretical foundation for the economic analysis of imperfect labor markets. She observed that a single employer of labor services could control the wage paid by adjusting the quantity employed. She coined the term *monopsony* as a label for the large employer facing a positively sloped labor supply function.

Despite those early efforts by prominent economists, not much progress was made until the late twentieth century, when economists began to

---

[4] Congressional Record 2457 (1890).
[5] A. C. Piguo, *The Economics of Welfare* (1924) at 512.
[6] J. R. Hicks, *The Theory of Wages* (1932) at 82.
[7] Robinson, *Economics of Imperfect Competition* at 293, 295.
[8] For example, Senator Amy Klobuchar (D. MN) has proposed antitrust challenges to mergers that enhance monopsony power.
[9] Randy Stutz, *The Evolving Antitrust Treatment of Labor-Market Restraints: From Theory to Practice* (2018) makes a convincing argument that antitrust policy should be used to protect labor from anticompetitive mergers and business conduct that unreasonably restricts employment and compensation.
[10] Piguo, *Economics of Welfare* at 512; Hicks, *Theory of Wages* at 82.
[11] Robinson, *Economics of Imperfect Competition* at 293, 295.

discover evidence that labor markets were far from perfect. Labor economists found widespread empirical evidence that labor supply functions were positively sloped and the exercise of some degree of monopsony power was pervasive.

In the early 1990s, Card and Krueger examined the effects of minimum wage laws on local fast-food labor markets.[12] Under competitive conditions, it was expected that these laws would lead to a reduction in employment as the theory would have suggested. To the surprise of many, the implementation of these minimum wage laws did not lead to any statistically significant evidence of job loss in the local market for fast-food workers. Card and Kreuger attributed this to monopsony power in the labor market.

This finding sparked a newfound interest in labor economists as they tried to determine the prevalence of monopsony power in the labor market. In his book *Monopsony in Motion*, Alan Manning estimated the pervasiveness of monopsony power in the U.S. labor market, finding an elasticity of labor supply equal to 1.38.[13] This fell far below infinity, which is what would be expected if the labor market were actually perfectly competitive. While Manning's estimate was not the first attempt at estimating the elasticity of supply in a labor market, his work provided the foundation for a variety of empirical studies attempting to estimate the elasticity of labor supply.[14]

Since Manning's work, there have been many examinations of monopsony power in the labor market. Some economists have tried to identify the sources of monopsony power. The literature has shown that sources of monopsony power can be attributed to a variety of factors, but these factors generally fall into one of three categories: (1) market concentration, (2) job differentiation, and (3) search frictions.

Other economists and legal scholars alike have focused on the policy implications of monopsony power in labor markets. For example, Alderman, Blair, and Saygin examined the effects of outlawing wage discrimination in monopsonistic labor markets with two equally productive groups of workers.[15] Angerhofer and Blair analyzed collusion among

---

[12] See David Card and Alan B. Krueger, Minimum Wages and Employment: A Case Study of the Fast Food Industry in New Jersey and Pennsylvania, 84 *American Economic Review* 772 (1994), and David Card and Alan B. Krueger, *A Reanalysis of the Effect of the New Jersey Minimum Wage Increase on the Fast-Food Industry with Representative Payroll Data*, unpublished (1998).

[13] Alan Manning, *Monopsony in Motion: Imperfect Competition in Labor Markets* (2003).

[14] For a more in-depth survey of empirical estimates of labor supply elasticities, see Chapter 3.

[15] Brianna L. Alderman, Roger D. Blair, and Perihan Saygin, Monopsony, Wage Discrimination, and Public Policy, 61 *Economic Inquiry* 572 (2023).

employers in the labor market and identified the intended consequences of lower compensation and improved profit.[16] They also identified some unintended consequences – lower prices for complementary inputs and higher output prices. Meanwhile, Naidu, Posner, and Weyl provided an overview of multiple issues affected by the presence of monopsony power, including minimum wage, mergers, and other antitrust policies.[17]

The study of monopsony and monopsony power in labor markets has led to a variety of survey pieces, including those done by Card,[18] and by Manning.[19] These surveys highlight the breadth and depth of the literature on monopsony in the labor market that has been written up to this point. Others have dedicated special issues to examining monopsony in the labor market.[20]

1.3 Monopsonistic Restraints in Labor Markets

The pervasive presence of monopsony power in labor markets has been exercised in several ways. In addition, there are practices that create monopsony power. We briefly describe these restraints and practices here.

1.3.1 Wage Fixing

Wage fixing is precisely what concerned Adam Smith nearly 250 years ago. A wage fixing cartel combines the employment needs of the firms in the local labor market and acts like a pure monopsonist. Wages, other forms of compensation, hours, and working conditions are set at monopsonistic levels rather than competitive levels.

The result is a decrease in the number of employees and a reduction in the compensation of those employees who are hired. Employee surplus falls below the competitive level. Employer profits are enhanced at the expense of the employees as employee surplus is converted to employer surplus.

---

[16] Tirza J. Angerhofer and Roger D. Blair, Collusion in the Labor Market: Intended and Unintended Consequences, *Competition Policy International, Antitrust Chronicle* (June 2020).

[17] Suresh Naidu, Eric A. Posner, and Glen Weyl, Antitrust Remedies for Labor Market Power, 132 *Harvard Law Review* 536 (2018).

[18] David Card, Who Set Your Wage?, 112 *American Economic Review* 1075 (2022).

[19] Alan Manning, Monopsony in Labor Markets: A Review, 74 *ILR Review* 3 (2021).

[20] For an example, in a recent special issue of the *Journal of Human Resources* (Volume 57, Supplement 2022), the focus was on monopsony in the labor market. For an overview, see Orley Ashenfelter, David Card, Henry Farber, and Michael R. Ransom, Monopsony in the Labor Market: New Empirical Results and New Public Policies, 57 *Journal of Human Resources* S1 (2022).

Social welfare is impaired as well owing to a misallocation of resources. At the cartel's optimal employment level, the incremental value of the output produced by the last unit of labor exceeds the worker's reservation wage. From society's perspective, too few workers are hired.[21]

1.3.2 No-Poaching Agreements

No-poaching agreements reduce competition in the labor market. While the specific terms of such agreements vary, the essence of no-poaching agreements is simple. Firm A agrees with Firm B to refrain from hiring Firm B's employees. Firm B reciprocates by making the same commitment to Firm A. The result is a reduction in the demand for the labor services of those workers employed by Firms A and B. The economic results are reduced compensation and fewer job opportunities for employees.[22]

1.3.3 Noncompete Agreements

In most instances, when an employee is hired, they fill out and sign several forms. At this time, the employee often signs a noncompete agreement (NCA). When an employee leaves their current job, they cannot work for a rival employer for some period of time. Typical time frames are as short as six months and as long as two years. The economic results of NCAs are ambiguous. For the worker, their job mobility is sharply curtailed. Consequently, they cannot seek better paying jobs with better opportunities. For the employers, NCAs protect their investment in developing human capital. In addition, they protect trade secrets. Currently, there are efforts to ban or severely limit the use of NCAs in employment contracts.[23]

1.4 Prevalence of Employer Collusion

There are many examples of employers colluding in the labor market. In some instances, the employers agree among themselves on wages, salaries, and other forms of compensation. In other instances, the employers agree not to poach one another's employees. The following examples provide some substance for our concerns regarding collusion.

---

[21] The undesirable economic consequences of monopsony are developed in Chapter 2. Wage fixing cartels are analyzed in Chapter 6.
[22] No-poaching agreements are examined in some detail in Chapter 7.
[23] NCAs receive close scrutiny in Chapter 8.

1.4.1 Collusion on Compensation

The Department of Justice (DOJ) filed a suit against Activision Blizzard for its imposition of a luxury tax on esports teams who pay a total team payroll that exceeds Activision's prescribed maximum.[24] There was a one dollar tax for every dollar that the total team compensation exceeded the maximum, that is, a 100 percent tax. Activision had argued that the tax was imposed to ensure competitive balance in the league, which allegedly increases fan interest.[25]

Only teams with the very best players are apt to earn salaries that invoke the luxury tax. Consequently, this tax will then depress the compensation that the best players will receive. For example, suppose that the so-called Competitive Balance Tax is triggered when a team's total payroll exceeds $1 million. Now assume a team is currently earning $900,000 but, given their talent, the market value of the team's players is $1.3 million. Paying the team their market value would trigger the luxury tax, and the resulting cost to the owner would be $1.6 million. Since the cost to the team's owner exceeds the value of the team, the owner will not pay the players their total market value. As a result, the team will be paid $400,000 less than they are worth.[26]

In another recent example, we can turn to the National Collegiate Athletic Association (NCAA) ban on academic achievement awards. For many years, the NCAA defined a "full ride," which they called a "grant-in-aid," as room, board, tuition, books, and related fees. Since this sum turns out to be quite a bit below the full cost of attendance, the NCAA responded to an antitrust suit by increasing the maximum compensation

[24] *U.S.* v. *Activision Blizzard, Inc.*, No. 1:23-cv-00895 (D.D.C. Apr. 3, 2023). See www.bloomberglaw.com/bloomberglawnews/exp/eyJpZCI6IjAwMDAwMTg3LTQ4NzktZGY0Yi1hYjk3LWNjN2JmZTliMDAwMCIsImN0eHQiOiJBVE5XIiwidXVpZCI6InJaM3lqZ3BGRmFFE0yK25paGJ3Nnc9PW9telAzMEJ0eWVVEaTdBBUEpHTGVOaGFFE9PSIsInRpbWUiOiIxNjgwNjA2ODk0ODAyYiIwic2lnIjoiZVFFFY2JPbDh4TkFSQkpTTTFNFFZlBwZFlBOWo4PSIsInYiOiIxIn0=?isAlert=false&item=headline&region=digest&source=newsletter&udvType=Alert and www.bloomberglaw.com/bloomberglawnews/exp/eyJpZCI6IjAwMDAwMTg3LTQ4NTAtZDU0Yi1hM2NmLWNmNWY1NDdmMDAwMCIsImN0eHQiOiJBVE5XIiwidXVpZCI6InQwVzRwRTluNngvYkQ4L2JJdHBPNGc9PTBDMTFyFySmVDU0g3YjFXSjR5NUdMVVE9PSIsInRpbWUiOiIxNjgwNTQ2NjkwMTMxIiwic2lnIjoiTGhRSSklSWEZoUzhlMkVkVkcVBrVW05eDNPRVVlFPSIsInYiOiIxIn0=?isAlert=false&item=headline&region=digest&source=breaking-news&udvType=Alert.
[25] Activision claimed that the collected taxes were redistributed to teams that did not exceed the maximum compensation level.
[26] This case has since been settled. Activision has discontinued its Competitive Balance Tax at the DOJ's urging.

that an athlete can receive to the full cost of attendance. But the NCAA did not permit academic achievement awards for athletes.

There are, however, many athletes who are on the Dean's List and deserve any academic achievement award for which they are qualified. For whatever reason, the NCAA did not permit the athletes that they should have been most proud of to receive such awards. Following the *Alston* decision by the Supreme Court,[27] the NCAA began permitting such awards up to $5,980. The NCAA and the major conferences are currently (2023) being sued in a class action antitrust suit on behalf of athletes who did not receive academic achievement awards despite meeting the qualifications for such awards.[28]

1.4.2 No-Poaching Agreements

No-poaching agreements became "breaking news" with two important antitrust suits filed by the DOJ: *Adobe Systems*,[29] and *Lucasfilm*.[30] In *Adobe Systems*, the major employers of hardware and software engineers – Adobe Systems, Apple, Google, Intel, Intuit, and Pixar – agreed not to solicit one another's employees. For example, if Intel spotted a talented engineer currently employed by, say, Apple, the agreement precluded Intel from cold calling that engineer in an effort to poach that person. This agreement was taken seriously. In one instance, a human resources person at Google was dismissed for inadvertently cold-calling an Apple employee.

In *Lucasfilm*, there was an agreement among movie studios that similarly precluded competition in the market for digital animators.

In both cases, the government obtained consent decrees that banned the use of no-poaching agreements in the future. But that was not the end of the defendant's woes. Private damage suits were filed on behalf of the employees.[31] Those two cases settled for a combined total of half a billion dollars.

In spite of clear warnings that no-poaching agreements may be the target of antitrust prosecution, they appear to be irresistible. The Attorney

---

[27] *National Collegiate Athletic Association* v. *Alston*, 594 U.S. ___ (2021).
[28] *Hubbard* v. *National Collegiate Athletic Association*, No. 4:23-cv-01593 (N.D. Cal. Apr. 4, 2023).
[29] *U.S.* v. *Adobe Systems, Inc.*, No. 1:10-cv-01629 (D.D.C. Sept. 24, 2010).
[30] *U.S.* v. *Lucasfilm Ltd.*, Case No. 1:10-cv-02220-RBW (D.D.C. Dec. 21, 2010).
[31] *In re: High-Tech Employee Antitrust Litigation*, Case No. 5:11-cv-02509-LHK (N.D. Cal. May 4, 2011) and *In re: Animation Workers Antitrust Litigation*, No. District of California, Case No. 14-cv-04062-LHK (123 F.Supp.3d 1175 (2015)).

General for the State of New York investigated no-poaching agreements among title insurers.[32] Fidelity National Financial Inc., the largest title insurer in the United States, agreed to pay $3.5 million to settle with the State of New York. There was verbal and written evidence of agreements to not solicit, recruit, or hire employees of rival companies.

1.5 Policy Proposals

As concern for the plight of workers has grown in the past decade, proposals for change have emerged from Congress, the White House, the DOJ, and the Federal Trade Commission (FTC). Although many of the proposals have not been implemented, it is clear that their focus has been on protecting workers from the exercise of monopsony power.

1.5.1 Congressional Proposals

There have been numerous proposals aimed at monopsony. Senator Amy Klobuchar (D. MN) suggested that Section 7 of the Clayton Act, which prohibits mergers that may be anticompetitive, be amended to remove any doubt that it applies to threats of monopsony. In some instances, a merger may easily pass muster because the firms compete in a national market for the sale of their output but have monopsony power in the local labor market. Although the amendment was not adopted, threats of enhanced monopsony power have been raised in two recent merger challenges.[33]

When the proposed merger of the second and third largest health insurers, Anthem and Cigna, respectively, was challenged, one of the counts dealt with monopsony.[34] In particular, the competitive concern was that the merged entity would be able to depress reimbursement rates for hospitals and physicians. Since the Court ruled in favor of the government on other grounds, it did not reach the monopsony issue.

When Penguin Random House, the largest book publisher in the relevant market, attempted to merge with Simon & Schuster, the third largest

---

[32] See www.bloomberglaw.com/bloomberglawnews/exp/eyJpZCI6IjAwMDAwMTg3LTJkYz UtZGQ0OC1hZDk3LWJkZDdkNjVjMDAwMyIsImN0eHQiOiJBVE5XIiwidXVpcZCI6 Ik9oaVJEVHl0QnRRYZU85a0RmZVFJeXc9PW16enVEcEslbUU0akEzbHlUdWNmN 2c9PSIsInRpbWUiOiIxNjgwMTc1MDA5OTIwIiwic2lnIjoia0tpcQkNoVzJLbmwlblglb DlFRng2WUsvUEVzPSIsInYiOiIxIn0=?isAlert=false&item=read-text&region=digest& source=newsletter&udvType=Alert.

[33] Mergers that create monopsony concerns are addressed in Chapter 10.

[34] *U.S.* v. *Anthem, Inc., and Cigna Corporation*, No. 1:16-cv-01493 (D.D.C. July 21, 2016).

book publisher, the proposed merger was blocked.[35] The government's challenge was posed solely on issues of monopsony related to advances to authors. In this case, the Court ruled in favor of the government.[36]

Senators Elizabeth Warren (D. MA) and Cory Booker (D. NJ) have tried to outlaw no-poaching agreements in the bill called the End Employer Collusion Act.[37] Booker went as far as to say:

> It's critically important that we ban these inequitable and anti-competitive agreements that leave workers without an opportunity to translate their value and skills into higher pay.

1.5.2 Policy Recommendations by the Council of Economic Advisers

In today's labor markets that are marred by anticompetitive conduct on the part of employers and labor market frictions, the Council of Economic Advisers (CEA) advocated a multipronged effort to improve wages and other forms of compensation.[38] After reviewing the empirical evidence and examining trends, the report contained several policy proposals.

First, the CEA urged vigorous antitrust enforcement. Stamping out collusion among employees can help to enhance competition. But the CEA also recognized that antitrust enforcement cannot resolve all the problems, so they recommended additional policy changes. Policies that facilitate job search, increase job options, and directly affect the wage-setting power of employers were mentioned specifically.[39]

The CEA recommended that the use of noncompete clauses in employment contracts be limited. More specifically, the CEA advocated the elimination of NCAs in employee contracts when they serve only to limit worker mobility and depress compensation below the level that would exist in the absence of a noncompete clause. The CEA also recommended that much future research be conducted on the economic consequences of noncompetes.

---

[35] *U.S. v. Bertelsmann SE & CO. KGAA*, No. 1:21-cv-02886 (D.D.C. Dec. 31, 2022).
[36] Penguin Random House decided not to appeal the Court's decision and abandoned the merger.
[37] This is not the first time Senator Booker has introduced legislation outlawing no-poaching agreements. In 2018, he proposed a bill that would give workers the ability to sue employers who threatened the use of no-poaching agreements.
[38] The CEA is not the only committee to comment on competition in the labor market. The anticompetitive consequences of monopsony in the labor market were identified by the Organisation for Economic Co-operation and Development. See *Executive Summary of the Roundtable on Competition Issues in Labour Markets* (June 5, 2019).
[39] The antitrust law and economics of NCAs are addressed in Chapter 8.

In spite of the fact that we live in the information age, the CEA expressed concern about the availability of information to workers regarding employment opportunities. It also endorsed transparency on wages and other forms of compensation. Increasing the flow of such information will permit workers to seek better job opportunities.

Finally, the CEA recommended that unnecessary licensing requirements be eliminated. Occupational licensing has been severely criticized by Nobel Laureate Milton Friedman. It restricts entry into those occupations where licenses are required. As a result, it limits competition, to the detriment of unlicensed workers and consumers, who will pay higher prices.

1.5.3 Enforcement Agencies

In their *Guidance,* the DOJ and FTC make it clear that collusion on any terms of employment will not be tolerated. They express a commitment to filing criminal suits, which expose individuals to fines of up to $1 million and prison sentences of up to ten years. Although these are maximum sanctions and are rarely, if ever, imposed, they should give pause to a business executive who would prefer to avoid the label of "convicted felon."

The Antitrust Division of the DOJ and the FTC encountered anticompetitive conduct in various labor markets. Concerned that human resources professionals may be engaged in unlawful conduct without being aware of the antitrust significance of their actions, the agencies issued their *Antitrust Guidance for Human Resource Professionals.*[40]

The document sets out the enforcement policies of the DOJ and the FTC regarding anticompetitive conduct in the labor market.[41] Their central message is crystal clear: Do not agree with rival employers to refrain from or limit competition for employees. Unilateral decisions to limit competitive involvement in the labor market are ordinarily legal, but agreements to do so are not. The *Guidance* warns that naked agreements to limit competition may result in criminal prosecution of both the firms and the individuals involved.[42]

The *Guidance* specifically addresses (1) agreements to fix wages, all forms of compensation, and working conditions, (2) agreements not to

---

[40] See www.justice.gov/atr/file/903511/download.

[41] It is not only in the United States that the anticompetitive consequences of monopsony have been recognized. In Kenya and South Africa, antitrust rules regarding the exercise of buyer power have been issued.

[42] An agreement is deemed to be "naked" if it is not part of a legitimate cooperative venture.

solicit or hire employees of a rival employer, that is, no-poaching agreements, and (3) information exchanges that involve competitively sensitive information on wages, benefits, hiring plans, and the like. The *Guidance* also points out that an employer's decision to reduce cost is not a defense. While monopsonistic collusion on wages does, in fact, lower average costs and thereby improve the employer's profit, it raises marginal cost, which leads to reduced output and higher prices for consumers.[43]

Additionally, the FTC and the National Labor Relations Board have signed a memorandum of understanding that commits the agencies to cooperate in promoting the well-being of workers.[44] The focus is on (1) labor market concentration that limits compensation and working conditions, (2) one-sided contract terms such as noncompete clauses, and (3) the classification of gig workers that prevents collective action. By joining forces, the agencies expect to promote the interests of labor.

1.6 A Preview of What Is to Come

Our treatment of monopsony in the labor market proceeds in the following fashion. The exposition throughout these theoretical chapters relies on line graphs, numerical examples, and verbal explanation. Algebra and calculus will be confined to footnotes and/or appendices.

1.6.1 Economic Theory of Monopsony

Chapter 2: We begin with the basic economic theory of monopsony. In this chapter, we present the economic models of (1) pure monopsony, (2) the dominant employer, and (3) oligopsony. In these cases, we show that profit maximization results in ill effects for workers. These include reduced compensation, reduced employment, and the redistribution of wealth. We also show that social welfare is reduced below the level that society would have experienced in the absence of monopsony.

1.6.2 Empirical Evidence

Chapter 3: Here we provide an overview of the empirical results with ample references to the literature. There is a substantial body of research that establishes the pervasive presence of monopsony in labor markets. The root

---

[43] These economic results are developed in Chapter 2.
[44] See www.ftc.gov/system/files/ftc_gov/pdf/ftcnlrb%20mou%2071922.pdf.

cause of monopsony power lies in the fact that labor markets are imperfect. In other words, labor supply functions are positively sloped, which allows the dominant employers to depress compensation by reducing employment. Moreover, there are various frictions that reduce an employee's ability to respond to alternative employment opportunities. These include costs of job search, turnover, mobility barriers, noncompete contracts, no-poaching agreements, legislation, and increased concentration.

1.6.3 Antitrust Policy

Chapter 4: The exercise of monopsony in labor markets is limited to one degree or another by public policy. Employer conduct aimed at creating monopsony power is governed by the Sherman Act of 1890, which forbids collusion among employers as well as competitively unreasonable conduct by a single employer.

Chapter 4 discusses private suits, the prohibition of Section 1, and the sanctions for violations. Corporations are subject to fines, while individuals may be fined and/or imprisoned. Section 1 forbids collusive restraints of trade. In the past, there was some confusion regarding the applicability of Section 1 to labor markets. These days are gone. The DOJ and FTC have issued their *Antitrust Guidance for Human Resource Professionals*, in which the agencies make it crystal clear that they will pursue criminal convictions for collusion in labor markets. In addition to public sanctions, Section 4 of the Clayton Act provides a private right of action for antitrust victims.

Chapter 5: In this chapter, we point out that private damage suits are not available to all victims of monopsonistic exploitation. In addition to the underpaid employees who have standing to sue, there are five groups that do not have standing: indirect suppliers, fringe suppliers, suppliers that are priced out of the market, suppliers of complementary inputs, and consumers of the final goods.

1.6.4 Public Policy in Action

Chapter 6: Here we present an economic model of employer collusion that explores the economic consequences of concerted efforts to depress wages and other forms of compensation. This chapter spells out the organizational challenges of building and implementing an employer cartel. It also examines the incentives to cheat on the cartel agreement. Our central focus is on the harm done to employees as well as the impact on social welfare.

In this chapter, we review an assortment of antitrust cases that alleged collusion on wages paid and other terms of employment. These examples include hospital nurses, temporary duty nurses, college athletes, and highly talented college students. Finally, we explore the unintended consequences of collusion in the labor market – higher prices for consumers.

Chapter 7: This deals with agreements among rivals not to hire one another's employees ("no-poaching" agreements). These have been found in a number of labor markets on numerous occasions. Such agreements, of course, depress the demand for these employees and thereby put a lid on compensation. In this chapter, we review some prominent cases involving (1) hardware and software engineers, (2) digital animators, (3) medical school faculty, (4) physical therapists, and (5) professional athletes.

For the most part, the suits filed by the DOJ have been resolved. Many of the private suits filed by the antitrust victims have been settled, but some are still pending. The chapter also explores the enforcement policies of the antitrust agencies that are provided in the *Antitrust Guidance for Human Resource Professionals*.

We provide an extended analysis of no-poaching agreements in professional sports. The four major sports leagues in North America – Major League Baseball (MLB), the National Basketball Association (NBA), the National Football League (NFL), and the National Hockey League (NHL) – all have antitampering provisions that apply to the athletes. The extent to which these provisions extend to coaches, front office personnel, and scouts varies in many ways and this is included in our coverage.

Chapter 8: Here, we focus on NCAs. These severely limit job mobility and reduce a worker's opportunities to exploit their human capital. Most NCAs preclude a worker from obtaining a position with a rival employer for six months to two years after separation. In addition, the former employee may not start their own business in the same industry. The economic result of these restrictions is to reduce labor supply elasticity, which enhances an employer's ability to depress employee compensation, other benefits, and working conditions.

Employers argue that they need NCAs for two primary reasons. First, upon separation, an employee could take the former employer's trade secrets to a rival employer. An NCA may solve this problem because many trade secrets, such as short-run production plans, are short-lived. Second, employers often invest in an employee's human capital with schooling or training. An NCA provides protection for such investments in human capital.

In Chapter 8, we examine the pros and cons of NCAs. We also examine the FTC's proposal to ban all NCAs completely.

Chapter 9: In this chapter, we turn our attention to labor unions and their role in providing countervailing power. Congress recognized the consequences of individual employees having to negotiate with large employers. For the most part, individual employees have no bargaining power and face all-or-nothing offers that reflect monopsony power. Consequently, Congress passed legislation that permits employees to unionize and thereby create a labor monopoly. The idea was to level the playing field so workers could not be abused. This chapter provides a brief review of the statutes and the scope of the labor exemption.

The formation of a union converts a monopsony into a bilateral monopoly. The economic effects of this are generally positive: Employment and output expand; thus, both employees and consumers are better off. We explain this analysis and illustrate it with references to professional sports. This chapter also explores the antitrust conundrum arising from bilateral monopoly.

Chapter 10: Mergers that involve issues of monopsony are addressed here. In some cases, a merger may be procompetitive or competitively neutral. In others, however, a merger may be anticompetitive and therefore should be barred. Horizontal mergers combine two (or more) firms that operate in the same output market. Since they employ similar workers, the merger may create monopsony power. Antitrust policy regarding horizontal mergers is provided by Section 7 of the Clayton Act and its judicial interpretation. Typically, the focus is on concentration in the output market, but there has been some recent recognition that a merger may have ill effects in the labor market. We examine this recent concern and provide some examples.

Chapter 11: In the final chapter, we summarize the antitrust law and economics of monopsony in the labor market. We provide some policy recommendations that are consistent with economic principles and empirical reality.

2

The Economics of Monopsony

2.1 Introduction

Monopsony is a market structure in which there is a single buyer of a well-specified good or service.[1] For decades, monopsony in the labor market was dismissed as a theoretical nicety without much – if any – empirical relevance. Recently, however, there has been a ground swell of concern due to wage stagnation, labor's shrinking share of GDP, and reports of collusion among employers.[2] Renewed interest in monopsony by academics, the antitrust agencies, and policy makers has been accompanied by legislative proposals to amend antitrust laws.[3] Complaints of monopsonistic abuse have been raised in the markets for hospital nurses, temporary duty nurses, physicians, hardware and software engineers, digital animators, and agricultural workers, among others.

To understand the source of the abuse and craft an economically sensible policy response, it is important to understand the economics of monopsony and monopsony power, that is, the power of the monopsonist to depress the wage it pays by curtailing employment. At first blush, one might suppose that lower labor costs enhance consumer welfare. But this is

---

[1] This chapter draws on Roger D. Blair and Jeffery L. Harrison, *Monopsony in Law and Economics* (2010); Roger D. Blair and Christine Piette Durrance, *The Economics of Monopsony in Issues in Competition Law and Policy*, W. Dale Collins, ed. (2008); and Roger D. Blair and Jessica Haynes, *Monopsony, Monopsony Power, and Antitrust Policy in Research Handbook on the Economics of Antitrust Law*, Einar Elhauge ed. (2012).

[2] There is a growing literature on monopsony power in labor markets. The next chapter provides a survey of this literature.

[3] Council of Economic Advisers, *Labor Market Monopsony: Trends, Consequences, and Policy Responses, Issue Brief* (2016). See also Alan B. Krueger and Eric A. Posner, *A Proposal for Protecting Low-Income Workers from Monopsony and Collusion*, The Hamilton Project (2018).

only true when lower labor costs flow from competition or productive efficiency – not when they result from monopsony. To avoid confused antitrust analysis, a clear understanding of monopsony is required. To this end,
this chapter will focus on an economic analysis of monopsony.

We begin with a discussion of pure monopsony, that is, the case of a single employer. This analysis provides the economic foundation for analyzing
other instances of disproportionate power in the labor market. In Section
2.3, we examine how monopsony in the input market influences marginal
and average cost in the output market. Section 2.4 explains all-or-nothing
offers in the labor market, and we then turn our attention to the dominant employer, which is a close cousin of pure monopsony in Section 2.5.
Oligopsony, which is a labor market with a few large employers, is the focus
of Section 2.6. In Section 2.7, we examine measures of monopsony power.
As an economic matter, our concern is with the effects on the wages paid,
the employment levels, the redistribution of wealth, and social welfare.

2.2 Basic Monopsony Model

If a firm is the only employer in a local labor market, it is a monopsonist
by definition. For example, if a hospital or a hospital system in a city is the
only employer of hospital nurses, it will be a monopsonist in that market.
Similarly, a coal mine in a company town may be the only employer in the
local labor market. To appreciate the economic consequences of monopsony, we begin with a competitive labor market and subsequently introduce monopsony.

2.2.1 Comparing Competition and Monopsony

All firms employ labor and other inputs to produce goods and services
which they sell, and thereby earn profit. A manager has a fiduciary responsibility to maximize the value of their firm. Since the firm is worth more the
higher its profit, a major responsibility of the manager is to make decisions
intended to maximize the firm's profits. These decisions include product
design and quality, system of distribution, number and location of production facilities, and employment decisions. When it comes to employment
decisions, the manager must do more than just arbitrarily pick the number
of employees since this decision is directly influenced by costs and benefits.

The demand for labor is determined by the contribution of labor to the
employer's profit, which depends on the price of the employer's output and
the increment in output that is attributed to labor services. This demand is

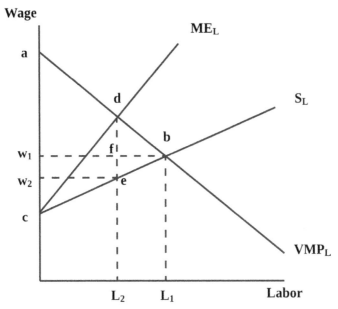

Figure 2.1 Profit maximization by a monopsonist

referred to as the value of the marginal product of labor, which is equal to the price of the firm's output times the increase in the units of output made possible by the increased employment of labor. We denote this demand as VMP_L in Figure 2.1. The supply of labor is the positively sloped function labeled S_L in Figure 2.1. The supply of labor reveals the reservation wage that must be paid to employ any given quantity of labor services.

In a competitive labor market, the employer will expand its employment of labor until the VMP_L is equal to the wage that must be paid.[4] This occurs at the intersection of the VMP_L and S_L. At that point, employer surplus, area abw_1 and employee surplus, area w_1bc, are maximized.[5] The sum of

---

[4] In other words, to maximize profits, the firm will expand the employment of labor until $P \cdot \frac{\partial Q}{\partial L} - w = 0$. The first term is the product of the output price (P) and the incremental increase in output flowing from increased employment, $\frac{\partial Q}{\partial L}$, which is the marginal product of labor (MP_L). That term is the value of the marginal product (VMP_L).

[5] At the point where the VMP_L equals S_L, the value of the last unit of labor services employed is just equal to the wage paid. For all other units of labor employed, the value of these services (VMP_L) exceeds the wage that is paid. The total amount of this surplus is employer surplus. Analogously, the last unit of labor employed receives a wage that is just equal to the reservation wage. All other units receive the market wage, which exceeds their reservation wage. This sum is employee surplus.

employer surplus and employee surplus is a measure of social welfare. In this labor market, no other combination of wage rate and employment will yield more total surplus than the w_1 and L_1 combination yields.

Things change if the labor market is monopsonistic. To maximize its profit, the monopsonist will expand its employment of labor such that the marginal (or incremental) value of the increased output is just equal to the marginal cost of expanding employment. In other words, the employer wants to hire the quantity of labor services where the value of the marginal product is equal to the marginal expenditure on labor (ME_L).[6]

The monopsonist will reduce employment to the point where the VMP_L is equal to the ME_L (which lies above S_L and is twice as steep).[7] The corresponding employment level is shown as L_2 in Figure 2.1 and the wage is w_2.

2.2.2 Economic Consequences of Monopsony

As we can see in Figure 2.1, the monopsonist depresses the wage that it pays by reducing its employment from L_1 to L_2. As a result, employee surplus falls from w_1bc to w_2ec. Employer surplus increases from abw_1 to $adew_2$. Employee surplus of w_1few_2 is redistributed from the employee to the employer. The triangular area dbe represents a reduction in social welfare due to the misallocation of resources resulting from monopsony. Because the monopsonist operates where the VMP_L equals the ME_L rather than where the VMP_L equals S_L, the employment level is allocatively inefficient. The social cost of employing another unit of labor is given by the height of the supply curve while the value to society of the added output that would be produced is given by the height of the demand for the input (i.e., the height of VMP_L). At L_2, the added social value of employing one more unit

---

[6] To get a sense of the relationship between the marginal expenditure and the wage, suppose that the supply of labor is $w = 10 + 0.2L$ where w is the wage and L is the number of hours of labor services. If the employer hires 50 hours of labor service, it will have to pay a wage of $w = 10 + 0.2(50) = \$20$. If the employer considers hiring an additional hour of labor services, they will have to pay a wage of $w = 10 + 0.2(51) = \$20.20$. That additional hour does not raise the total wage bill by only \$20.20 since the employer will have to pay \$20.20 for all hours of labor rather than just the one additional hour. Consequently, the wage bill will increase from $wL = (10 + 0.2(50))50 = \$1,000$ to $wL = (10 + 0.2(51))51 = \$1,030.20$. In other words, hiring one additional hour of labor will increase the total expenditure on labor by \$30.20, which is the ME_L.

[7] For example, if the supply of labor can be written as $w = 10 + 0.2L$, the total expenditure on labor would be $wL = 10L + 0.2L^2$ and the marginal expenditure would be $\frac{dw}{dL} = 10 + 0.4L$. Thus, ME_L an S_L have the same intercept $(w = 10)$ on the wage axis, but the slope of ME_L (0.4) is twice as steep as that of S_L (0.2).

exceeds the added social cost. From a *social* perspective, then, the employment of labor should expand beyond L_2, but it does not because L_2 maximizes the employer's profit.

2.3 Monopsony, Marginal Cost, and Average Cost

In Figure 2.1, we see that the competitive wage of labor is equal to w_1. The exercise of monopsony power reduces the wage paid from w_1 to w_2. In ordinary circumstances, one would think that reduced wages would be a good thing for everyone except the employees. After all, lower wages result in higher profits for employers. It would seem that at least part of the cost savings will be passed on to consumers in the form of lower output prices. As a result, it appears that the monopsonist makes more profit and consumers are better off. So why is there an economic objection to monopsony?

The rosy scenario we just described is wrong. It is based on a fundamental misunderstanding of the relationship between the exercise of monopsony power and the resulting cost functions. The truth is that monopsony leads to lower *average* cost for some ranges of output, which provides the profit incentive for monopsonistic behavior, but monopsony causes *marginal* cost to shift upward, which leads to reduced output and a consequent decrease in consumer surplus.[8] We believe that it is important to understand these effects if antitrust policy is to be sound.

2.3.1 Impact on Average Cost and Marginal Cost

It can be shown that the presence of monopsony power causes the employer's marginal cost curve to shift upward.[9] Whether the firm has market power in the output market or not, an upward shift in the firm's marginal cost curve leads to a reduction in its profit maximizing output. Accordingly, there is no improvement in consumer welfare. In fact, the opposite will be the case regardless of whether the employer has market power in its output market. In either event, the effect of a reduction in the employer's output is to increase price, reduce consumption, and thereby reduce social welfare.

In Figure 2.2, a firm that is a competitor in its output market and has no monopsony power in the labor market will be in equilibrium by producing

---

[8] Analogous results can be found in Roger D. Blair and Richard E. Romano, Collusive Monopsony in Theory and Practice: The NCAA, 42 *Antitrust Bulletin* 681 (1997).
[9] See Roger D. Blair and Christine Piette Durrance, *The Economics of Monopsony in Issues in Competition Law and Policy*, W. Dale Collins ed. (2008).

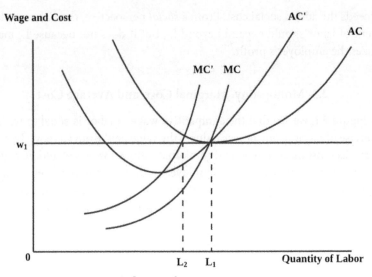

Figure 2.2 Influence of monopsony on cost curves

Q_1 units of output. It sells its output for the market determined price P_1. In equilibrium, P_1 equals MC and AC. If this firm becomes a monopsonist in the local labor market, its marginal cost will shift upward from MC to MC'. To maximize its profit, the firm will hire less labor and produce less output. In Figure 2.2, output falls from Q_1 to Q_2. Despite the shift in marginal cost, the monopsonist enjoys higher profits as a result of curtailing its employment of labor.

The average cost of production also changes with the introduction of monopsony at all points except Q_1. At an output of Q_1, there will be no change in the employment of labor and, therefore, no change in the wage paid. As a result, the average cost with and without monopsony power is the same. If the employer increases the firm's output beyond Q_1, it will have to hire more labor, which will cause the wage rate to rise. This, in turn, will cause the average cost (AC') to rise above the average cost (AC). In contrast, if the employer reduces the firm's output below Q_1, it will reduce the amount of labor employed, which will cause the wage paid to fall. The result is that average cost falls and AC' will be below AC. This results in a general shift downward and to the left of the minimum point on the average cost curve, from AC to AC'. The employer's average cost will be below the price of its output and the firm will earn economic profits equal to $(P_1-AC')Q_2 > 0$. The reduction in average cost resulting from a reduced employment of labor and the corresponding decrease in output provides the profit incentive for the monopsonist's restricted employment of labor.

For antitrust policy purposes, it is important to understand that the reduced wages flowing from an exercise of monopsony power are *not* socially beneficial. While they result in lower *average* cost and, therefore, higher profits for the monopsonist, they result in higher *marginal* cost. This, in turn, leads to no benefit for the consumer. On the other hand, if wages are reduced due to greater efficiency, both marginal and average costs will fall, output will expand, and consumer welfare will increase.

2.4 All-or-Nothing Offers

In the simple model of monopsony, the firm reduces its employment of labor to depress the wage. In this way, it converts some employee surplus into profit for itself. But some employee surplus remains with the employee. In principle, the employer could make all-or-nothing offers that can extract all the employee surplus. This is possible because the monopsonist can make an offer that requires the same number of hours but at a lower hourly wage.

To get a sense of all-or-nothing offers, suppose that the labor supply curve is $w = 10 + 0.5L$ where L is the number of hours worked. To induce this worker to provide 40 hours of labor services per week, they must be paid $30 per hour. The labor surplus is calculated as $\frac{1}{2}(30-10)(40)$ which is $400.

Suppose the employer offered to pay $29 per hour, but required 40 hours per week or the worker would not be hired. At $29 per hour, the worker would prefer to work only 38 hours, but this is not an option. If the worker accepts the offer, they will work 40 hours, earn $1,160, and enjoy labor surplus of $360.[10] Despite the extraction of some employee surplus by the employer, the employee is still better off accepting the offer than not because some positive surplus is better than the alternative of receiving no pay at all.

The usual supply curve tells us how much labor will be provided at any given wage. The management decision of a particular employer is how much labor to employ at any given wage. The all-or-nothing supply curve, however, is a different matter. It answers the question: what is the maximum number of labor services employees will make available at each wage

---

[10] Employee surplus after all-or-nothing offer: $\frac{1}{2}(29-10)(38) - \frac{1}{2}(30-29)(40-38) = \$360$.

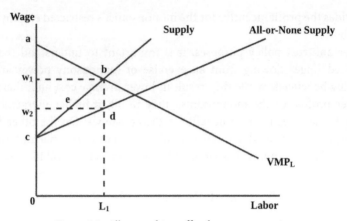

Figure 2.3 All-or-nothing offers by a monopsonist

when the alternative is to earn nothing at all?[11] Accordingly, the all-or-nothing supply curve lies below the usual supply curve.[12] Knowledge of the all-or-nothing supply curve enables the monopsonist to fully exploit its monopsony power by extracting all the employee surplus.[13]

Consider the demand that a monopsonist has for labor as shown in Figure 2.3. The usual supply curve is shown, and the interaction of supply and demand determines an equilibrium wage and employment level in a competitive labor market of w_1 and L_1. The monopsonist could exploit its power in the usual way by restricting its employment below L_1, thereby depressing the wage below w_1. Alternatively, however, the monopsonist could make all-or-nothing offers to its employees. In effect, the monopsonist can push the employees off the traditional supply curve and onto the all-or-nothing supply curve at the employment level L_1, which is the privately optimal employment level for the monopsonist.[14] The wage actually paid falls from w_1 to w_2 without any reduction in the employment level.

The short-run consequences of the all-or-nothing scenario are purely distributive rather than allocative. In the limit, all the employee surplus is transferred to the employer. In Figure 2.3, under competitive conditions, the employer surplus is the area abw_1, and the employee surplus is

[11] P. Richard, G. Layard, and Alan A. Walters, *Microeconomic Theory* (1978) at 244: "Lying below the supply curve is the seller's all-or-nothing price, showing the minimum price per unit at which he is willing to sell each quantity."
[12] See Milton Friedman, *Price Theory* (1976) at 118.
[13] All – or nearly all – employment opportunities have an all-or-nothing character.
[14] This is the privately (as opposed to socially) optimal employment level in the sense that the employer's profits are maximized with quantity L_1 and wage w_2.

cbw_1. After imposing all-or-nothing conditions upon the employees, the employer increases surplus by the rectangular area w_1bdw_2. This comes at the expense of employees, whose employee surplus has been reduced by the same amount.[15] Note that the area above the supply curve and below w_2 (i.e., area cew_2) is equal to area deb, and therefore, employee surplus is zero.[16] Thus, the monopsonist will have extracted all the employee surplus through its all-or-nothing offers. Although this exercise of monopsony does not reduce employment in the short run, it may in the long run as employees may not want to enter this particular market.

In our earlier numerical example, the employee's labor supply function was $w = 10 + 0.5L$. With an all-or-nothing offer, the employer could reduce the wage from \$30 per hour to \$20 per hour for a 40-hour work week.[17] This would leave the employee with no surplus.

The all-or-nothing model seems to fit recent cases in which health care providers challenged the monopsonistic pricing practices of health care insurers.[18] The providers typically object to the maximum price the insurer has offered.[19] The insurers probably prefer not to reduce the quantity of medical services available. The long-run consequences are, however, difficult to predict. For example, in *Kartell* v. *Blue Shield*,[20] a group of physicians

---

[15] This is easily proven. Triangles cew_2 and deb are similar right triangles with equal bases ($w_2e = ed$). Thus, the triangles are congruent and, therefore, the areas are the same. Because triangle cew_2 lies above the supply curve, it represents positive employee surplus since the reservation wage lies below the actual wage paid. Triangle deb, however, lies below the supply curve and, thus, represents negative employee surplus since the reservation wage exceeds the actual wage paid. Because these two triangles are congruent, all employee surplus has been extracted.

[16] There is no employee surplus above the all-or-nothing supply curve. For example, area cdw_2 does *not* represent employee surplus. The all-or-nothing supply represents – by construction – the supply response when all employee surplus has been extracted by the monopsonist.

[17] The positive surplus for the first 20 hours is $\frac{1}{2}(20-10)(20)=100$, while the deficit from the second 20 hours is $\frac{1}{2}(30-20)20=100$.

[18] See, for example, *Kartell* v. *Blue Shield*, 749 F. 2d 922 (1st Cir. 1984), cert. denied, 471 U.S. 1029 (1985); *Medical Arts Pharmacy, Inc.* v. *Blue Cross, Inc.*, 675 F. 2d 502 (2d Cir. 1982); *Travelers Insurance Co.* v. *Blue Cross*, 481 F. 2d 80 (3d Cir.), *cert denied,* 414 U.S. 1093 (1973); *Pennsylvania Dentist Association* v. *Medical Service Association*, 574 F. Supp. 457 (M.D. Pa. 1983).

[19] See Jill Boylston Herndon, Health Insurer Monopsony Power: The All-or-None Model, 21 *Journal of Health Economics* 197 (2002).

[20] *Kartell* v. *Blue Shield*, 749 F. 2d 922 (1st Cir. 1984), cert. denied, 471 U.S. 1029 (1985). Challenges such as this, brought under Section 1 of the Sherman Act, usually fail because an insurer is a single employer and can unilaterally shop for favorable terms. See Phillip Areeda and Louis Kaplow, *Antitrust Analysis* (1988) at 251, n. 27.

challenged the pricing policies of Blue Shield, which offered reimbursement on a take-it-or-leave-it basis.[21] The plaintiffs contended that the rates were so low that they discouraged entry into the physician services market.[22]

2.5 The Dominant Employer

The dominant employer is a close cousin of the pure monopsonist.[23] In this model, a single large employer is surrounded by a collection of small employers, which are termed fringe employers. Due to its size, the dominant employer recognizes that its employment level will influence the market wage. As a result, this firm will act as a wage setter. Each fringe employer is small enough that it acts as a wage taker because its employment level is too small to influence the market. In essence, the fringe of competitive employers accepts the wage that the dominant employer pays as the market determined wage. Behaving competitively, the fringe firms will employ labor up to the point where their collective demand equals the wage set by the dominant employer.

Now, the dominant employer's problem is to adjust its employment to maximize profit subject to the competitive behavior of the fringe employers. This is shown in Figure 2.4 where VMP_f represents the demand for labor by the competitive fringe, VMP_{df} represents the demand of the dominant employer, and S is the supply curve. The dominant employer recognizes that at any wage that it sets, the fringe will employ labor where VMP_f equals the wage. The dominant employer incorporates this behavior into its decision calculus by subtracting VMP_f from S to obtain the residual supply of labor, which is denoted by S_r in Figure 2.4. At every wage level, the residual supply plots the difference between the total labor supplied and the quantity hired by the fringe employers. The curve marginal to S_r, which is labeled me, represents the marginal expenditure for the dominant employer. The balance of the analysis is familiar – the dominant employer hires L_{df} where me equals VMP_{df}, which determines the wage equal to w_1 from the residual supply. At a wage of w_1, the fringe will hire L_f where w_1 equals VMP_f. At w_1, total employment will equal L_1, which is equal to the sum of L_{df} and L_f. As we can see, the marginal expenditure (me) exceeds

---

[21] *Kartell* v. *Blue Shield*, 749 F. 2d 922, 923–24 (1st Cir. 1984). Another example of an all-or-nothing situation appears to be *Kartell* v. *Blue Shield Inc.*, 887 F. 2d 1535 (11th Cir. 1989).

[22] *Kartell* v. *Blue Shield*, 749 F. 2d 922, 924 (1st Cir. 1984).

[23] The dominant firm model was developed to examine the pricing behavior of a large *seller*. See Karl Forchheimer, Theoretisches zum unvollständigen Monopole, 1 *Schmollers Jahbuch* 12 (1908). We have adapted this model to the dominant employer analog.

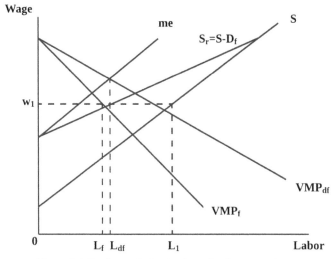

Figure 2.4 Profit maximization by a dominant employer

the wage paid (w_1), which means that the value of the marginal product of labor for the dominant employer (VMP_{df}) exceeds the wage paid.

The profit maximizing behavior of the dominant employer leads to the same sort of allocative inefficiency that results from pure monopsony. Since the value of the marginal product exceeds the wage, the value created by employing one more unit of labor exceeds the social cost of doing so. Consequently, dominant employer behavior leads to a deadweight social welfare loss analogous to that of pure monopsony. The deleterious effects of the dominant employer's profit maximizing conduct are muted, but not eliminated, by the competitive fringe employers. The more important the fringe's presence in the labor market, the smaller will be the reduction in wages, employment, and social welfare.

2.6 Oligopsony

When there are several large employers in the labor market, the market structure is referred to as oligopsony. Individual efforts to depress the wage paid by restricting employment may be impaired by the conduct of the employer's rivals. This market structure is a bit perplexing. Unlike the pure monopsony and its dominant employer variant, oligopsony may yield quite different outcomes. At one extreme, we may observe the pure monopsony solution, while the perfectly competitive solution may emerge at the other extreme. This range of outcomes is dismaying because it makes prediction quite difficult and, therefore, muddles antitrust policy.

2.6.1 Tacit Collusion

If the employers recognize that a fair share of the monopsony profit is larger than a fair share of any other profit, they may reach the pure monopsony outcome by accommodating one another's presence in the labor market. This conduct is referred to as tacit collusion because this outcome can be achieved without any actual agreement or even any direct communication.[24] As we will see in Chapter 4, tacit collusion is beyond the reach of the antitrust laws. Since the economic results may be the same as those of pure monopsony, tacit collusion is a source of frustration.

2.6.2 Cournot Oligopsonists

If the firms set their employment levels, the result in the labor market will be a wage and employment level that falls between the pure monopsony outcome and the perfectly competitive outcome. As the number of employers increases, the wage and employment level will approach the perfectly competitive results. The reverse is also true – as the number of employers falls, the economic results worsen. Moreover, it makes tacit collusion more likely. This relationship between the number of employers and the economic results provides the foundation for considerations of monopsony in merger analysis.[25]

2.6.3 Bertrand Oligopsonists

If the employers announced the wages they offered, as long as that wage is below the VMP_L, there is an incentive to bid up the wage and scoop up all the labor supply.[26] Consequently, competition on the wage being offered will result ultimately in the competitive wage and employment level.

---

[24] For an experimental demonstration, see Katerina Sherstyuk, Collusion Without Conspiracy: An Experimental Study of One-Sided Auctions, 2 *Experimental Economics* 59 (1999). Edward Chamberlin introduced the idea of "tacit agreement" in a duopoly setting. See Edward Chamberlin, *The Theory of Monopolistic Competition* (8th ed. 1963) at 47. As we noted in Chapter 1, Adam Smith observed that employers might engage in tacit collusion.

[25] See Tirza J. Angerhofer and Roger D. Blair, Considerations of Buyer Power in Merger Review, 10 *Journal of Antitrust Enforcement* 260 (2022). Additionally, we examine mergers in the labor market in Chapter 10.

[26] Josef Bertrand, Recherches sur les Principes Mathématiques de la Théorie des Richesses, Book review of *Theorie Mathematique de la Richesse Sociale* and of

2.7 Measuring Monopsony Power

Monopsony power is the ability of a large employer to influence wages by adjusting its employment level. In essence, the monopsonist recognizes that the supply function is positively sloped and that it can slide along that supply curve to a lower wage by decreasing its employment. This is why the monopsony wage deviates from the competitive wage. A measure of monopsony power should reflect this deviation. One way to do this is to adapt the Lerner Index of monopoly power to the case of monopsony.[27]

2.7.1 Lerner Index of Monopsony Power

Following Lerner, we define the monopsony power index as the VMP_L – wage gap relative to the wage paid:[28]

$$\lambda = \frac{VMP_L - w}{w}.$$

In Appendix A2.2, we show that the Lerner Index is the reciprocal of the elasticity of supply of labor:

$$\lambda = \frac{1}{\varepsilon_L}.$$

Since the elasticity of the labor supply measures the responsiveness of the labor services supplied to changes in the wage, this is an appealing result. The more elastic the supply, the greater is the reduction in employment necessary to achieve any specific wage reduction. The effect of ε_L on λ can be seen in several numerical examples, which are illustrated in Table 2.1 below.

Recherches sur les Principles Mathematiques de la Theorie des Richesses, 67 *Journal de Savants* 499 (1883).

[27] See Abba Lerner, The Concept of Monopoly and the Measurement of Monopoly Power, 1 *Review of Economic Studies* 157 (1934). For an adaptation to monopsony, see Roger D. Blair and Jeffrey L. Harrison, Cooperative Buying, Monopsony Power, and Antitrust Policy, 86 *Northwestern University Law Review* 331 (1991).

[28] This adaptation of the Lerner Index is static. For a more sophisticated measure of monopsony power, see Monica Langella and Alan Manning, The Measure of Monopsony, 19 *Journal of the European Economic Association* 2929 (2021). Their approach identified instances in which the true measure of monopsony exceeded or fell short of the value of the Lerner Index. Additionally, see David Berger, Kyle Herkenhoff, and Simon Mongey, Labor Market Power, 112 *American Economic Review* 114 (2022). Using a structural model, the authors used administrative U.S. Census Bureau data to estimate measures of oligopsony in the labor market.

Table 2.1 *The effect of elasticity on the Lerner Index*

ε_L	0.5	1.0	2.0	5.0	∞
λ	2.0	1.0	0.5	0.2	0

Thus, when supply is inelastic ($\varepsilon_L = 0.5$), there is a substantial deviation from the competitive result (200%). But the more elastic the supply, the smaller the deviation. In the limit, when $\varepsilon_L = \infty$, the buyer is essentially in a competitive market and the deviation is zero.

2.7.2 Dominant Employers

The monopsony power of a dominant employer is mitigated by the demand response of the competitive fringe. The Lerner Index can be adapted to this case. In Appendix A2.2, we show that the Lerner Index may be written as $\lambda = \dfrac{s}{\varepsilon - \eta(1-s)}$. Now, monopsony power is a function of the dominant employer's share of total employment (s), the overall elasticity of labor market supply (ε), and the elasticity of the fringe employer's demand (η).

To evaluate monopsony power, we may consider how each variable influences λ.[29] First, we may observe that the larger the dominant employer's share is of employment, the greater is its monopsony power. This makes economic sense and is consistent with our intuition. The more important the dominant employer is in the market, the greater the firm's ability is to depress the wage by restricting its employment, which leads to greater monopsony power. Second, increases in ε will decrease λ. This result also makes economic sense. The elasticity of supply measures the relative responsiveness of the labor employed to changes in the wage paid. As the employment level becomes more responsive to changes in the wage paid (i.e., as ε increases), the dominant employer's monopsony power falls. This is because the employees can redirect their efforts to other firms where wages may be higher. In the limit, the elasticity of supply goes to infinity (i.e., the supply curve is flat and therefore, perfectly elastic) and the value of λ goes to zero. Finally, we may examine the influence of the demand elasticity of the fringe employers. As this elasticity increases, the monopsony power of the dominant employer falls. This follows because any reduction

[29] Several numerical examples are provided in Roger D. Blair and Jeffrey L. Harrison, The Measurement of Monopsony Power, 37 *Antitrust Bulletin* 133 (1992).

in the wage paid implemented by the dominant employer's curtailed level of employment is offset to some extent by the enhanced employment of the fringe. The more responsive they are to wage decreases, the more difficult it is for the dominant employer to make such a decrease stick. In the limit, the elasticity of fringe demand goes to infinity and the dominant employer's monopsony power goes to zero.

2.7.3 Oligopsony and the Lerner Index

The monopsony power of oligopsony can be measured by the Lerner Indices developed in Section 2.7.1. Oligopsony is complicated because it depends on how a small number of large buyers behave. If they tacitly collude, we get one result. If they adopt Cournot or Bertrand behavior, we get another. Moreover, it will also depend on whether there is a competitive fringe or not.

2.8 Concluding Remarks

There is nothing good about monopsony in the labor market. The exercise of monopsony power leads to a social welfare loss because employment is suboptimal – too few labor services are being employed. This means that too little output is being produced. The economic results are unfortunately lower wages, reduced employment, higher output prices, consumer welfare losses, and a redistribution of wealth from employees to employers. The employer is the only winner. Everyone else loses.

APPENDICES

A2.1 Profit Maximization

If the firm is competitive in the output market, but a monopsonist in the local labor market, its profit function will be:

$$\Pi = PQ(L,K) - w(L)L - rK,$$

where P is the output price, $Q(L,K)$ is the production function, L is labor, K is capital, w is the wage paid, and r is the price of capital.

Profit maximization requires employing labor such that the first partial derivative of Π equals:

$$\frac{\partial \Pi}{\partial L} = P\frac{\partial Q}{\partial L} - \left(w + L\frac{\partial w}{\partial L} \right) = 0.$$

The first term on the right-hand side is the VMP_L while the second is the ME_L.

A2.2 Lerner Index of Monopsony

The rate of monopsonistic exploitation can be written as:

$$\frac{\text{VMP}_L - w}{w} = \frac{w + L\dfrac{dw}{dL} - w}{w} = \frac{L}{w} \cdot \frac{dw}{dL} = \frac{1}{\varepsilon_L},$$

where ε_L is the elasticity of labor supply.

A2.2.1 Dominant Employer Application

The first thing to do is find the elasticity of the residual supply. Recall that the residual supply is:

$$L_{df} = L - L_f,$$

where L_{df} is the quantity of labor employed by the dominant firm, L is the total quantity of labor employed in the market, and L_f is the employment level of the fringe firms. Differentiating both sides with respect to w yields:

$$\frac{dL_{df}}{dw} = \frac{dL}{dw} - \frac{dL_f}{dw}.$$

After multiplying both sides by $\dfrac{w}{L_{df}}$, we have an expression for ε_D, the elasticity of the residual supply.

$$\frac{w}{L_{df}}\left(\frac{dL_{df}}{dw} = \frac{dL}{dw} - \frac{dL_f}{dw} \right)$$

$\Rightarrow$

$$\frac{w}{L_{df}} \cdot \frac{dL_{df}}{dw} = \frac{w}{L_{df}} \cdot \frac{dL}{dw} - \frac{w}{L_{df}} \cdot \frac{dL_f}{dw}$$

$\Rightarrow$

$$\varepsilon_D = \left(\frac{L}{L} \cdot \frac{w}{L_{df}} \cdot \frac{dL}{dw} \right) - \left(\frac{L}{L} \cdot \frac{L_f}{L_f} \cdot \frac{w}{L_{df}} \cdot \frac{dL_f}{dw} \right)$$

$\Rightarrow$

$$\varepsilon_D = \left(\frac{L}{L_{df}} \cdot \frac{w}{L} \cdot \frac{dL}{dw} \right) - \left(\frac{L_f}{L_{df}} \cdot \frac{w}{L_f} \cdot \frac{dL_f}{dw} \right)$$

$\Rightarrow$

$$\varepsilon_D = \frac{\varepsilon}{s} - \frac{(1-s)\eta}{s}$$

$\Rightarrow$

$$\varepsilon_D = \frac{\varepsilon - \eta(1-s)}{s},$$

where s is the market share of the dominant employer, ε is the labor market supply elasticity, and η is the elasticity of the fringe employer's demand. The Lerner Index is the reciprocal of the elasticity of the residual supply:

$$\lambda = \frac{s}{\varepsilon - \eta(1-s)}.$$

3

Empirical Evidence of Monopsony
in Labor Markets

3.1 Introduction

For many years, it was assumed that most labor markets could be characterized as perfectly competitive. In other words, employers could hire as much or as little labor as they wanted at the competitive wage. The prevailing thought was that monopsony power only existed in specialized markets consisting of a single buyer in an isolated geographic market, that is, the proverbial "company town." These cases were treated as theoretical curiosities without much – if any – empirical significance. Accordingly, the case of monopsony in the labor market was largely ignored for nearly half a century.[1]

Recently, however, there has been ample empirical evidence showing that elements of monopsony power are pervasive in the labor market.[2] A survey of the empirical literature reveals that there are many sources of labor market imperfections. In this chapter, we provide an overview of this extensive literature.[3]

---

[1] David Card, Who Set Your Wage?, 112 *American Economic Review* 1075 (2022), explains briefly why Joan Robinson's seminal contributions had been ignored. Card provides four main reasons: (1) Robinson describes perfect monopoly and perfect monopsony without offering much guidance on other forms of market imperfection, (2) economists did not find the model particularly useful in other contexts, (3) proposing a model in which employers are choosing not to hire more workers did not sit well during the Great Depression, and (4) Robinson's public persona portrayed her as a far-leftist, which may have dismayed other economists during the Cold War era.

[2] See, for example, Alan Manning, *Monopsony in Motion: Imperfect Competition in Labor Markets* (2003).

[3] This chapter draws on a variety of empirical surveys, including Alan Manning, Monopsony in Labor Markets: A Review, 74 *ILR Review* 3 (2021); Council of Economic Advisors, *Labor Market Monopsony: Trends, Consequences, and Policy Responses, Issue Brief* (2016); Douglas O. Staiger, Joanne Spetz, and Ciaran S. Phibbs, Is There Monopsony

In Section 3.2, we explain the difference between perfect labor markets, in which there is no monopsony power, and imperfect labor markets, which involve some degree of monopsony. In Section 3.3, we turn our attention to some of the sources of labor market imperfections and how they result in market power for employers. In Section 3.4, we discuss the policy implications of monopsony power in the labor market. We close with some concluding remarks in Section 3.5.

3.2 Perfect and Imperfect Labor Markets

Initially, economists assumed that firms had downward sloping demands for labor services, but that supply functions of labor were perfectly elastic. As can be seen in Figure 3.1, the demand for labor services (VMP_L) is downward sloping, while the supply of labor services (S_L) has a slope of zero. At any given quantity of labor services, the reservation wage of the workers remains at w_1, that is, the competitive wage. This means that the employer could choose to employ any quantity of labor, including L_1 or L_2, and the wage would remain unchanged. The firm will simply employ the quantity of labor that equates the demand and supply of labor, hiring L_1 units of labor services.

In the 1930s, Joan Robinson questioned the idea of these perfect labor markets, and used the term "monopsony" to define a market in which a single employer faced a labor supply that is positively sloped, rather than perfectly elastic.[4] Robinson explained that in competitively structured labor markets, like that shown in Figure 3.1, workers could not be exploited. She argued that employee exploitation could not exist because an employee would simply offer their labor to another firm at a higher wage if they were unhappy with their current position. This led her to conclude that labor supply functions must be positively sloped.

For many years, Robinson's idea of an imperfect labor market was largely ignored. Recently, however, studies of monopsony power have found it to be of much more empirical relevance than previously thought. Many

in the Labor Market? Evidence From a Natural Experiment, 28 *Journal of Labor Economics* 211 (2010); Suresh Naidu, Eric A. Posner, and Glen Weyl, Antitrust Remedies for Labor Market Power, 132 *Harvard Law Review* 536 (2018); and Ihsaan Bassier, Arindrajit Dube, and Suresh Naidu, Monopsony in Movers: The Elasticity of Labor Supply to Firm Wage Policies, 57 *Journal of Human Resources* S50 (2022).

4 Joan Robinson, *The Economics of Imperfect Competition* (1933). Interestingly, Robinson was not the only person to believe there was some relationship between wages and employment. Near the time of her publication, Karl Marx pointed out the presence of employee exploitation in the labor market. See Karl Marx, *Capital*, 320–329 (1867, Translated 1990).

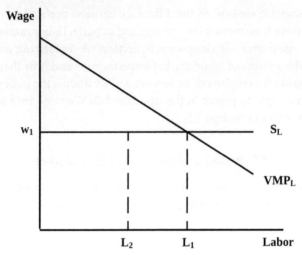

Figure 3.1 A competitive labor market

empirical studies have found that labor supply curves are upward sloping. These include Burdett and Mortensen,[5] Manning,[6] Card, Rute Cardoso, Heining, and Kline,[7] and Lamadon, Mogstad, and Setzler.[8] These empirical findings are consistent with the concept of "imperfect" labor markets, which allow for the existence of monopsony power.

When the supply of labor is positively sloped, the associated marginal expenditure necessarily lies above the labor supply. Consequently, a monopsonist will choose to employ labor services up to the point where the marginal expenditure equals the demand for labor, rather than equating supply and demand, as in the case of a perfect labor market. Because the slope of the marginal expenditure is necessarily steeper than the corresponding supply when the supply is positively sloped, the resulting employment is restricted below the level at which the labor contribution (VMP_L) equals the wage paid. Due to the positive slope of the supply, this results in a lower wage paid to employed workers, as can be seen in Figure 3.2.

[5] Kenneth Burdett and Dale T. Mortensen, Wage Differentials, Employer Size, and Unemployment, 39 *International Economic Review* 257 (1998).

[6] Manning, *Monopsony in Motion*.

[7] David Card, Ana Rute Cardoso, Joerg Heining, and Patrick Kline, Firms and Labor Market Inequality: Evidence and Some Theory, 36 *Journal of Labor Economics* S13 (2018).

[8] Thibaut Lamadon, Magne Mogstad, and Bradley Setzler, Imperfect Competition, Compensating Differentials and Rent Sharing in the U.S. Labor Market, 112 *American Economic Review* 169 (2022).

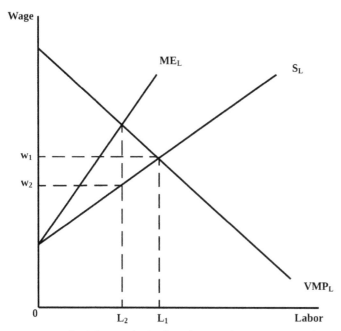

Figure 3.2 An imperfect labor market leads to decreased employment and suppressed wages

As the concept of monopsony power has become more widely accepted, many labor economists have set out to determine the elasticity of labor supply and have found a variety of results. One of the first noteworthy attempts to establish a numerical measure of the elasticity of supply was performed by Alan Manning. Using panel data, Manning found the elasticity of labor supply in the U.S. to be 1.38 by applying the Burdett and Mortensen model,[9] which attributes the power to establish wages to search frictions.[10]

Since then, several labor economists have used Manning's methodology as a foundational work to obtain additional estimates of the elasticity of labor supply. Table 3.1 shows estimates of the elasticity of supply determined in a variety of studies conducted between 2015 and 2022.

Some studies, like that conducted by Sokolova and Sorensen,[11] determined the elasticity to fall within the range of 1.0 to 2.0. Others, like that

[9] Burdett and Mortensen, Wage Differentials.
[10] Manning, *Monopsony in Motion.*
[11] Anna Sokolova and Todd Sorensen, Monopsony in Labor Markets: A Meta-Analysis, 74 *ILR Review* 27 (2021).

Table 3.1 *Estimates of the elasticity of supply*

Empirical study	Estimated labor supply elasticity
Azar, Berry, and Marinescu (2019)[a]	4.8
Bassier, Dube, and Naidu (2022)[b]	4.2
Cho (2018)[c]	4.8
Kroft et al. (2020)[d]	4.1
Sokolova and Sorensen (2018)[e]	1.68
Webber (2015)[f]	1.08

[a] Azar José, Berry Steven T., and Marinescu Ioana Elena, *Estimating Labor Market Power*. Working Paper (2019).

[b] Ihsaan Bassier, Arindrajit Dube, and Suresh Naidu, Monopsony in Movers: The Elasticity of Labor Supply to Firm Wage Policies, 57 *Journal of Human Resources* S50 (2022).

[c] David Cho, The Labor Market Effects of Demand Shocks: Firm-Level Evidence from the Recovery Act. Unpublished Paper (2018).

[d] Kory Kroft, Yao Luo, Magne Mogstad & Bradley Setzler, *Imperfect Competition and Rents in Labor and Product Markets: The Case of the Construction Industry*. NBER Working Paper No. 27325 (2020).

[e] Anna Sokolova and Todd Sorensen, Monopsony in Labor Markets: A Meta-Analysis, 74 *ILR Review* 27 (2021).

[f] Douglas A. Webber, Firm Market Power and the Earnings Distribution, 35 *Labour Economics* 123 (2015).

conducted by Bassier, Dube, and Naidu,[12] found that the elasticity of labor fell within the range of 4.0 to 5.0. In any case, it is clear that the elasticity of supply is far from infinite, which would be the case in a perfect labor market. The magnitude of the effect, however, is still being analyzed to this day.

These differences in estimated elasticities can be attributed to different empirical methodologies and different data sets. Sokolova and Sorensen examined 53 studies which provided over 1,300 estimates. They found the unweighted mean of elasticity to be 10.58, while the unweighted median elasticity is much lower at 1.68.[13]

Meanwhile, Bassier, Dube, and Naidu utilized a model proposed by Abowd, Kramarz, and Margolis (AKM),[14] as well as a matched event study approach. They found "that the firm components of wage – as measured using either AKM or our matched event study approach – are clearly negatively correlated with the overall separation rate and particularly the

---

[12] Bassier, Dube, and Naidu, Monopsony in Movers.

[13] Sokolova and Sorensen provided a table of average weighted and unweighted elasticities that are organized by data and data methods. See Table 3.1.

[14] John M. Abowd, Francis Kramarz, and David N. Margolis, High Wage Workers and High Wage Firms, 67 *Econometrica* 251 (1999).

job-to-job separation rate, consistent with the firm effects reflecting 'better jobs.'"[15] This led to a separation elasticity of –2.1, which implies a labor supply elasticity of approximately 4.7.

Estimates of labor supply elasticity can become even more complex when we look at individual markets, rather than the labor market as a whole. Studies across more specialized labor markets have yielded mixed results.

For example, many studies have attempted to estimate the elasticity of supply in the nurse labor market. Yett found a wage elasticity in the nurse labor market of 0.2 for the period of 1949 to 1952,[16] and an elasticity of 0.34 for the period of 1950 to 1960. Hixson estimated the wage elasticity to be 0.28 for Michigan nurses.[17] Altman,[18] however, found wage elasticities ranging between 0.7 to 1.0. Ault and Rutman estimated the elasticity for annual hours to be 0.39 in 1981 and 0.24 in 1988,[19] and Askildsen, Baltagi, and Holmas,[20] utilizing the basic ordinary least squares model, identified a wage elasticity of 0.254.

More recently, however, Staiger, Spetz, and Phibbs found "estimates of the short-run elasticity of labor supply to an individual hospital average around 0.1,"[21] while Hanel, Kalb, and Scott altered the parameters of their study to include entry and exit into the market,[22] rather than just changes in hours worked, and found an elasticity of supply equal to 1.37.

Studies of labor supply elasticities have also found varying magnitudes across gender groups. Using methods of survival analysis and a large, linked employer–employee data set for Germany, Hirsch, Schank, and Schnabel found that their estimate for the elasticity of supply fell in a range of 1.9 to 3.7, but was always lower for women.[23]

[15] Bassier, Dube, and Naidu, Monopsony in Movers at S52.

[16] Donald E. Yett, *An Economic Analysis of the Nurse Shortage* (1975).

[17] Jesse S. Hixson, *The Demand and Supply of Professional Hospital Nurses: Intra-Hospital Resource Allocation*. PhD Dissertation, Michigan State University (1969).

[18] Stuart H. Altman, *Present and Future Supply of Registered Nurses* (1971).

[19] David E. Ault and Gilbert L. Rutman, On Selecting a Measure of Labour Activity: Evidence from Registered Nurses, 1981 and 1989, 26 *Applied Economics* 851 (1994).

[20] Jan Erik Askildsen, Badi H. Baltagi, and Tor Helge Holmas, Will Increased Wages Reduce Shortage of Nurses? A Panel Data Analysis of Nurses' Labour Supply, 12 *Health Economics* 70 (2003).

[21] Staiger, Spetz, and Phibbs, Is There Monopsony in the Labor Market?, p. 213.

[22] Barbara Hanel, Guyonne Kalb, Anthony Scott, Nurses' Labour Supply Elasticities: The Importance of Accounting for Extensive Margins, 33 *Journal of Health Economics* 94 (2014).

[23] Boris Hirsch, Thorsten Schank, and Claus Schnabel, Differences in Labor Supply to Monopsonistic Firms and the Gender Pay Gap: An Empirical Analysis Using Linked Employer–Employee Data from Germany, 28 *Journal of Labor Economics* 291 (2010).

Other studies, including that conducted by Ransom and Oaxaca found elasticities in the range of 2.4 to 3 for men and about 1.5 to 2.5 for women.[24] Collecting year-end payroll files from grocery stores, they pooled workers between 1977 and 1985 in an attempt to calculate an estimate of the elasticities of labor supply for men and women. Utilizing two methods of calculating elasticity, they were able to determine the elasticity ranges mentioned earlier.

This suggests that, while monopsony in the labor market is generally acknowledged to be at least somewhat pervasive, the measure of elasticity varies due to a variety of factors such as the specific labor market and the gender of the workers. Other factors can amplify the effects of monopsony power in a market. We examine some of those factors in our next section.

3.3 Sources of Labor Market Imperfections

If labor markets were perfectly competitive, there would be a large number of relatively small employers offering identical terms of employment. There would also be a large number of workers willing to supply their labor services at the same wage. However, labor markets are decidedly imperfect. For one thing, labor supply functions are positively sloped rather than flat. Consequently, the elasticity of labor supply functions is far from infinite as it would be if labor markets were perfect.

At the same time, many labor markets are dominated by one or a small number of large employers. This is especially true in local labor markets. In this section, we examine the sources of labor market imperfection to improve our understanding of monopsony in the labor market. According to David Card's survey, the primary sources of monopsony appear to be search frictions and idiosyncratic preferences for different jobs.[25] Additionally, monopsony power has been attributed to employer concentration.

3.3.1 Imperfect Labor Supply

Labor supply functions are positively sloped because reservation wages are not uniform across all individuals. Workers differ in their willingness to work due to a variety of factors: age, gender, marital status, education, experience, residence, and so on. Reservation wages may differ due to the

---

[24] Michael R. Ransom and Ronald L. Oaxaca, New Market Power Models and Sex Differences in Pay, 28 *Journal of Labor Economics* 267 (2010).
[25] Card, Who Set Your Wage?

characteristics of specific jobs. For example, a salesclerk may require a higher wage to work in a grocery store than in a sporting goods store – or vice versa.

Not all jobs are created equal. In fact, nearly all jobs have some unique characteristics that make one job more or less attractive to a candidate than another job. For those who prefer one employer over another, the preferred employer has some measure of monopsony power.

Consider two jobs for car repair mechanics that require the same labor services. Both jobs will pay the mechanic $25 per hour and require 40 hours of labor, but Job A is 3.0 miles from the mechanic's home with 8 AM to 5 PM shifts Monday through Friday, and Job B is five miles away with shifts from 7 AM to 3 PM Monday through Friday, and 7 AM to 12 PM on Saturday.[26] Moreover, Job A provides the mechanic with free coffee throughout the shift, but Job B is closer to the mechanic's favorite lunch-time restaurant.

These two jobs are different. While the job tasks, the total hours worked, and the wage rate remain the same at either job, the differences in location, shift timing, and additional amenities (both internal like the coffee bar with Job A, and external like the restaurant near Job B) create different incentives for individuals to work at different places. If the mechanic wants to be home early to help their children with homework after school, they may prefer Job B due to the timing of the shift even though it is further away from home. These preferences are not uniform across individuals in the workforce, which makes determining the exact boundaries for each unique labor market a challenge for labor economists.

Even economists face the impacts of differentiation in their job choice. Economists who have earned a PhD have many job options that differ in terms of compensation and working conditions. Teaching positions at universities differ in terms of teaching and research obligations. Outside academics, economists can work for consulting firms and earn more income but have no contact with students and no scholarly research duties. Businesses and government agencies provide additional differentiated job opportunities.

These alternatives vary in terms of compensation and the job responsibilities. An individual will select the job option that maximizes their utility. Since individual preferences differ, one job may be more or less appealing across individuals.

---

[26] By assumption, both of these jobs receive a one-hour lunch break from 12 PM to 1 PM during the week.

Empirical evidence suggests that these preferences do have impacts on our job choices. For example, Manning noted that women are limited in choice and job mobility by family responsibility.[27] Marinescu and Rathelot found that physical location plays a large role in which jobs we are willing to apply for.[28] The authors found that U.S. job seekers are 35 percent less likely to apply to a job 10 miles away from their own zip code of residence than one in their own ZIP code.

Differentiation means that fewer jobs are perfect substitutes, meaning that labor markets are smaller than may have been initially perceived.

The second major source of monopsony power has been characterized as search frictions. Alan Manning introduced the dynamic monopsony model in his book *Monopsony in Motion*,[29] which assumes that searching for better job opportunities is costly. This means that an employer may reduce wages or, at the very least, fail to increase wages because it knows that, while an employee has the opportunity to leave their job, there are costs to doing so. Not only are there costs associated with the search itself but leaving a job for another means finding a better opportunity, which is not always easy.

Workers will search for better job opportunities until the expected marginal benefit is equal to the marginal cost of additional search. Search frictions compound the marginal cost and, therefore, reduce the amount of search. This, of course, means that workers may not find their ideal position.

As a general proposition, search frictions are things that impede a worker's ability to find better job opportunities. One major friction is important information. In many cases, a worker may be unaware of open positions that pay better or provide better working conditions. To the extent that something prevents, or at least hinders a worker's ability to become aware of the more desirable job, there is a search friction.

3.3.2 Concentration of Employers

A firm need not be the only employer in town to have monopsony power. As we saw in the Chapter 2, a dominant employer may wield monopsony power. In addition, a small group of large employers may engage in tacit

---

[27] Manning, *Monopsony in Motion*.
[28] Ioana Marinescu and Roland Rathelot, Mismatch Unemployment and the Geography of Job Search, 10 *American Economic Journal: Macroeconomics* 4 (2018).
[29] Manning, *Monopsony in Motion*.

or overt collusion and behave as an employer cartel. Finally, if the large employers behave as Cournot oligopsonists in the local labor market, they can exercise some monopsony power.

The number and size distribution of potential employers in the local labor market are important determinants of the wage-setting power of the employers. In fact, it was originally believed that employees had a variety of potential job opportunities in a market, so the market power of employers was small. However, recent studies have found this to be less true for a variety of reasons. Some employers are not actively looking for new workers, while others are outside the appropriate geographic range for the prospective employee. Clearly, defining the geographic boundaries of a labor market for an individual can have effects on the degree of concentration within a labor market since this impacts the number and size of the firms in the defined labor market.

The degree of market concentration is often measured through the Herfindahl-Hirschman index (HHI), which is the sum of the squared market shares.[30] To eliminate confusing decimals, the DOJ and the FTC multiply the sum of the squared market shares by 10,000, which is equivalent to treating the market share as a whole number.[31] An interesting characteristic of the HHI is that:

$$N = \frac{1}{\text{HHI}},$$

where N is the number of equal-sized employers that will generate the given value of the HHI. For example, the actual value of the HHI, 0.125, is based on the actual market shares and number of employers, but N will be eight. Thus, eight firms of identical size will generate an HHI of 0.125, or 1,250 as the DOJ and FTC would express it.

A study by Azar, Marinescu, Steinbaum, and Taska found[32] the average labor market to have an HHI of approximately 4,300,[33] which corresponds to 2.3 equal sized recruiting firms in a market.[34] It would seem,

---

[30] If s_i is the market share of employer i, then the HHI is $\text{HHI} = \sum_{i=1}^{n} S_i^2$, where n is the number of employers in the labor market.

[31] For example, a share of 0.10, which is 10 percent, is treated as 10 in calculating HHI.

[32] See José Azar, Ioana Marinescu, Marshall I. Steinbaum, and Bledi Taska, Concentration of US Labor Markets: Evidence from Online Vacancy Data, 66 *Labour Economics* 101886.

[33] This figure employs the DOJ/FTC convention of removing decimals.

[34] According to the DOJ and the FTC, an HHI above 2,500 is considered a highly concentrated market since N would be four.

then, that high HHI values should correspond to high monopsony power in that labor market. In many empirical studies, however, researchers have found that measures of concentration are not necessarily a clear indicator of market power, including those conducted by Berry, Gaynor, and Scott Morton,[35] and Syverson.[36]

While concentration may not directly correlate to market power, recent studies have shown negative effects of higher concentration on wages. For example, Azar, Marinescu, and Steinbaum (AMS) calculated labor market concentration through posted vacancies (or job openings) and applications to those jobs to determine the value of the HHI.[37] They found a strong, negatively correlated relationship between log real wages and log HHI values determined through vacancies. The authors found the elasticity between real wages and HHI to be − 0.14, so a 1.0 percent increase in the HHI will lead to a 0.14 percent decrease in real wages.[38] Other studies have found similar results, with elasticities between HHI and wages ranging between − 0.05 and − 0.15.[39]

This raises questions regarding merger enforcement in the labor market. While we cannot directly conclude that higher concentration leads to higher market power in labor markets, it does appear to have a negative effect on wages.[40]

---

[35] Steven Berry, Martin Gaynor, and Fiona Scott Morton, Do Increasing Markups Matter? Lessons from Empirical Industrial Organization, 33 *Journal of Economic Perspectives* 44 (2019).

[36] Chad Syverson, Macroeconomics and Market Power: Context, Implications, and Open Questions, 33 *Journal of Economic Perspectives* 23 (2019).

[37] See José Azar, Ioana Marinescu, and Marshall I. Steinbaum, Labor Market Concentration, 57 *Journal of Human Resources* S167 (2022).

[38] When the employers merge, the change in the HHI will be equal to twice the product of the merging employers market shares. The delta (Δ) is $\Delta = 2s_1s_2$. For example, is $s_1 = 3$ and $s_2 = 5$, then the Δ will be 30. Given the estimates found by AMS, if the pre-merger HHI were, say, 1,500, the change would be 2 percent, which would indicate a wage reduction of about 0.03 percent. If the pre-merger wage were, say, \$20, the merger would then cause a reduction of about \$0.06 per hour.

[39] See Kevin Rinz, Labor Market Concentration, Earnings, and Inequality, 57 *Journal of Human Resources* S251 (2022), David Arnold, *Mergers and Acquisitions, Local Labor Market Concentration, and Worker Outcomes,* unpublished (2019), Elena Prager and Matt Schmitt, Employer Consolidation and Wages: Evidence from Hospitals, 111 *American Economic Review* 397 (2021), and Efraim Benmelech, Nittai K. Bergman, and Hyunseob Kim, Strong Employers and Weak Employees: How Does Employer Concentration Affect Wages?, 57 *Journal of Human Resources* S200 (2022).

[40] The influence of monopsony in labor markets on merger policy is examined in Chapter 10.

3.3.3 Additional Employer Actions

A variety of additional firm behaviors can impact, and more specifically, depress wages and employment. These include collusive agreements on wages,[41] no-poaching agreements,[42] and non-compete agreements.[43] Each of these arrangements will be examined more closely in later chapters.

3.4 Policy Implications of Monopsony Power

The existence of monopsony power in the labor market has implications for a variety of policies, including minimum wage legislation, antitrust policy, and merger policy. We will examine each of these areas in turn.

3.4.1 Minimum Wage Legislation

In the absence of monopsony power, minimum wage legislation is a mixed blessing for workers. Since the demand for labor is negatively sloped, a binding minimum wage will cause employment to fall. Those who remain employed are better off as their wage rises, but those who have been employed and now are unemployed are obviously worse off.

Interestingly, however, labor economists have found that employment does not always fall following the imposition of a minimum wage. In an empirical study, Card and Krueger found that implementing a binding minimum wage policy did not have a negative effect on employment.[44] Further studies have even found that employment may in fact rise with the introduction of a minimum wage.[45] A reasonable explanation for these empirical results is monopsony in the labor market.

If an employer has monopsony power in the labor market, a minimum wage that exceeds the current wage may be extremely welcome by the labor community. In these circumstances, both the wage and employment may

---

[41] Collusion on wages and other terms of employment are examined in Chapter 6.
[42] We dive into no-poaching agreements in Chapter 7.
[43] Non-compete agreements are the focus of Chapter 8.
[44] See David Card and Alan B. Krueger, Minimum Wages and Employment: A Case Study of the Fast Food Industry in New Jersey and Pennsylvania, 84 *American Economic Review* 772 (1994), and David Card and Alan B. Krueger, *A Reanalysis of the Effect of the New Jersey Minimum Wage Increase on the Fast-Food Industry with Representative Payroll Data*, unpublished (1998).
[45] See Arindrajit Dube, Suresh Naidu, and Michael Reich, The Economic Effects of a Citywide Minimum Wage, 60 *ILR Review* 522 (2007).

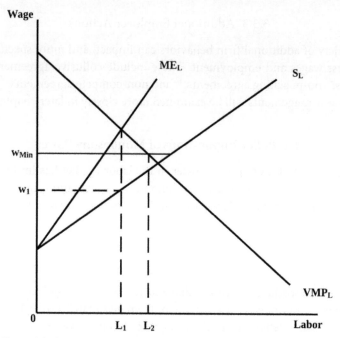

Figure 3.3 A minimum wage may increase a monopsonist's employment

rise. Consider the demand for labor (VMP_L) and the supply of labor (S_L) displayed in Figure 3.3. Prior to the minimum wage legislation, L_1 units of labor were employed at a wage of w_1. Following the minimum wage legislation, the employer's marginal expenditure on labor is altered. It is flat at the height of the minimum wage between the origin and S_L. Since the employer's demand for labor (VMP_L) intersects the horizontal portion of the marginal expenditure, employment expands from L_1 to L_2 even though the wage paid rises from w_1 to w_{min}.

Beyond the work of Card and Krueger, there is a good deal of empirical evidence that minimum wages do not lead to reduced employment.[46] For

---

[46] David Card, Do Minimum Wages Reduce Employment? A Case Study of California, 1987–89, 46 *ILR Review* 38 (1992); David Card, Using Regional Variation in Wages to Measure the Effects of the Federal Minimum Wage, 46 *ILR Review* 22 (1992); Lawrence F. Katz and Alan B. Krueger, The Effect of the Minimum Wage on the Fast-Food Industry, 46 *ILR Review* 6 (1992); and Stephen Machin and Alan Manning, The Effects of Minimum Wages on Wage Dispersion and Employment: Evidence from the UK Wages Councils, 47 *ILR Review* 319 (1994). A more recent paper by Jesse Wursten and Michael Reich, *Small Businesses and the Minimum Wage*, IRLE Working Paper No. 102–123 (2023) has found that raises in minimum wage had no statistically significant effect on employment levels

example, Manning examined the effects of introducing equal pay legislation on the employment of women.[47] By implementing equal pay legislation, the British government essentially instituted a minimum wage for women by requiring that the government raise the wage of women to that of men if they were initially paid less.[48] Similar to other empirical findings, there was no statistically significant decrease in the employment of women. Manning attributed this lack of an effect to monopsony power in the labor market.

Bhaskar and To explained this result with a model of monopsonistic competition.[49] The welfare results turned out to be somewhat ambiguous since firm employment rises while total employment may fall due to the possible exit of employers.

3.4.2 Downstream Effects

The existence and exploitation of monopsony power creates negative effects in the input market that can spill over into the output market.[50] Consider a monopsonist in a local labor market. By restricting employment of workers, the firm is necessarily restricting the quantity of output that can be produced.

The effects of this restriction depend on the structure of the labor market. If the monopsonist is a dominant employer, they will depress wages, but not as much as they would if they were a pure monopsonist. This also means that there is a restricted number of workers in either case, but less so in the case of a dominant employer. Hence, the adverse economic effects in the output market should be somewhat mitigated by the presence of the fringe.

In Figure 3.4, it is easy to see that monopsony in the labor market has harmed consumers in the output market. Let D be the demand for the firm's

---

in low wage industries including the fast-food industry and grocery stores. They attribute these economic results to monopsony in these labor markets.

[47] Alan Manning, The Equal Pay Act as an Experiment to Test Theories of the Labour Market, 63 *Economica* 191 (1996).

[48] For a theoretical analysis, see Brianna L. Alderman, Roger D. Blair, and Perihan Saygin, Monopsony, Wage Discrimination, and Public Policy, 61 *Economic Inquiry* 572 (2023).

[49] Venkataraman Bhaskar and Ted To, Minimum Wages for Ronald McDonald Monopsonies: A Theory of Monopsonistic Competition, 109 *Economic Journal* 190 (1999).

[50] The magnitude of the adverse effect in the output market depends on the market structure. If the output market is competitive, the impact will be negligible. In contrast, the impact will be significant if the output market is also imperfect.

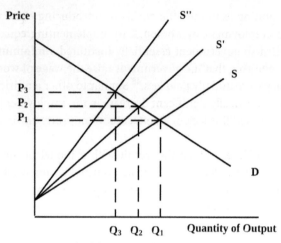

Figure 3.4 Monopsony in the labor market harms consumers in the output market

output and S be the supply of the output before the employer restricts the quantity of labor employed. In a competitive setting, the firm will produce Q_1 units of its output at a price of P_1.

Pure monopsony and a dominant employer both lead to reductions in supply of output, but the effect is greater in the case of pure monopsony. Hence, S' represents the supply of the goods sold in the case of a dominant employer, and S'' represents the supply when the employer is a pure monopsonist.

When the firm is a dominant employer, the result is a decrease in output to Q_2 and an increase in the output price to P_2. The pure monopsonist will decrease output even further to Q_3, resulting in an even higher output price of P_3.

Each case reduces consumer welfare and creates a social welfare loss in the market. The source of this deadweight loss differs when the market structure differs.

The pure monopsonist creates a social welfare loss that is entirely attributed to an inefficiency in the market. The value of the goods to consumers exceeds its cost to the sellers. If the firm were to expand its quantity of the goods sold, the firm would approach and eventually reach the quantity that equates these two values. However, because the firm has suppressed its employment, the supply shrinks, and an inefficiency is created. This inefficiency leads to a social welfare loss in the output market. The welfare losses are more complicated in the case of a dominant employer.

In the case of a dominant employer, the deadweight loss is a combination of an inefficiency in the market, as well as a misallocation of resources.

Again, the value of the goods to consumers is greater than its cost to the sellers, but the difference is smaller than in the case of pure monopsony, which creates the inefficiency. But there is some additional loss due to the fact that employees who could be more productive working at the dominant employer may be hired by a fringe employer where they are less effective.

Consider a larger firm, like a hospital, with monopsony power in the nurse labor market. This hospital can suppress the wages paid to its nurses. Now, let's introduce a smaller private practice with no market power. A more qualified nurse may be more productive and save more lives in the larger hospital, but they may be hired by the private practice because they are unable to get a job at the hospital. The nurse is still working in the market, and still receiving the suppressed wage, but they are not as effective as they would have been at the hospital.

Berger, Herkenhoff, and Mongey found that this theoretical misallocation of resources was consistent with empirical findings.[51] Relative to the efficient allocation of resources, monopsony resulted in welfare losses from labor market power by 7.6 percent. Moreover, output decreased by 20.9 percent. They attributed 60 percent of welfare losses to misallocation, 30 percent to pure markdowns, and the remaining 10 percent to their interactions.

The economic effects of monopsony power are clearly harmful to employees and consumers alike. Monopsony, however, is not necessarily illegal *per se*. As we will see in the next chapter, monopsony power that emanates from collusion among employers is unlawful. In contrast, the unilateral exercise of monopsony power is only unlawful if it exists due to competitively unreasonable conduct.

3.4.3 Merger Policy

The Department of Justice and Federal Trade Commission attempt to determine the economic effects of permitting various kinds of mergers. This includes horizontal mergers, that is, mergers among firms within the same market. One difficulty that the antitrust authorities face is determining what exactly defines the boundaries of the market. One tool that the Agencies use is the SSNIP test. They select a candidate set of products. Then they ask whether a hypothetical monopolist could increase the price by a small but significant amount without losing so many sales that the

---

[51] David Berger, Kyle Herkenhoff, and Simon Mongey, Labor Market Power, 112 *American Economic Review* 114 (2022).

price increase would be unprofitable. If so, that set of products constitutes a relevant product market.[52] The goal is to find the smallest set of products and smallest area that satisfies the SSNIP test.

Analogously, the SSNRW test asks whether a monopsonist could impose a "small, but significant non-transitory reduction in wages" without losing so many employees that the wage decrease would be unprofitable. Azar, Berry, and Marinescu suggested using this modified SSNIP test as a means of drawing boundaries around the relevant antitrust labor market.[53] They defined "small but significant" to be 5.0 percent and "non-transitory" to be one year.[54] Through their estimates of elasticities across a variety of occupations, they found that most estimates of elasticities fell below their critical values, implying that most occupations are relevant antitrust markets.

The SSNRW implies a critical value of elasticity of 20, which is large, but well below infinite. Referring back to Table 3.1, it is clear that most labor supply elasticities fall far below 20, which means that nearly all labor markets are vulnerable to monopsony. This creates another challenge for the antitrust authorities as they struggle to determine which mergers pose the most imminent and drastic effects to various labor markets.[55]

This is especially important because mergers of employers do have effects on the earnings of the employed workers. David Arnold found that, while mergers that had negligible effects on the local labor market do not appear to affect the annual earnings of workers, those workers who were employed by merging firms with substantial effects on the labor market found their earnings decreased by over 2.0 percent.[56]

3.5 Concluding Remarks

Despite being initially overlooked, monopsony power is an empirically relevant characteristic of the labor market. It is exploited by reducing employment and thereby reducing the wage paid to employees. Although the estimates of labor supply elasticities vary across occupation and over time, all estimates are far from infinite. Measures of overall supply elasticity appear to fall loosely in a range of 1.0 to 6.0, but this measure is easily altered by refining the labor market or characteristics of the employees in

---

[52] A similar question is posed to define the relevant geographic market.

[53] José A. Azar, Steven T. Berry, and Ioana Marinescu, *Estimating Labor Market Power*, NBER Working Paper No. w30365 (2022).

[54] These definitions are analogous to those used in the more familiar SSNIP test.

[55] Further discussions of monopsony and merger policy can be found in Chapter 10.

[56] Arnold, *Mergers and Acquisitions*.

said market (e.g., by gender). All this evidence suggests that the concept of a perfect labor market may be the true theoretical curiosity.

It is difficult to attribute one cause as the absolute source of monopsony power. There are in fact many sources that can work together and compound the effects of monopsony power in the labor market. The effects of monopsony power in the labor market have a variety of implications for policymakers, including the antitrust authorities. How the agencies treat monopsony in the labor market is a complex endeavor, and the focus of our next chapter.

4

Antitrust Policy in the United States

4.1 Introduction

The cornerstone of antitrust policy in the United States is the Sherman Act, which was passed in 1890.[1] Its central goal is to protect competition and the competitive process. The economic rationale for these twin concerns resides in the fact that competition results in the maximization of social welfare. In most cases, consumer welfare will be maximized as well.

In the next section, we will examine the statutory language of the Sherman Act along with its implementation. We will turn to the Clayton Act of 1914, which was designed to address some specific competitive concerns with the Sherman Act's broad prohibitions, in Section 4.4. Section 4.5 deals with antitrust enforcement and the sanctions for violations. In Section 4.6, we review the enforcement policies of the Department of Justice and the Federal Trade Commission regarding collusion among employers in the labor market. We close this chapter with some concluding remarks in Section 4.7.

4.2 The Sherman Act

In the wake of the Civil War, there was widespread dissatisfaction with the current economic environment. Farmers were plagued by low output prices, high interest rates, and high prices for farm equipment and other essential inputs. Consumers found price fixing conspiracies in a wide assortment of important products. Public sentiment flared over protective

---

[1] For a compact survey, see Herbert Hovenkamp, *Federal Antitrust Policy: The Law of Competition and Its Practice*, 6th ed. (2020). For an extensive treatment, see Phillip Areeda and Herbert Hovenkamp, *Antitrust Law Vol. I–XIV*.

tariffs and political corruption in Big Business.[2] Something had to be done. The result was the Sherman Act of 1890.[3]

4.2.1 Sherman Act

The major prohibitions of the Sherman Act are contained in Sections 1 and 2. Section 1 addresses collaboration among competitors. In contrast, Section 2 deals with unilateral efforts to displace competition with monopoly.

Section I: Every contract, combination in the form of trust or otherwise, or conspiracy, in restraint of trade or commerce among the several States, or with foreign nations, is declared to be illegal. Every person who shall make any contract or engage in any combination or conspiracy hereby declared to be illegal shall be deemed guilty of a felony, and, on conviction thereof, shall be punished by fine not exceeding $100,000,000 if a corporation, or, if any other person, $1,000,000, or by imprisonment not exceeding 10 years, or by both said punishments, in the discretion of the court.

Whenever rival firms agree to refrain from competing with one another, they run afoul of Section 1 of the Sherman Act. Agreements to limit price competition,[4] rig bids,[5] reduce either quality or quantity,[6] divide markets,[7] and allocate customers, among other things, have all been declared unlawful under Section 1 of the Sherman Act.[8]

Section II: Every person who shall monopolize, or attempt to monopolize, or combine or conspire with any other person or persons, to monopolize any part of the trade or commerce among the several States, or with foreign nations, shall be deemed guilty of a felony, and, on conviction thereof, shall be punished by fine not exceeding $100,000,000 if a corporation, or, if any other person, $1,000,000, or by imprisonment not exceeding 10 years, or by both said punishments, in the discretion of the court.

It is important to recognize that the structural condition of monopoly is not unlawful. Instead, taking steps to become a monopolist is what violates

---

[2] An extremely useful historical account of the conditions that resulted in the Sherman Act can be found in Hans B. Thorelli, *The Federal Antitrust Policy* (1955).

[3] 15 U.S.C. §1 and 15 U.S.C. §2.

[4] *U.S. v. Trenton Potteries Co.*, 273 U.S. 392 (1927).

[5] *Addyston Pipe and Steel Co. v. United States*, 175 U.S. 211 (1899).

[6] See Roger D. Blair and Christine Piette Durrance, Restraints on Quality Competition, 10 *Journal of Competition Law and Economics* 27 (2014).

[7] *Palmer v. BRG of Georgia, Inc.*, 498 U.S. 46 (1990).

[8] For a compact survey of antitrust law and economics, see Roger D. Blair and David L. Kaserman, *Antitrust Economics* (2nd ed. 2009).

Section 2. In its Grinnell decision, the Supreme Court summarized its opinion of what constitutes unlawful monopolization:[9]

The offense of monopoly under section 2 of the Sherman Act has 2 elements: (1) the possession of monopoly power in the relevant market; and (2) the willful acquisition and maintenance of that power as distinguished from growth or development as a consequence of a superior product, business acumen, or historic accident.

The first prong of the *Grinnell* test establishes the structural condition of monopoly, which is not necessarily unlawful.

There is a good reason for this – monopoly can emerge from desirable conduct. These include research and development expenditures that result in important innovations that are protected by patents. In some instances, managerial efficiency makes it impossible for others to compete. Finally, where demand is small relative to the efficient scale of production, competition may lead to the survival of a single firm, that is, a "natural" monopoly.

What makes the structural condition of monopoly unlawful is the way the firm acquired its monopoly. In other words, if a firm dominates an industry, or a market, through competitively objectionable conduct, that firm will violate Section 2.

Predatory pricing, that is, pricing below cost to drive out competition, is the paradigmatic example of monopolizing conduct.[10] This practice involves short-run losses by the predator to bankrupt rivals and subsequent recoupment after the demise of the rival through monopoly pricing.

In its *Brooke Group* decision,[11] the Supreme Court condemned below cost pricing where the alleged predator had a reasonable expectation of recouping its investment in excluding rivals.

4.2.2 Sanctions for Sherman Act Violations

The Sherman Act's sanction for violations of Sections 1 and 2 are the same. For corporations, a fine of up to $100 million per offense may be imposed. In many instances, the actual fine is less than the maximum, which may be necessary for smaller firms to avoid bankruptcy.

The maximum fine for an individual who violates either Section 1 or Section 2 is $1 million. Individuals normally do not pay substantial fines, but they may be subject to a prison sentence. The maximum prison sentence

[9] *U.S.* v. *Grinnell Corp.*, 384 U.S. 563 (1966).
[10] For a compact survey, see Blair and Kaserman, *Antitrust Economics* in Chapter 7.
[11] *Brooke Group Ltd.* v. *Brown & Williamson Tobacco Corp.*, 509 U.S. 209 (1993).

is 10 years, but no one has received the maximum. In fact, the longest sentence to be imposed was five years.

4.3 Monopsony and the Sherman Act

During our 130-year experience with antitrust enforcement, the focus has been on monopoly rather than monopsony. But this does not mean that monopsony is exempt from antitrust prosecution. In its opinion in *Anderson* v. *Shipowners' Association of Pacific Coast*,[12] the Supreme Court found that Section 1's prohibition of collusive restraints of trade applied to labor markets.

In its *Mandeville Island Farms* opinion,[13] the Supreme Court made it clear that sellers were protected from collusion among buyers. This case involved an agreement among refiners of sugar beets to use a pricing formula that depressed the prices paid to growers below their but for levels. The growers filed suit to recover antitrust damages pursuant to Section 4 of the Clayton Act.[14] The refiners argued that the growers lacked standing to sue because they were sellers rather than consumers. The Supreme Court rejected this argument:

The refiners' conspiracy was of the type forbidden, even though the price- fixing was by purchasers and though the claimants of treble damages are sellers instead of customers or consumers.

The prohibition of monopsony is analogous to that of monopoly. First, a successful plaintiff will have to prove that the defendant has monopsony power in the relevant market. In addition, the plaintiff will have to prove that the defendant acquired its monopsony status through competitively unreasonable conduct.

Allegations of monopsonizing conduct were at the core of the *Weyerhaeuser* case.[15] The dispute involved an allegation that Weyerhaeuser had engaged in predatory conduct in the alder sawlog market. Unlike most predatory price claims, Ross-Simmons did not allege pricing below cost in an effort to drive rivals out of the market. Instead, it involved claims that Weyerhaeuser overpaid for alder sawlogs and, thereby, denied an essential input to Ross-Simmons. In essence, Ross-Simmons alleged that Weyerhaeuser's purchasing practices were aimed at denying

[12] *Anderson* v. *Shipowners' Association of Pacific Coast*, 272 U.S. 359 (1926).
[13] *Mandeville Island Farms* v. *American Crystal Sugar*, 334 U.S. 219 (1948).
[14] 15 U.S.C. §15 provides a private right of action for anyone injured by an antitrust violation.
[15] *Weyerhaeuser Co.* v. *Ross-Simmons Hardwood Lumber Co.*, 549 U.S. 312 (2007).

Ross-Simmons and other hardwood lumber companies access to the inputs that were essential for their continued vitality as competitors in the hardwood lumber market.

At the District Court, the jury found Weyerhaeuser guilty and awarded damages to Ross-Simmons which were trebled to $78.8 million. In its appeal to the Ninth Circuit, Weyerhaeuser argued that Ross-Simmons had failed to satisfy the *Brooke Group* test for predatory pricing.[16] The Ninth Circuit rejected Weyerhaeuser's appeal and affirmed the District Court's ruling, but the tide turned at the Supreme Court.

The Supreme Court found that monopsony and monopoly should be treated symmetrically.[17] Consequently, allegations of predatory bidding (or overbuying) would have to meet the standards set out in *Brooke Group*.[18] More specifically, a successful plaintiff would have to prove two things. First, the plaintiff would have to prove the existence of predatory bidding. This requires proof that the defendant overpaid for the input in question such that the average cost of its finished product exceeded the market determined price.[19] In essence, the overbidding resulted in unprofitable sales. Second, the plaintiff had to prove that the defendant had a reasonable probability of recouping its losses after the plaintiff's demise as a rival.[20] In the case of Ross-Simmons, they had to prove that Weyerhaeuser paid so much for the sawlogs that the prices that it could realize in the output market were below its costs, and that Weyerhaeuser has a reasonable probability of recouping the losses that it experienced during the period of predation. Since Ross-Simmons failed to satisfy this modified *Brooke Group* test, the Supreme Court reversed the judgement of the lower court.[21]

Recently, there has been considerable private litigation against buyers by input suppliers that have been underpaid due to collusion among buyers or employers.

---

[16] *Brooke Group Ltd.* v. *Brown & Williamson Tobacco Corp.*, 509 U.S. 209 (1993).

[17] "[M]onopoly and monopsony are symmetrical distortions of competition from an economic standpoint.... The kinship suggests that similar legal standards should apply to claims of monopolization and claims of monopsonization." *Weyerhaeuser Co.* v. *Ross-Simmons Hardwood Lumber Co.*, 549 U.S. 312, 322 (2007).

[18] There is no distinction between overbidding and overbuying. The only way to buy too much is to stand ready to bid too much; if one bids too much, one must stand ready to buy too much. Identifying what constitutes "too much" is no mean feat.

[19] *Weyerhaeuser Co.* v. *Ross-Simmons Hardwood Lumber Co.*, 549 U.S. 312, 325 (2007).

[20] *Id.* at 325–326.

[21] *Id.* at 326 (2007). For a compact analysis of the Weyerhaeuser case, see Brianna L. Alderman and Roger D. Blair, Predation by the Dominant Buyer, *Competition Policy International Antitrust Chronicle* (2022).

4.3.1 Recent Litigation

There has been a good deal of antitrust litigation involving monopsony. In most instances, it has involved allegations of collusion among buyers or employers.

No-poaching agreements among rival employers are agreements not to hire one another's employees.[22] Such agreements have involved hardware and software engineers,[23] digital animators,[24] medical school faculty,[25] and others. In addition, there have been wage-fixing agreements among rival employers. These have arisen in the markets for hospital nurses,[26] fashion models,[27] meatpacking employees,[28] and temporary duty nurses.[29]

4.4 The Clayton Act of 1914

For two decades, there was concern within the business community and the consuming public that the vague prohibitions in the Sherman Act would prove to be ineffective in dealing with the "monopoly problem." The business community was concerned by the statutory language since it was open to interpretation. Consequently, the line between permissible and impermissible conduct was unclear. Consumers were concerned that the judiciary might favor the business community in drawing that line.

The Clayton Act was aimed at providing some specificity and extending the reach of the antitrust laws.

4.4.1 Price Discrimination

There was some evidence that Standard Oil (now Exxon) demanded lower prices than those that were offered to its rivals in the petroleum industry. These lower prices gave Standard Oil a competitive advantage over its competition. The result was Standard Oil's dominance of the petroleum industry in the late 1800s and early 1900s. To curtail such efforts to monopolize,

---

22 This is the subject of Chapter 7.
23 *U.S.* v. *Adobe Systems, Inc.*, No. 1:10-cv-01629 (D.D.C. Sept. 24, 2010).
24 *U.S.* v. *Lucasfilm Ltd.*, Case No. 1:10-cv-02220-RBW (D.D.C. Dec. 21, 2010).
25 *Seaman* v. *Duke University*, No. 1:15-cv-462 (M.D.N.C. Sep. 25, 2019).
26 *Cason-Merenda* v. *Detroit Medical Center*, No. 2:06-cv-15601 (E.D. Mich. Dec. 13, 2006).
27 See www.ftc.gov/news-events/news/press-releases/1995/06/council-fashion-designers-america.
28 *Brown* v. *JBS USA Food Company*, No. 1:22-cv-02946 (U.S.D.C. Colorado Nov. 11, 2022).
29 *Doe* v. *Arizona Hospital Healthcare Association*, No. cv 07-1292-PHX-SRB (D. Ariz. Mar. 19, 2009).

Section 2 of the Clayton Act prohibits price discrimination under certain circumstances.

Section 2a: [I]t shall be unlawful for any person engaged in commerce ... either directly or indirectly, to discriminate in price between different purchasers of commodities of like grade and quality ... where the effect of such discrimination may be substantially to lessen competition or tend to create a monopoly in any line of commerce.

The basic prohibition is clear: When price discrimination may result in a substantial lessening of competition or a tendency to monopolize, it is forbidden. The sub-sections are there to close loopholes. Interestingly, there are two defenses. First, irrespective of the competitive effect, if a price reduction is necessary to meet an equally low price of a rival, it is permissible. Second, if a price reduction can be justified on the basis of lower costs, the reduction is lawful. For our purposes, Section 2f is important because it addresses the exercise of monopsony power.

Section 2f: [I]t shall be unlawful for any person engaged in commerce, in the course of such commerce, knowingly to induce or receive a discrimination in price which is prohibited by this section.

This prohibition has been difficult to implement because it requires proof that the buyer actually knows that the price that it is demanding is discriminatory. During the bargaining with a supplier, the large buyer may simply insist on a price below that offered by the seller without regard to the price that the buyer's rivals are paying.

4.4.2　Conditional Contracts

In some contracts, a seller or a buyer imposes conditions that limit competition. Some of these are procompetitive while others may be anticompetitive. Section 3 of the Clayton Act bars conditional sales when the effects may be a substantial lessening of competition or a tendency to create a monopoly.

Section 3: That it shall be unlawful for any person engaged in commerce, in the course of such commerce, to lease or make a sale or contract for sale of goods, wares, merchandise, machinery, supplies or other commodities, whether patented or unpatented, for use, consumption or resale ... or fix a price charged therefor, or discount from, or rebate upon, such price, on the condition, agreement or understanding that the lessee or purchaser thereof shall not use or deal in the goods, wares, merchandise, machinery, supplies or other commodities of a competitor or competitors of the lessor or seller, where the effect of such lease, sale, or contract for sale or such condition, agreement or under-standing may be to substantially lessen competition or tend to create a monopoly in any line of commerce.

A wide array of conditional sales fall under Section 3 of the Clayton Act.

Tying Contracts: A seller agrees to sell product A, but only under the condition that the buyer also purchases product B. In other words, the seller uses the tying good (A) to sell the tied good (B).

Requirements Contracts: A seller agrees to supply its product, but only on the condition that the buyer purchases all its requirements for that product from the supplier. This contract forecloses the seller's rivals from supplying any of the buyer's input needs.

Territorial Confinement: A seller agrees to supply its product, but only on the condition that the buyer not resell the product outside its designated area.

Exclusive Dealing: A seller agrees to supply its product but only on the condition that the buyers not distribute rival products.

4.4.3 Mergers

A merger joins together the assets of two or more previously independent firms. Depending on the specific competitive environment, a merger may be procompetitive, anticompetitive, or competitively neutral. Antitrust policy regarding mergers is contained in Section 7 of the Clayton Act.

Section 7: That no person engaged in commerce or in any activity affecting commerce shall acquire, directly or indirectly, the whole or any part of the stock or other share capital and no person subject to the jurisdiction of the Federal Trade Commission shall acquire the whole or any part of the assets of another person engaged also in commerce or in any activity affecting commerce, where in any line of commerce or in any activity affecting commerce in any section of the country, the effect of such acquisition may be substantially to lessen competition, or to tend to create a monopoly.

Section 7 of the Clayton Act applies to horizontal mergers, which involve the combination of two competing firms. For example, if a hospital in a local market acquires another hospital in that market, the merger would be horizontal. Section 7 also covers vertical mergers. If a supplier acquires its customer, the merger would be vertical.

Both horizontal and vertical mergers are unlawful only if they result in a substantial lessening of competition or a tendency to create a monopoly. The language of Section 7 does not appear to apply to monopsony power that could result from a merger. Senator Amy Klobuchar (D. Minn.) tried to amend Section 7 to include explicitly "or monopsony." It turns out that the judiciary has taken care of this.

4.5 Private Enforcement

Antitrust enforcement by the antitrust agencies (the Department of Justice and the Federal Trade Commission) is supplemented by private enforcement.[30] Section 4 of the Clayton Act provides a private right of action to those who have been injured by the antitrust violation.[31]

Section 4: [A]ny person who shall be injured in his business or property by reason of anything forbidden in the antitrust laws may sue therefor in any district court of the United States in the district in which the defendant resides or is found or has an agent, without respect to the amount in controversy, and shall recover three-fold the damages by him sustained, and the cost of suit, including a reasonable attorney's fee.

Although Section 4 clearly says "any" person, the judiciary has confined any person to any person *directly* injured by an antitrust violation. There are several reasons why this restriction may be necessary. When an antitrust violation occurs, its economic effects ripple through the economy. If every injured party had decided to sue for damages, the judicial system would be swamped.

For example, consider the economic effects of a price fixing conspiracy that raises the price of chicken. The immediate result is a decrease in the quantity of chicken consumed by overcharged consumers. Suppliers of chicken are injured as the sellers of processed chicken reduce their output and, therefore, demand for the birds. In addition, the growers will demand less feed, less labor, and less transportation services. The suppliers of processed chicken will also need fewer inputs. The rippling effect goes on and on. The demands of the cartel members for inputs – feed, farm labor, and transportation, are reduced. On the output side, the processed chicken suppliers will purchase less packaging and transportation. They will also hire fewer workers. But this is not the end. Restaurants and grocery stores will buy less chicken, and this will have adverse effects on the input suppliers. This seems to have no end.

---

[30] For a thorough treatment of private enforcement, see Phillip Areeda, Herbert Hovenkamp, Roger D. Blair, and Christine Piette Durrance, *Antitrust Law IIA* 390–399 (2021). For a more compact treatment, see Roger D. Blair and Wenche Wang, Buyer Cartels and Private Enforcement of Antitrust Policy, 38 *Managerial and Decision Economics* 1185 (2017).
[31] 15 U.S.C. §15.

As interpreted by the Supreme Court, the plain language of Section 4 does not mean precisely what it says. For example, "any person" is limited to those who have been directly injured. To be compensable, injuries must be "antitrust injuries" as defined by the Supreme Court in its *Brunswick* decision.[32]

In its *Bigelow* decision, the Supreme Court explained that antitrust damages are correctly measured:

by comparison of profits, prices and values as affected by the [antitrust violation], with what they would have been in its absence under freely competitive conditions.[33]

Thus, the measure of damages is a comparison of the actual state of affairs with the antitrust violation and what they would have been in the absence of the violation. Any differences that are due to exogenous factors unrelated to the antitrust violation must be controlled for.

In its *Reiter* decision, the Supreme Court made it clear that consumers who have been directly overcharged by a price fixing cartel have suffered in their property and, consequently, have standing to pursue antitrust damages.

In a monopsony case the usual concern is with an underpayment, that is, the price actually paid is below the competitive price.

The Supreme Court's *Mandeville Island Farms* decision dealt with a case involving collusive monopsony. As we mentioned earlier, the refiners of sugar beets in northern California agreed among themselves to employ a price formula in buying sugar beets that depressed the price that they paid. This resulted in a group of sugar beet growers filing suit under Section 4 of the Clayton Act. The Supreme Court found that:

[t]he refiners' conspiracy was of the type forbidden, even though the price-fixing was by purchasers and though the claimants of treble damages are sellers instead of customers or consumers.

In a labor market setting, the damage (Δ) would be:

$$\Delta = \left(w_{bf} - w_a \right) L_a,$$

---

[32] *Brunswick Co.* v. *Pueblo Bowl-O-Mat, Inc.*, 429 U.S. 477 (1977) defines antitrust injury as "injury, which is to say injury of the type the antitrust laws were intended to prevent and that flows from that which makes defendants' acts unlawful. The injury should reflect the anticompetitive effect either of the violation or anticompetitive acts made possible by the violation." Roger D. Blair and Jeffery L. Harrison, Rethinking Antitrust Injury, 42 *Vanderbilt Law Review* 1539 (1989), argues that victims of monopsony suffer antitrust injury due to depressed prices that they receive. Chapter 5 provides an examination of which victims of antitrust injury are entitled to damages.

[33] *Bigelow* v. *RKO Radio Pictures, Inc.*, 327 U.S. 251, 264 (1946).

where w_{bf} is the wage that would have been paid but for the violation, w_a is the actual wage paid, and L_a is the actual quantity of labor services employed.

In estimating the damages, the plaintiffs can rely on business record for w_a and L_a, but w_{bf} must be estimated. The estimation of w_{bf} must account for all the factors that influence wages. The plaintiff is only entitled to recover the difference due to the antitrust violation.

4.6 DOJ–FTC Antitrust Guidance

The federal Antitrust Agencies became concerned that impermissible, monopsonistic conduct was misunderstood by employers. In 2016, the DOJ and the FTC jointly issued their *Antitrust Guidance for Human Resource Professionals*.[34] This document put employers on notice that collusive activity in the labor market among employers was considered to be *per se* unlawful under Section 1 of the Sherman Act.

The Agencies seemed to be concerned with two specific restraints: (1) collusion among employers on the wages to be paid and (2) agreements not to hire one another's employees, that is, "no-poaching" agreements. We will examine the *Guidance* on these agreements in turn.

4.6.1 Collusion on Wages and Benefits

Naked wage-fixing agreements are agreements to limit competition in the labor market.[35] They have no redeeming virtues and, therefore, are *per se* violations of Section 1 of the Sherman Act. This prohibition extends to all terms of employment including wages and salaries, bonus plans, shift differentials, benefits such as retirement plans, health insurance, vacation and sick leave, family leave, and any other terms of employment upon which employers may compete.

The *Guidance* also warned that the DOJ would begin to file criminal charges for those engaged in wage fixing. For the employers, this could result in substantial fines. For HR professionals convicted of a Section 1 violation, their sanctions could include prison sentences as well as fines.[36] Moreover, the employees who were undercompensated as a result of a Section 1 violation could sue the employer for treble damages pursuant to Section 4 of the Clayton Act.

---

[34] See www.justice.gov/atr/file/903511/download.
[35] For a more extensive review of collusion on wages and other terms of employment, see Chapter 6.
[36] See Chapter 6.

4.6.2 No-Poaching Agreements

In broad strokes, a no-poaching agreement is an agreement among rival employers to not hire one another's employees.[37] The terms of such agreements may vary to some extent. In some cases, the firms simply agree not to make cold calls to another firm's employees. But if an employee initiates the inquiry, then it is permissible to hire that person. In other cases, hiring another firm's employees is forbidden. In one case, lateral hires were forbidden, but hires involving a promotion were permitted. In all cases, the demand for labor is depressed and wages are lower than they would be in the absence of no-poaching agreements.

In their *Guidance*, the DOJ and FTC have clearly condemned no-poaching agreements. In the absence of extenuating circumstances, no-poaching agreements are considered to be *per se* violations of Section 1 of the Sherman Act. As with wage-fixing agreements, employees who have been disadvantaged by no-poaching agreements may sue their employer for being under-compensated.

4.7 Concluding Remarks

As a broad generalization, the Sherman Act and the Clayton Act are aimed at preserving competition and protecting competitive processes in all markets. This includes the labor market. The market structure of monopsony is only unlawful if it results from competitively objectionable conduct. Collusion among employers, however, is usually unlawful *per se*. Whether the collusion is aimed at decreasing compensation or at no-poaching agreements, employers should expect a hostile reception in court. Violators may face fines, imprisonment, and private damage suits.

Recently, there has been considerable private litigation by input suppliers that have been underpaid due to collusion among buyers or employers. In these labor markets, the complaints involve collusive agreements on their compensation to be paid or agreements not to hire one another's employees. These collusive strategies will be examined in Chapters 6 and 7, respectively.

---

[37] No-poaching agreements are the focus of Chapter 7.

5

The Intended and Unintended
Victims of Monopsony

5.1 Introduction

Monopsony in the labor market – sometimes legal, sometimes illegal – is pervasive in the U.S. economy.[1] Nearly all empirical studies of the labor market find positively sloped labor supply functions, which means that wages can be depressed by reducing employment.[2] In that event, employees are subject to monopsonistic exploitation, that is, their compensation will fall below their contribution to the employer's profit. If the monopsony is lawful, the underpaid employees have no antitrust remedy.[3]

There are, however, antitrust remedies for victims of employer cartels. Employer cartels have been found in many labor markets. These include markets for digital animators,[4] hardware and software engineers,[5] hospital nurses,[6] temporary duty nurses,[7] physical therapists,[8] employees of the major meatpackers,[9] university faculty,[10] and others.

When the threat of public enforcement deters unlawful monopsonization and collusion, everyone is protected. When monopsonistic exploitation is not deterred, however, there may be many victims – some intended,

---

[1] This chapter draws on Brianna L. Alderman and Roger D. Blair, The Antitrust Victims of Monopsony, *Journal of Antitrust Enforcement* (2023).
[2] For a survey, see Anna Sokolova and Todd Sorensen, Monopsony in Labor Markets: A Meta-Analysis, 74 *Industrial and Labor Relations Review* 27 (2021).
[3] The employees may unionize to create countervailing power. See Chapter 8.
[4] *U.S.* v. *Lucasfilm Ltd.*, Case No. 1:10-cv-02220-RBW (D.D.C. Dec. 21, 2010).
[5] *U.S.* v. *Adobe Systems, Inc.*, No. 1:10-cv-01629 (D.D.C. Sept. 24, 2010).
[6] *Cason-Merenda* v. *Detroit Medical Center*, No. 2:06-cv-15601 (E.D. Mich. Dec. 13, 2006).
[7] *Doe* v. *Arizona Hospital Healthcare Association*, No. cv 07-1292-PHX-SRB (D. Ariz. Mar. 19, 2009).
[8] *U.S.* v. *Jindal*, No. 4:20-cr-358 (E.D. Tex. Dec. 09, 2020).
[9] *Brown* v. *JBS USA Food Company*, No. 1:22-cv-02946 (U.S.D.C. Colorado Nov. 11, 2022).
[10] *Seaman* v. *Duke University*, No. 1:15-cv-462 (M.D.N.C. Sep. 25, 2019).

some unintended. By and large, the unintended victims will lack antitrust standing and, therefore, their injuries will go uncompensated. In this chapter, we identify those uncompensated injuries and argue that granting standing to those groups of victims will improve both the compensatory and deterrent functions of Section 4 of the Clayton Act.

In this chapter, we identify six classes of victims along with their injuries and explore the legal precedents that preclude recovery for five of the victim classes.

In Section 5.2, we begin with a review of the economic consequences of pure and partial monopsony, while Section 5.3 focuses on antitrust's only protected class – direct victims. Section 5.4 discusses the five unprotected classes of victims and offers some suggestions for reform to expand the number of protected classes. In Section 5.5, we discuss some additional concerns that may arise due to an expansion in the number of protected individuals. Finally, Section 5.6 offers some concluding remarks.

5.2 Economic Consequences of Monopsony

To identify the victims of monopsony in the labor market, we will employ a hypothetical cartel of employers. We begin with the competitive benchmark. The collective demand for employees by all employers is the value of the marginal product (VMP_L) of employees.[11] The supply (S_L) of employees will be equal to the demand in competitive equilibrium. In Figure 5.1, the wage (w) and quantity of labor hired (L) that equates supply and demand are w_1 and L_1, respectively.

In this competitive equilibrium, employer surplus is the difference between the value of the marginal product and the price that must be paid for labor. In Figure 5.1, employer surplus is captured by the triangular area abw_1. Employee surplus is the difference between the reservation wage, that is, the minimum wage that must be paid to induce the worker to enter the labor market, and the wage paid. In Figure 5.1, employee surplus is equal to the triangular area w_1bc.

Together, the sum of employer surplus and employee surplus – area abc – is a measure of social (or total) welfare. This sum is maximized in competitive equilibrium. Any change in the wage paid and quantity of labor

[11] Labor is emloyed to produce output. The change in total output due to an incremental change in employment is the marginal product of that input. The incremental value to the employer is the marginal product times the price of the output – P • MP = VMP – which is the value of the marginal product. Thus, the demand for the input is its VMP.

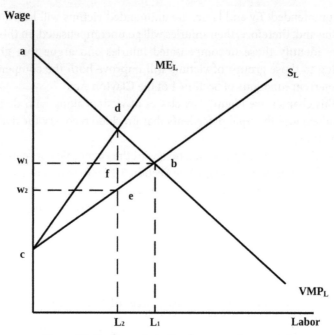

Figure 5.1 Profit maximization by an employer cartel

employed will decrease social welfare. The maximization of consumer welfare (or social welfare) is the economic rationale for our antitrust policy.[12]

If there is a single employer in the market, then there will be a pure monopsony. If all the employers in a labor market form a cartel, the economic results will be the same as those of pure monopsony. To maximize profits, the monopsonist (or the cartel) will restrict its employment of labor to the quantity that equates the marginal expenditure of labor (ME_L) to the value of the marginal product.[13] This is shown in Figure 5.1 as L_2. At that quantity, the wage is w_2.

In comparison to the competitive equilibrium, the wage paid falls from w_1 to w_2, the quantity of labor employed falls from L_1 to L_2, and

---

[12] Phillip Areeda and Herbert Hovenkamp, *Antitrust Law*, 5th ed., ¶ 100a (2022), state: "[T]he general goal of the antitrust laws is to promote 'competition' as the economist understands that term. Thus, we say that the principal objective of antitrust policy is to maximize consumer welfare by encouraging firms to behave competitively while yet permitting them to take advantage of every available economy that comes from internal or jointly created production efficiencies, or from innovation producing new processes or new or improved products."

[13] For the mathematics supporting this calculation, see Chapter 2.

social welfare falls by the triangular area dbe. Surplus is redistributed from employees to the employers. The rectangular area w_1few_2 had been employee surplus, but is now employer surplus.

5.2.1 Numerical Example

A numerical example is useful in gaining an appreciation for the impact of monopsony. Suppose that the demand for hours of labor services can be written as:

$$w = 70 - 0.0001L,$$

while the supply is given as:

$$w = 10 + 0.0002L.$$

In competitive equilibrium, the wage will be $50 and the number of hours worked will equal 200,000.

If the employers form a cartel, they will maximize their collective profits by employing the quantity of labor where the marginal expenditure on labor is equal to the value of the marginal product, that is, where ME_L equals VMP_L. Since the marginal expenditure will be equal to:

$$ME = 10 + 0.0004Q,$$

the cartel will employ 120,000 hours of work at a wage of $34.

The formation of a cartel has now led to a reduction of employment and the exclusion of laborers who were priced out of the market. For those workers who were not priced out, they received an underpayment totaling $1,920,000.[14] The loss in employee surplus for those priced out of the market is $640,000.[15] These are substantial values and could be significantly compounded in situations where the cartel exploits its monopsony power for many years before being stopped.

5.2.2 Partial Conspiracy

Many cartels do not involve every single employer. For example, there are four meatpackers that account for 85 percent of domestic purchases of fed cattle in the U.S. There are some 700 smaller meatpackers that account for

---

[14] The underpayment on actual employment is equal to $(w_1 - w_2)L_2 = (\$50 - 34)120,000 = \$1,920,000$.

[15] The loss in employee surplus due to being priced out of the market is equal to $\frac{1}{2}(w_1 - w_2)(L_1 - L_2) = \frac{1}{2}(\$50 - 34)(200,000 - 120,000) = \$640,000$.

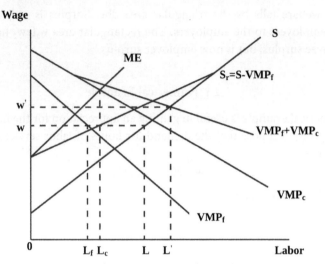

Figure 5.2 Profit maximization with partial conspiracy

the remaining 15 percent. Allegedly, the four large buyers conspired with one another while the remaining 700 did not. In that event, it is useful to adopt the collusive variant of the dominant buyer model.

If the employers did not form an employer cartel, the market price would be found at the intersection of the total market demand ($VMP_f + VMP_c$) and the market supply of labor. At this point, the market will clear at a wage of w' and L' units of labor employed.

It may be the case, however, that only some of the employers form a cartel. If there are many firms in the labor market, it is likely that not all these firms will be members of the cartel. Assuming that there are a few major employers hiring a large share of labor in the market, these employers may agree to work in concert to suppress the market wage. The demand for these employers will be denoted as VMP_c in Figure 5.2. Those employers who are independent of the cartel will be referred to as the fringe, and their demand is VMP_f. The function S represents the supply of labor in the whole market.

The cartel will need to take the fringe employers' demand into account to maximize its collective profit. The members will determine the residual supply of labor (S_r) in the market by subtracting the fringe's demand from the total market supply: $S_r = S - VMP_f$. Using the residual supply, the cartel will find the profit maximizing quantity of labor employed by equating the demand function (VMP_c) with its marginal expenditure (ME).

At this equality, the cartel will employ the profit maximizing quantity, L_c, at a wage of w. The non-colluding employers will act as price takers, paying w and employing L_f units of labor, as seen in Figure 5.2. The total quantity of labor employed will equal L.

5.2.3 Numerical Example

To illustrate the economic effect of a competitive fringe, consider the following numerical example. Suppose that some, but not all, employers have decided to collude. The cartel's demand for labor is:

$$w = 70 - 0.000125L,$$

while the demand for labor for the non-member firms is:

$$w = 70 - 0.0005L.$$

The market supply for labor is still:

$$w = 10 + 0.0002Q.$$

The aggregate market demand remains the same as that of the single firm monopsony model. Thus, if the employers behave competitively, the market will clear where 200,000 hours of labor are employed at a wage of $50 each. However, if there is a partial conspiracy, the total quantity of labor employed in the market is suppressed to 160,249 hours, while the wage paid falls to $42.[16] The members of the cartel employ 104,349 hours of labor, while the fringe employers hire the remaining 55,900 hours of labor.

This example illustrates an interesting result of a partial conspiracy. Because the non-cartel employers have no obligation to reduce their employment, profit maximization will lead them to expand, rather than contract, their level of employment. This offsets, to an extent, the efforts of the cartel members to depress the wage paid in the market. Consequently, the wage falls from $50 to $42, rather than $34. Although the wage is still higher than it would be if all employers were members of the cartel, that does not make this the ideal case. There is still a loss in social welfare, and many workers are injured because of the collusive agreement.

---

[16] These numbers have been rounded for mathematical ease. The derivation of these results is available from the authors upon request.

The existence of a partial conspiracy prices some potential workers out of the market. In this example, that loss equals $159,004.[17] In this setting, there is also an underpayment of $1,281,992.[18]

The arguably more interesting result of a partial conspiracy is that for umbrella victims. The only employees entitled to damages under current federal statutes are those who were hired by members of the cartel. This means that damages amounting to $447,200 are not recoverable by those who work for non-cartel employers.[19] Despite accounting for over one third of the total injury, these victims will not be compensated for their losses.

5.2.4 Summary

Through the analysis of our numerical examples, we can see that there are many victims when employers decide to act in concert. While many individuals may be injured because of the formation of a cartel, not all have standing to sue. In fact, only one group is entitled to damages in federal cases. Our next section shines some light on this privileged set of victims.

5.3 Antitrust's Only Protected Class

In our example of a wage-fixing conspiracy among all employers in a labor market, the employees are obviously the victims. The wage that they receive for their labor falls from w_1 to w_2. Thus, they experience an underpayment on the quantity of labor employed equal to $(w_1 - w_2)L_2$. In our first numerical example, the unlawful underpayment is equal to $1,920,000.

Section 4 of the Clayton Act permits private damage suits in antitrust cases.[20] Specifically, Section 4 holds that:

any person who shall be injured in his business or property by reason of anything forbidden in the antitrust laws may sue therefor … and shall recover threefold the damages by him sustained, and the cost of suit, including a reasonable attorney's fee.[21]

---

[17] The loss in employee surplus due to being priced out of the market is equal to ½($50 − 42) (200,000 − 160,249) = $159,004.

[18] The underpayment on actual employment is equal to ($50 − 42)160,249 = $1,281,992.

[19] The underpayment suffered by employees who were hired by the fringe is equal to ($50 − 42)55,900 = $447,200.

[20] 15 U.S.C. Section 15.

[21] 15 U.S.C. Section 15.

In *Mandeville Island Farms*,[22] the U.S. Supreme Court made it clear that sellers enjoyed the same protection as buyers:

It is clear that the agreement is the sort of combination condemned by the Act, even though the price-fixing was by purchasers, and the persons specially injured under the treble damage claim are sellers, not customers or consumers.[23]

The Supreme Court's decision in *Bigelow*[24] established that the extent of the antitrust damages caused by a cartel's existence can be found:

by comparison of profits, prices and values as affected by the [antitrust violation], with what they would have been in its absence under freely competitive conditions.[25]

Accordingly, the damages (Δ) suffered by those employees that were not priced out of the market would be the difference between the wage that would have been paid but for the antitrust violation (w_{bf}) and the wage actually paid (w_a) times the actual quantity of labor supplied (L_a):

$$\Delta = \left(w_{bf} - w_a \right) L_a.$$

Ordinary business records can be used to find w_a and L_a. The econometric challenge resides in estimating w_{bf} while controlling for exogenous influences on the wage. This, of course, is precisely what multivariate econometrics is designed to do.[26] If the plaintiffs are successful, they will receive treble damages plus their costs of litigation.[27]

To have antitrust standing to pursue damages under Section 4 of the Clayton Act, a plaintiff must have suffered antitrust injury, which the Supreme Court defined in its *Brunswick* decision as:[28]

---

[22] *Mandeville Island Farms* v. *American Crystal Sugar Co.*, 334 U.S. 219 (1948).
[23] *Mandeville Island Farms* v. *American Crystal Sugar Co.*, 334 U.S. 235 (1948).
[24] *Bigelow* v. *RKO Radio Pictures, Inc.*, 327 U.S. 251 (1946).
[25] *Bigelow* v. *RKO Radio Pictures, Inc.*, 327 U.S. 264 (1946).
[26] See Phillip Areeda, Herbert Hovenkamp, Roger D. Blair, and Christine Piette Durrance, *Antitrust Law IIA*, ¶394 (2021), for a brief treatment. Also see Jonathan B. Baker and Daniel L. Rubenfeld, Empirical Methods in Antitrust Litigation: Review and Critique, 1 *American Law and Economics Review* 386 (1999), Franklin M. Fischer, Multiple Regression in Legal Proceedings, 80 *Columbia Law Review* 702 (1980), and Pierre Cremieux, Ian Simmons, and Edward A. Snyder, Proof of Common Impact in Antitrust Litigation: The Value of Regression Analysis, 17 *George Mason Law Review* 939 (2010). Also, see Mark A. Allen, Robert E. Hall, and Victoria A. Lazear, *Reference Guide on Estimation of Economic Damages in* Reference Manual on Scientific Evidence (3rd ed. 2011), Daniel L. Rubenfeld, *Reference Guide on Multiple Regression in* Reference Manual on Scientific Evidence (3rd ed. 2011), and James F. Nieberding, Estimating Overcharges in Antitrust Cases Using a Reduced-Form Approach: Methods and Issues, 9 *Applied Economics* 361 (2006).
[27] 15 U.S.C. Section 15.
[28] *Brunswick Company* v. *Pueblo Bowl-O-Mat*, 429 U.S. 477 (1977).

injury of the type the antitrust laws were intended to prevent and that flows from that which makes defendants' acts unlawful. The injury should reflect the anticompetitive effect either of the violation or anticompetitive acts made possible by the violation.[29]

The cartel's employees' injury amounts to the underemployment resulting from the employer collusion. Thus, their injury clearly satisfies the requirements to be *antitrust* injury. Moreover, since the employees were directly injured by the employer cartel, they satisfy the standing requirements of *Illinois Brick*.[30]

In our second numerical example, we determined that the total underpayment in the market was equal to $1,281,992. However, as was previously stated, not all of this is recoverable. This is because judicial precedent has confined the protected class to those who are direct victims of the conspiracy. As a result, the employees who were hired by the fringe employers will not be entitled to damages, despite suffering the same underpayment as the direct employees.[31]

We will now take a closer look at this class of victims, and others who are not currently entitled to damages under Section 4 of the Clayton Act, but who may deserve to be.

5.4 Unprotected Victims

Section 4 of the Clayton Act appears to apply to literally "any person" who has experienced an economic loss due to an antitrust violation.[32]

The Supreme Court, however, has confined the coverage of Section 4 to direct victims, that is, the underpaid employees. This leaves at least five groups of antitrust victims without a remedy. These groups are (1) those employees who were priced out of the market, (2) indirect suppliers of labor services, (3) "umbrella" employees, (4) suppliers of complementary inputs, and (5) direct buyers of the cartel's output. We will examine each of these in more detail.

5.4.1 Excluded Employees

When the exercise of monopsony power depresses the wage paid below the competitive level, some employees will be priced out of the market. Returning to the market depicted in Figure 5.1, those employees on the

---

[29] *Brunswick Company* v. *Pueblo Bowl-O-Mat*, 429 U.S. 489 (1977).

[30] *Illinois Brick Co.* v. *Illinois*, 431 U.S. 720 (1977).

[31] These employees are often referred to as "umbrella" victims and will be discussed in further detail in Section 5.4.

[32] *Illinois Brick Co.* v. *Illinois*, 431 U.S. 720 (1977).

supply curve between L_1 and L_2 would have worked at the competitive wage of w_1, but w_2 was below their reservation wages. In other words, they were priced out of the market.

They have lost employee surplus equal to area fbe in Figure 5.1. Their injury is very real, but nearly impossible to prove on an individual basis. First, even if we could identify those who are on the supply curve between L_1 and L_2, it matters a great deal where one is on that segment of the supply curve. The extent of the excluded employee's injury is the difference between the competitive wage and the employee's reservation wage, which is the height of the supply curve. As is plain to see in Figure 5.1, this gap narrows from ($w_1 - w_2$) to nothing as we move along the supply curve from L_2 to L_1. No one can prove precisely what his or her reservation wage actually is. This problem leads to our second point – everyone who did not work at a wage of w_2 can argue that they would have been pleased to work at a wage of w_1. Accordingly, their injury would be the full difference of ($w_1 - w_2$).

Although their loss may be difficult to measure, area fbe may be quite large. In the first numerical example, this area was equal to ½($w_1 - w_2$)($L_1 - L_2$) or $640,000. This is not a trivial uncompensated loss. In this case, the total underpayment equals $1,920,000, so the uncompensated loss is 34.88 percent of the actual underpayment.

The bottom line is that those who are priced out of the market cannot have antitrust standing due to practical problems of proof.[33] Any individual damage claim would be speculative, which is a fatal flaw.[34] Damages must be the product of just and reasonable inference – not sheer speculation.

Although individual claims seem problematic, it should be possible to estimate the total injury to those priced out of the market. The difference between the collusive and non-collusive wages must already be known. The only other sum required is the difference between the collusive and non-collusive quantities of labor employed.[35]

If the injury can be estimated that sum could be awarded to the class. Those who can prove their individual claims could recover that amount.

---

[33] William M. Landes, Optimal Sanctions for Antitrust Violations, 50 *University of Chicago Law Review* 652 (1983), has argued that optimal antitrust sanctions should equal the harm done to others. In the case of monopsony, this would include losses experienced by those priced out of the market.

[34] Roger D. Blair and William H. Page, Speculative Antitrust Damages, 70 *Washington Law Review* 423 (1995).

[35] For this calculation to be a precise measure of lost employee surplus, one must assume that supply of labor services is linear over this range of employment.

Any undistributed funds could then be used for some beneficial purpose. This, of course, is not an ideal solution, but it does force antitrust wrongdoers to recognize the injury that they cause to this class of victims.

5.4.2 Indirect Suppliers of Labor Services

In its opinion in *Illinois Brick Company* v. *Illinois*,[36] the Supreme Court held that only the direct buyer of a price-fixed good or service had antitrust standing to pursue damages under Section 4 of the Clayton Act. Its rationale for this limitation on just who "any person" is was reasonably straight forward.

In *Illinois Brick*, the Supreme Court confined antitrust standing to the direct buyers from a seller cartel. To the extent that unlawful overcharges were passed on to the more remote customers, those customers were out of luck. A number of reasons were given for this restriction, but two seem to be most prominent. First, the Court was troubled by the possibility of duplicative awards. This concern arose because the Court's earlier *Hanover Shoe* decision did not permit a defendant to reduce its damage liability by arguing that the plaintiff had passed on part or all of any overcharge to its customers.[37] If the downstream customers were entitled to claim the amount that had been passed on and the plaintiffs were also entitled to recover the full overcharge, there would be duplicative damages. To avoid this possibility, the Court denied antitrust standing to downstream customers.

The Supreme Court was also concerned that a single overcharge would require complex apportioning among plaintiffs down the distribution chain. The seriousness of this problem depends upon how many steps there are in the distribution chain. Symmetry demands that indirect suppliers of

---

[36] *Illinois Brick Co.* v. *Illinois*, 431 U.S. 720 (1977).

[37] *Hanover Shoe, Inc.* v. *United Shoe Machinery Corp.*, 392 U.S. 481 (1968). The prospect of duplicative damages apparently does not bother the Supreme Court when they are due to state legislation that permits recovery by indirect purchasers. In *California* v. *ARC America Corp.*, 490 U.S. 93, 103 (1989), Justice White held that "[i]t is one thing to consider the congressional policies identified in Illinois Brick and Hanover Shoe in defining what sort of recovery federal antitrust law authorizes; it is something altogether different, and in our view inappropriate, to consider them as defining what federal law allows States to do under their own antitrust law. As construed in Illinois Brick, Section 4 of the Clayton Act authorizes only direct purchasers to recover monopoly overcharges under federal law. We construed Section 4 as not authorizing indirect purchasers to recover under federal law because that would be contrary to the purposes of Congress. But nothing in Illinois Brick suggests that it would be contrary to congressional purposes for States to allow indirect purchasers to recover under their own antitrust laws." For a somewhat skeptical view of the Court's ruling in *ARC America*, see Ronald W. Davis, Indirect

labor services also be denied standing to recover unlawful underpayments to suppliers.[38]

This is not the place to argue that *Illinois Brick*'s policy on antitrust standing for indirect victims should be reversed.[39] Our point is that the Supreme Court's concern regarding any complex apportionment may have been relevant in 1977 but should be much less so now.[40] In extremely complex cases, efforts to estimate damages for indirect victims may be futile, i.e., speculative. In those cases, there will be a failure of proof. Recognizing this possibility, however, is no reason to deny standing to all indirect victims.[41]

In *Zinser* v. *Continental Grain Company*,[42] wheat farmers in Texas, Oklahoma, and New Mexico filed suits under Section 4 of the Clayton Act as indirect suppliers of wheat. Apparently, there was an impending sale of wheat to the Soviet Union that was kept secret. As a result, grain prices were lower than they would have been had that information been known. This, in turn, caused the prices paid to wheat farmers to be lower than they would have been. The wheat farmers did not sell to the defendants – a USDA official and a collection of grain exporters. Instead, they sold to middlemen who then sold to the defendants.

The District Court and the Circuit Court found that the plaintiffs were indirect suppliers and, as such, were denied standing under *Illinois Brick*. The Supreme Court recognized an exception for pre-existing

---

Purchaser Litigation: ARC America's Chickens Come Home to Roost on the Illinois Brick Wall, 65 *Antitrust Law Journal* 375 (1997). For a positive view regarding indirect purchasers, see Roger D. Blair and Jeffrey L. Harrison, Reexamining the Role of Illinois Brick in Modern Antitrust Standing Analysis, 68 *George Washington Law Review* 1 (1999).

[38] This is precisely what Areeda, Hovenkamp, Blair, and Durrance, *Antitrust Law IIA* ¶346g have concluded.

[39] This is addressed by Gregory Leonard, The Illinois Brick Damages Edifice: Demolition or Deconstruction?, 84 *Antitrust Law Journal* 315 (2022), and Joshua P. Davis and Anupama K. Reddy, Unintended Consequences of Repealing the Direct Purchaser Rule, 84 *Antitrust Law Journal* 341 (2022). The dispute in *Apple, Inc.* v. *Pepper*, 139 S. Ct. 1514 (2019), and the Supreme Court's confusion regarding economic reality raised the question of overturning *Illinois Brick Co.* v. *Illinois*, 431 U.S. 720 (1977). But there were neither indirect buyers nor indirect sellers in that case. App developers sold directly to iPhone owners. The transaction took place in Apple's App Store, but Apple did not buy and resell apps. For an in-depth economic analysis of the App Store, see Tirza J. Angerhofer and Roger D. Blair, Economic Reality at the Core of Apple, 66 *Antitrust Bulletin* 308 (2021).

[40] Richard M. Brunell and Andrew J. Gavil, Perspectives on Indirect Purchaser Litigation: Time for Reform? 84 *Antitrust Law Journal* 309 (2022).

[41] In fact, there are 37 states that have enacted *Illinois Brick* repealer statutes. See State Illinois Brick Repealer Laws Chart, Practical Law Checklist 8-521-6152.

[42] *Zinser* v. *Continental Grain Co.*, 660 F.2d 754 (1981).

cost-plus-fixed-quantity contracts.[43] Under this exception, there is no risk of duplicative recovery nor is there an apportionment problem. But this exception is extremely narrow.[44] Much the same can be said for suppliers.

In *Winters* v. *Ocean Spray Cranberries, Inc.*,[45] one group of plaintiffs were indirect suppliers of cranberries. Ordinarily, they would have been denied standing on the *Illinois Brick* logic. In this instance, however, they were entitled to the exception offered under fixed-quantity-cost-plus contracts.

In *In re Beef Industry Antitrust Litigation*,[46] the suppliers of fed cattle alleged that they were injured by a conspiracy to depress the price paid for carcass beef to the meatpackers. The plaintiffs alleged that the meatpackers used a pricing formula to determine the price that they paid for fed cattle that was driven by the wholesale price paid by customers of the meatpackers. The fifth circuit recognized this as the functional equivalent of *Illinois Brick*'s cost-plus exception.

In *Doe* v. *Arizona Hospital and Health Care Association*,[47] a class of temporary duty nurses alleged that nearly all the hospitals in Arizona had conspired to depress the wages of temporary duty nurses. The colluding hospitals negotiated with a nursing agency, which then paid the nurses. The nurses were indirect suppliers of nursing services. The Court, however, acknowledged that the nurses might qualify for *Illinois Brick*'s cost-plus exception. It could not determine this without explicitly examining the contracts between the nurses and the agency.

Based on the scenario in this case, an interesting "pass-back" question arises. Suppose that the non-collusive wage for a temporary duty nurse would have been $50 per hour, but the collusive wage was $40. The contract between the nurse and the agency calls for a 10 percent commission. The result is that the agency receives $40 per hour, retains a $4 fee, and passes on $36 to the nurse. In the absence of the collusion, the agency would have received $5, and the nurses would have earned $45.

In this example, there would be no duplicative damages, nor would there be a need for complex apportioning. The damage to the agency is $1 per hour while the damage to the nurses is $9 per hour. The underpayment of $10 is precisely equal to the sum of the agency damages and the nurse

[43] *Illinois Brick Co.* v. *Illinois*, 431 U.S. 720 (1977).
[44] *Kansas* v. *Utilicorp United*, 497 U.S. 199 (1990). For an analysis, see Herbert Hovenkamp, The Indirect Purchaser Rule and Cost-Plus Sales, 103 *Harvard Law Review* 1717 (1990).
[45] *Winters* v. *Ocean Spray Cranberries, Inc.*, 296 F. Supp. 3d 311 (2017).
[46] *In re Beef Industry Antitrust Litigation*, 600 F.2d 1148 (5th Cir. 1979).
[47] *Doe* v. *Arizona Hospital and Healthcare Association*, Not Reported in F. Supp. 2d (2009).

damages. In cases like this, there is no obvious reason to deny the under-paid nurses their day in court.

5.4.3 Umbrella Employees

In a partial conspiracy among sellers, some consumers buy from non-participants in the cartel. These consumers were charged more than the competitive price because the price charged by the non-participants is driven by the price charged by the cartel members. Those prices are raised under the "umbrella" provided by the cartel.

Analogously, the sellers who deal with non-participant buyers receive less for their wares than they would have received in the absence of the collusion, and this clearly holds in the case of an employer cartel.

In Figure 5.2, it is clear that L_f was provided at a wage of w, which is below the but for wage of w′. These employees have suffered antitrust injury since the depressed wage flowed from the consequences of the collusion. This injury is equal to the area $(w - w′)L_f$. In our second numerical example, this value was approximately one-third of all damages directly resulting from the cartel's formation.

Those who were hired by the colluding firms at unlawfully depressed wages suffer antitrust injury since this is the type of injury that the antitrust laws were intended to prevent. Precisely the same can be said of the employees of the non-participating firms. The Supreme Court has not ruled on the umbrella issue for buyers.[48]

But there is no sound economic rationale for denying compensatory damages to umbrella employees. The injury to the umbrella employees is precisely the same underpayment per unit as that suffered by the direct employees to the cartel. It is true that the quantities are different, but that is just a matter of arithmetic.

In the numerical example, the but for wage is $50 and the collusive wage is $42, so the per unit underpayment is $8. Suppose that 5,000 laborers were hired at the collusive wage of $42 by a cartel member and 3,000 workers were hired by a non-member at that same wage. It seems illogical that only the 5,000 workers who were hired by the cartel can receive damages, given that the other 3,000 workers are clearly undercompensated for injury caused by the cartel.

---

[48] At this time, there is a split in the Circuits. See Roger D. Blair and Christine Piette Durrance, *Umbrella Pricing: Antitrust Injury and Standing in Issues in Competition Law and Policy*, W. Dale Collins, ed. (2008).

Furthermore, extending antitrust standing to the umbrella employees will increase the deterrent effect of private damage actions. The umbrella employees would not sue the firms that hired them since those fringe employers did not participate in the alleged collusion. Instead, they simply responded to what appeared to be market-determined prices. Accordingly, the cartel members would be liable for the antitrust injury suffered by the umbrella employees. One might object that the cartel did not directly profit from the reduced wage paid to the employees of the non-participants.[49] But there is no denying that all the underpayments were due to unlawful collaboration among the cartel members.

5.4.4 Suppliers of Complementary Inputs

When an employer cartel restricts employment to depress the wage that it must pay to its employees, it also reduces its need for complementary inputs. For example, collusion in the market for temporary duty nurses reduces their employment and compensation. But it also reduces the demand for complementary labor services and other complementary inputs to nursing services, orderlies, linen services, food services, pharmacy services, and so on.

Those providing complementary labor services are obviously worse off since their employment is reduced. Their lost income would seem to be antitrust injury since it results from the anticompetitive conduct of the employer cartel. If these suppliers of complementary labor services sued for lost income, there would be no duplicative damages nor would there be a complex apportionment problem. Nonetheless, these individuals have been denied standing. Much the same is true for suppliers of other complementary inputs.

In many, but not all, circumstances, denying standing to suppliers of complementary inputs makes sense. For example, if the employment of hardware and software engineers is reduced by a smartphone manufacturer, there are so many complementary components that it would be nearly impossible to isolate individual damages for such a complex product.

In other cases, however, it may be much simpler. For example, suppose that the producers of hammers simply assemble each hammer by attaching

---

[49] The cartel members do, however, receive some benefit from the reduced wage paid by the non-participants through reduced likelihood of detection. As more fringe firms adopt the reduced wage established by the cartel, it becomes harder to detect the existence of collusion because it appears that the entire market is adopting this lower wage. Thus, it may appear to be the result of market forces instead of intentional wage suppression.

a hammer head to a handle. If the producers agree to depress the wage paid to the assemblers by agreeing to reduce the quantities of labor employed, they will obviously impose losses on the handle suppliers since the firms will purchase fewer inputs due to restricted employment. In a simple, fixed-proportions case like this one, it should be relatively easy to estimate the losses suffered by the handle supplier. Moreover, there appears to be no real reason for denying them standing.

Clearly, some judgement must be employed. Rather than having a blanket denial of standing for suppliers of complements, those who can provide a reasonable estimate of the damages should be permitted to do so. We recognize that this policy could lead to many more antitrust suits being filed but reject the notion that injured parties should be denied their day in court for the convenience of the judiciary.

5.4.5 Consumers of the Employer Cartel's Output

The final group that seemingly has no recovery for the injury flowing from the unlawful monopsony is the one that purchases the output produced by the employer cartel.

For the most part, the economic effects of a challenged practice are determined in a partial equilibrium analysis. In the case of an employer cartel, the challenged practice is collusion on the quantities of labor that will be hired. The economic impact of the conduct is confined to wage and quantity of labor employed. The economic consequences of the collusion in the market that the firm supplies are ignored. This may be fine for determining liability, but it fails to provide compensation for consumers who arguably experience antitrust injury.

In both Figures 5.1 and 5.2, it is apparent that the quantity of output produced by the firm is smaller with monopsony than with competition, given the reduced level of employment. This, in turn, means that the monopsonist's output is necessarily reduced. Since demand functions are negatively sloped, the consumer will pay a higher price and buy a smaller quantity of the goods produced by the firm. Consequently, consumer welfare must fall.[50]

---

[50] Roger D. Blair and Richard E. Romano, Collusive Monopsony in Theory and Practice: The NCAA, 42 *Antitrust Bulletin* 681 (1997), and Roger D. Blair and Kelsey A. Clemons, Is Monopsony the New Monopoly? Yes!, 34 *Antitrust* 84 (2019). For an analytical treatment of these results, see Tirza J. Angerhofer and Roger D. Blair, Monopoly and Monopsony: Antitrust Standing, Injury, and Damages, 89 *University of Cincinnati Law Review* 256 (2021).

5.5 Additional Considerations

Although we believe that our economic analysis and proposals for reform
are sound, we recognize that there are some thorny issues that remain.
These include the possibility of over-deterrence, squeezing of employees,
and the economic impacts of mergers. We address each of these in turn.

5.5.1 Compensation and Deterrence

As we have argued above, the exercise of unlawful monopsony power
injures several classes of victims. Only the direct employees of an unlawful monopsonist or an employer cartel have standing to sue for antitrust
damages under Section 4 of the Clayton Act. The aim of our proposal is to
expand antitrust standing to include the other victims. Implementation of
our proposal would greatly improve the compensatory goal of the Clayton
Act's provision for private damage awards. It also enhances deterrence.

Committing an antitrust violation is risky. There is some probability of
escaping sanctions and enjoying enhanced profit, but there is a complementary probability of detection and subsequent conviction and punishment. Recognizing this fact, the deterrent function (Δ) can be written as:

$$\Delta = \Pi_0 - E[\Pi],$$

where Π_0 is the firm's profit without an antitrust violation and $E[\Pi]$ is the
expected value of profit with an antitrust violation. If a firm's profit without committing an antitrust violation exceeds the expected profit when
committing an antitrust violation, Δ will be positive and the antitrust violation will be deterred.

For any given probability of being convicted of an antitrust violation,
expanding the firm's exposure to damage recovery will reduce the expected
profit. Thus, such an expansion increases Δ. As a result, both goals – compensation and deterrence – are served by our proposal.

5.5.2 Over-Deterrence

Our proposal substantially increases the damage exposure for an unlawful
monopsonist, or a cartel, that exercises monopsony power. This raises the
issue of over-deterrence. In other words, would a firm or a group of firms
refrain from engaging in procompetitive conduct that is socially beneficial
due to the fear of heavy economic sanctions? The possibility exists but only
in limited circumstances.

For unlawful monopsonization due to competitively unreasonable conduct, over-deterrence is really not an issue. Much the same is true for collusion among ostensible rivals that is designed to emulate monopsony. There are no redeeming virtues to be lost due to over-deterrence.

One possibility involves the Williamson Tradeoff as modified for the merger of buyers rather than sellers.[51] From the standpoint of social welfare, however, the problem lies in the interpretation of Section 7 of the Clayton Act that does not permit such tradeoffs. It does not reside in our proposal for antitrust damages.

5.5.3 "Squeezing" of Employees

If a merger permits the new firm to "squeeze" its employees, this may be deemed anticompetitive. The merged firm may exercise monopsony power in the usual way by restricting employment and thereby depressing wages. This, however, reduces output, so there is harm in the downstream market.

There is an alternative – making and "all-or-nothing" offer.[52] Such offers push the employee off their supply curve. The monopsonist will want the quantity that maximizes the sum of employee surplus and employer surplus, which occurs at the quantity where the value of the marginal product of labor equals the marginal cost of labor. The monopsonist then offers to employ that quantity of labor at a reduced wage. In principle, the monopsonist could structure an all-or-nothing offer in such a way that it would extract all the employee surplus. In this event, there would be no harm to consumers because output of the final good would not change.

5.5.4 Merger to Monopsony

To justify a merger that appears to be anticompetitive in the output market on efficiency grounds, the merger must pose no harm to consumers.[53] In

---

[51] Oliver E. Williamson, Economies as an Antitrust Defense: The Welfare Tradeoffs, 58 *American Economic Review* 18 (1968), analyzed an efficiency-enhancing merger that increased price to consumers while reducing the costs of production and distribution. His proposal has not been implemented. See Germán Bet and Roger D. Blair, Williamson's Welfare Trade-Off Around the World, 55 *Review of Industrial Organization* 9 (2019).

[52] A more detailed discussion of all-or-nothing offers is provided in Chapter 2.

[53] Merger policy that raises concerns related to monopsony is addressed by a variety of scholars. See Roger D. Blair, Merger to Monopsony: An Efficiencies Defense, 55 *Antitrust Bulletin* 689 (2010), Ioana Marinescu and Herbert J. Hovenkamp, Anticompetitive Mergers in Labor Markets, 94 *Indiana Law Journal* 1031 (2019), and Suresh Naidu, Eric A. Posner, and Glen Weyl, Antitrust Remedies for Labor Market Power, 132 *Harvard Law*

other words, price in the output market must not rise, which means output cannot fall. Consequently, the quantities of intermediate goods must not decline unless the decline is directly due to the efficiency introduced after the merger. Thus, any decline in inputs employed by the firm is not a result of monopsony power being exercised in input markets.

In other words, if the efficiency merely reduces the demand for labor and/or other intermediate goods, quantities and prices may fall, but that is not due to the exercise of monopsony power.

5.6 Concluding Remarks

Private damage actions under Section 4 of the Clayton Act serve two purposes. First, they provide compensation to some – but not all – victims of antitrust violations. Second, the provision for private recovery of antitrust damages increases deterrence beyond that provided by the public sanctions.[54] In our view, both are important. In *Illinois Brick*, however, the Supreme Court limited antitrust standing in the (perhaps mistaken) belief that this would enhance the deterrent effect of private enforcement. In our view, both goals would be furthered by expanding the number of victims with antitrust standing. This can be seen clearly in the case of monopsonistic exploitation by an employer cartel.

The exercise of monopsony power by an employer cartel increases employer profits but imposes losses on the victimized employees. The antitrust victims are not limited to underpaid employees. There are five other groups whose members have been hurt by the unlawful agreement. These include (1) employees who have been priced out of the market, (2) indirect suppliers of labor services, (3) umbrella employees, (4) suppliers of complementary inputs, and (5) buyers from the cartel. We have explained the costs and benefits of permitting antitrust damage suits by those victims.

Review 536 (2018). For a European view, see Ariel Ezrachi and Maria Ioannidou, Buyer Power in European Union Merger Control, 10 *European Competition Journal* 69 (2014). A more extensive discussion of merger to monopsony can also be found in Chapter 10.
[54] These involve corporate and individual fines as well as prison sentences.

6

Collusion on Wages and Terms of Employment

6.1 Introduction

Recently, David Card asked what seems to be a simple question: "Who sets your wage?"[1] Based on an exhaustive survey of the literature, he concluded that your employer sets your wage due to evidence of pervasive monopsony power.

In most instances, employers compete in the labor market through the terms of employment that they offer: wages and salaries, health and life insurance, annual and sick leave, among other things. In some situations, however, rival employers find that cooperation is more profitable than competition. By agreeing to restrict employment, the colluding employers can reduce the wages that they pay and thereby increase their profit. The cost savings enjoyed by the employers are not passed on to consumers in the form of lower output prices. In fact, the opposite occurs: reducing the employment of labor causes output to fall and prices to rise.

In this chapter, we provide an economic analysis of collusion in the labor market. In doing so, we show that collusion results in lower wages, lower employment, and a reduction in social welfare.

In Section 6.2, we provide a simple economic model of an employer cartel that illustrates the ill effects of collusion in the labor market.[2] In Section 6.3, we discuss the incentives that individual firms may have to cheat on a monopsonistic agreement. Section 6.4 focuses on the antitrust treatment of collusion in the labor market. In Section 6.5, we examine allegations of collusion in the nurse labor market, and we discuss the alleged collusion in

---

[1] David Card, Who Set Your Wage?, 112 *American Economic Review* 1075 (2022).
[2] In Section 2.3, we illustrated the effects of monopsony on marginal and average costs, which should dispel any notion that collusive wage reduction will be passed on to consumers.

the market for broiler chickens in Section 6.6. In Section 6.7, we turn our attention to the NCAA cartel whose members collude in the market for athletes and coaches. The subject of Section 6.8 is the collusion among several elite universities in recruiting elite students. Section 6.9 focuses on the measurement and estimation of antitrust damages for victims of collusive monopsony, and we close with some concluding remarks in Section 6.10.

6.2 The Economics of Collusion in the Labor Market

In some instances, employers cooperate rather than compete in the labor market. The motivation is simple – the lure of higher profit. In this section, we explore a simple employer cartel model and examine the economic consequences for the employer, the employees, and consumers.

6.2.1 Competitive Benchmark

An employer's demand for labor services is derived from its efforts to maximize profit in the output market. If the employer has some power in its output market, but none in the labor market, its profit function (Π) is:

$$\Pi = P(Q)Q(L,K) - wL - rK,$$

where P is the output price, Q is the production function, w is the wage of labor (L), and r is the price of capital (K). To maximize its profit, the employer will hire labor such that:

$$\frac{\partial \Pi}{\partial L} = \left(P + Q\frac{dP}{dQ}\right)\frac{\partial Q}{\partial L} - w = 0.$$

The first term on the right-hand side is the marginal revenue product of labor (MRP_L). The MRP_L is the firm's derived demand for labor.[3]

In Figure 6.1, the aggregate demand for labor is shown as MRP_L. This is the sum of the individual firm labor demand functions. The supply of labor is shown as S_L. The competitive equilibrium employment is found where the firm will employ L_1 units of labor services, and the wage will be w_1.

Employer surplus is the difference between labor's contribution to profit (MRP_L) and the wage that is paid. In Figure 6.1, this is area abw_1. The employee surplus is the difference between the wage received and

---

[3] The demand for an input is derived from the consumer demand for the firm's output. This differs from the value of the marginal product of labor (VMP_L) owing to the employer's power in the output market.

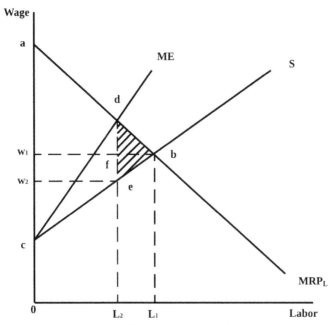

Figure 6.1 Monopsonistic profit maximization results in a social welfare loss

the reservation wage of the workers as measured by the height of the supply (S_L). In Figure 6.1, this is area w_1bc. The sum of employer surplus and employee surplus is a measure of social welfare. In Figure 6.1, this is the triangular area abc. No other wage and employment level yields a higher social welfare, which is why the goal of the antitrust laws is to protect competition and the competitive process.

6.2.2 Collusion in the Labor Market

The employers may agree among themselves to collude in the labor market to enhance their profits. Acting as one, the cartel profit function becomes:

$$\Pi = P(Q)Q(L,K) - w(L)L - rK.$$

The wage is now a function of how much labor is employed. To maximize cartel profits, the employers will limit their employment to the point where:

$$\frac{\partial \Pi}{\partial L} = \left(P + Q\frac{dP}{dQ} \right)\frac{\partial Q}{\partial L} - \left(w + L\frac{dw}{dL} \right) = 0.$$

That is, labor will be employed to the point where the marginal revenue product of labor (MRP_L) is equal to the marginal expenditure on labor (ME_L). The latter is the increase in the total wage bill that accompanies a small increase in employment.[4]

In Figure 6.1, profit maximization results in a reduction in employment from L_1 to L_2 and a reduction in the wage from w_1 to w_2. Between L_1 and L_2, the value of labor services exceeds the reservation wages of the employees. From a private perspective, it is not profit maximizing to expand employment beyond L_2. Consequently, employment will be restricted below the socially optimal level.

6.2.3 Welfare Implications of Collusive Monopsony

Figure 6.1 illustrates the effect of collusive monopsony on economic welfare. Employer surplus is the difference between their willingness to pay as reflected in the demand and the wage that the market requires. At the competitive solution, this is given by area abw_1. Employee surplus, however, is the difference between the minimum wage at which the employees will work, as reflected in the supply curve and the wage that the market dictates. At the competitive solution, the employer surplus is given by area w_1bc in Figure 6.1.

Competition in this market leads to the maximum sum of employer and employee surplus, which is area abc in Figure 6.1. No other wage and employment level will generate a larger total surplus.

Collusive monopsony has an adverse effect on the welfare of the employees and on social welfare. Profit maximization by the colluding firms reduces employee surplus by the area w_1bew_2. Part of this reduction, area w_1few_2, is converted into employer surplus (or profit) and part of it, area fbe, is simply lost. This results in a reduction in employee surplus from the triangular area w_1bc to the triangular area w_2ec.

Due to the reduction in employment, there is a total social welfare loss equal to the striped triangle dbe. This welfare loss is due to the misallocation of resources. As Figure 6.1 illustrates, the social cost of hiring the employees, as measured by the height of the supply curve, is below the value that these employees provide, as measured by the height of the

---

[4] The total wage bill is $w(L)L$, so ME_L equals $w + L\left(\dfrac{dw}{dL}\right)$. For example, suppose that the supply of labor is $w = 10 + 0.01L$, this means that the wage bill is $(10 + 0.01L)L$. If employment is increased by one, then the incremental wage paid would be $10 + 0.02L$, which is higher than the wage.

demand curve, between L_2 and L_1. From a social perspective, too few laborers are being employed. The collusive monopsony solution is allocatively inefficient due to under-employment. This allocative inefficiency is what causes the reduction in social welfare.

6.3 The Incentive to Cheat

Collusion among employers to restrict employment and thereby depress the compensation of the employees creates an incentive for each cartel member to cheat on the agreement.

When the employers are competing, the individual employer will maximize its profit by hiring l_1 units of labor at the competitive wage (w_1). At that employment level, the firm's marginal revenue product (mrp_L) is equal to the wage. Following the formation of the employer cartel, the wage falls to w_2. At that wage, each employer would prefer to hire l_3 units of labor since its mrp_L equals w_2 at that employment level. This is shown in Figure 6.2.

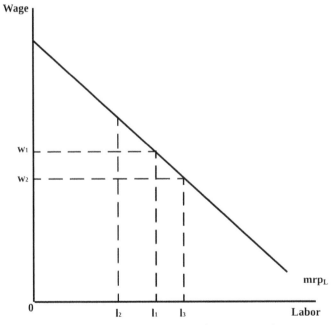

Figure 6.2 The cartel member has an incentive to cheat since profit is greater at l_3 than at l_2

To make this collusive wage stick, the employer should reduce its employ-ment to l_2. It is plain to see that the firm's mrp_L exceeds w_2 at l_2. This, of course, provides an incentive for each employer to cheat on the agreement and hire l_3 units of labor instead. Consequently, the cartel must monitor the conduct of its members and figure out how to discipline cheaters.[5]

Stigler pointed out that members of a price fixing cartel can infer that someone is cheating on the agreement if customer traffic is outside the usual bounds.[6] Here, we have adapted his reasoning to collusion among employers.

All members of an employer cartel recognize that there is bound to be some labor turnover. If an employer begins losing an unexpectedly large number of current employees, however, it may suggest that someone in the cartel is cheating. If it appears that a disproportionate number of the departing employees are going to a specific employer, one might infer that that specific employer is cheating by offering a wage above the agreed upon level.

Ordinarily, a certain number of employees will leave a rival and opt to switch employers. If an employer fails to attract the expected number of transfers, that employer may suspect that someone is cheating.

Finally, new workers enter the labor force on a continuing basis. If an employer attracts an unexpectedly low number of new entrants, that may also be due to some cartel member or members failing to follow the cartel agreement.

Some employers will use third parties to monitor cheating. In some cases, information sharing services are used to monitor the behavior of other participating firms.[7] In other cases, firms may use their customers to share information among the colluding firms.[8]

---

[5] Ian Ayres, How Cartels Punish: A Structural Theory of Self-Enforcing Collusion, 87 *Columbia Law Review* 295 (1987).

[6] George J. Stigler, A Theory of Oligopoly, 72 *Journal of Political Economy* 44 (1964).

[7] For example, the major poultry producers are accused of using an information sharing service to collude and suppress the wages of their plant employees. See Section 6.6 for a more detailed discussion.

[8] For example, in the fed cattle market ranchers allege that four major meatpackers are using contractual agreements between ranchers and meatpackers to facilitate collusion. When a rancher agrees to a contractual "queuing agreement" with the major meatpack-ers, ranchers who want to receive bids from other meatpackers must report the bid prices they have previously received from other firms. In this way, the meatpackers can utilize their customers, that is, ranchers, to monitor the pricing behavior of other cartel mem-bers. For a more in-depth analysis of collusion in the fed cattle market, see Brianna L. Alderman, Meatpackers Feed on Fed Cattle, 68 *Antitrust Bulletin* 88 (2023).

In any event, firms who discover cheating must punish the cheaters. If cheating goes unpunished, there is no reason for every single cartel member to adhere to the cartel agreement. Since cheating pays, the employers will cheat on one another if left unchecked. Widespread cheating is bound to impair cartel stability, so it would be desirable to forestall cheating. To deter cheating, the cartel must make cheating unprofitable. This, however, is no mean feat.

If Employer A cheats and, consequently, Employer B experiences reduced profit, Employer B could retaliate in a so-called "tit-for-tat" response.[9] That is, Employer B "cheats" on Employer A, so they are even. If this behavior continues, this can result in a breakdown of the cartel agreement.

6.4 Antitrust Treatment of Collusion in the Labor Market

Section 1 of the Sherman Act forbids any "conspiracy in restraint of trade or commerce." But does this apply to labor? The answer is "absolutely." At one time, colluding employers tried to argue that employment decisions did not involve trade or commerce and, therefore, Section 1 did not apply to collusion in the labor market.

The application of Section 1 of the Sherman Act to employer collusion on wages began almost 100 years ago with the Supreme Court's decision in *Anderson* v. *Shipowners' Association of Pacific Coast.*[10] The Court held that the antitrust laws apply to wage fixing conspiracies and it is unnecessary "to inquire whether, as contended by respondents, the object of the combination was merely to regulate employment of men, and not to restrain commerce."[11] In spite of this early decision, there had not been much antitrust activity challenging wage fixing by employers. This is no longer the case. Beginning in the 1990s, there have been both public and private suits aimed at wage fixing.[12]

[9] Note that a "tit-for-tat" strategy is not the only response strategy for punishment. For example, the firms could also implement a "grim trigger" strategy where Employer B will never cooperate with Employer A again after Employer A cheats on the agreement.
[10] *Anderson* v. *Shipowners Association of Pacific Coast*, 272 U.S. 359 (1926).
[11] *Id.* at 363.
[12] For example, see *McNeil* v. *National Football League*, 790 F. Supp. 871, 880–881 (D. Minn. 1992). In this case, the court made it very clear that Section 1 applies to labor markets. More recently, in *U.S.* v. *Lopez*, 2:23-cr-00055-CDS-DJA (D. Nev. May 18, 2023), the DOJ charged Lopez with fixing the hourly wages paid to RNs and LPNs who were employed by home healthcare agencies in the Las Vegas area. The DOJ filed a criminal indictment charging Lopez and his co-conspirators with a *per se* violation of Section 1 of the Sherman Act.

Colluding employers have also tried to argue that depressing the compensation of labor reduces costs, and therefore, is socially beneficial. As we have seen in the preceding sections, however, this claim is false. In fact, the opposite is true – collusion leads to a reduction in output and a corresponding increase in the price to consumers. Consequently, both consumer welfare and social welfare decline when the compensation of labor is depressed through collusive monopsony.

6.4.1 Judicial Treatment of Collusion in the Labor Market

The judiciary treats collusion in the labor market with the same hostility that it treats collusion in other markets. While some defendants may argue that their agreements warrant rule of reason treatment due to some procompetitive intentions, naked restraints in labor markets will usually receive *per se* treatment. This is precisely what the DOJ and the FTC believe is the appropriate antitrust policy.

6.4.2 Advice from the Agencies

In 2016, the DOJ and the FTC issued their *Antitrust Guidance for Human Resource Professionals* to advise employers that collusion in the labor market would be treated as a *per se* violation of Section 1 of the Sherman Act.[13] The Agencies began by pointing out that:

[a]n agreement among competing employers to limit or fix the terms of employment for potential hires may violate the antitrust laws if the agreement constrains individual firm decision-making with regard to wages, salaries, or benefits; terms of employment; or even job opportunities.[14]

They reinforce this admonition with an unqualified warning:

It is unlawful for competitors to expressly or implicitly agree not to compete with one another, even if they are motivated by a desire to reduce costs.[15]

The Agencies warn that:

[a]greements among employers ... not to compete on the terms of compensation are illegal.[16]

---

[13] See www.justice.gov/atr/file/903511/download (*Guidance*).
[14] See *Guidance* at p. 1.
[15] See *Guidance* at p. 2. As we have shown, any cost reduction enhances profits, but harms employees and consumers.
[16] See *Guidance* at p. 3.

The Agencies also warn in their *Guidance* that wage fixing agreements expose the members of such agreements to criminal prosecution, which could result in substantial fines and/or imprisonment.[17] In addition, those who have been injured by these unlawful agreements may file treble damage suits against the employers.

6.5 Collusion in the Nurse Labor Market

Hospital nurses play a vital role in the care of patients.[18] They monitor the patient's progress, administer medicine, help patients get in and out of bed, and provide a host of other health care services. If a hospital is understaffed, the quality of patient care suffers. Unfortunately, that seems to be the norm in the United States. For decades, there has been a persistent and ubiquitous shortage of nurses. As an economic matter, this is perplexing. Ordinarily, we would expect compensation to rise, thereby increasing the number of nurses until the shortage disappears. But this market adjustment is not happening. One explanation for the persistent shortage is collusion among the hospitals to depress the compensation of hospital nurses.

6.5.1 Recent Antitrust Litigation

There have been several class action antitrust suits filed by nurses alleging collusion in the local nurse labor markets, including suits filed in Albany,[19] Chicago,[20] Detroit,[21] Memphis,[22] and San Antonio.[23] In these cases, nurses alleged that the defendants wielded collusive monopsony power in the local markets for hospital nurses and conspired to use that power to depress the wages of nurses in violation of Section 1 of the Sherman Act.[24] Second, the nurses alleged that the defendants had

---

[17] Interestingly, in *U.S.* v. *Jindal*, No. 4:20-cr-358 (E.D. Tex. Dec. 09, 2020), the DOJ alleged that Niraj Jindal was engaged in a wage fixing conspiracy to suppress nurses' pay. However, both Jindal and the alleged co-conspirators were found "not guilty."

[18] This section relies heavily on Chapter 15 in Tirza J. Angerhofer, Roger D. Blair, and Christine Piette Durrance, *Antitrust Policy in Healthcare Markets* (2023).

[19] *Fleischman* v. *Albany Medical Center*, No. 06-cv-0765 (N.D.N.Y. July 22, 2010).

[20] *Reed* v. *Advocate Health Care*, No. 06C3337 (N.D. Ill. Sept. 28, 2009).

[21] *Cason-Merenda* v. *Detroit Medical Center*, No. 2:06-cv-15601 (E.D. Mich. Dec. 13, 2006).

[22] *Clarke* v. *Baptist Memorial Healthcare Corp.*, No. 264 F.R.D. 375, 377 (W.D. Tenn. 2009).

[23] *Maderazo* v. *VHA San Antonio Partners, L.P.*, No. 5:06-cv-00535 (W.D. Tex. 2006).

[24] Antitrust allegations of wage-fixing are not limited to the market for nurses. For example, there have been similar allegations in the labor market for physical therapists and physical therapist assistants.

entered into a conspiracy to regularly exchange "detailed and non-public information about compensation being paid or to be paid to their [registered nurse (RN)] employees," which facilitated the suppression of RN compensation.[25] The plaintiff nurses alleged that the area hospitals eliminated, or at least impaired, competition for nurses, avoided competition in the nurse labor market, and thereby depressed RN wages below the non-collusive level.

In the Detroit case, there were allegations of frequent telephone exchanges of competitively sensitive information by hospital human resource (HR) professionals regarding RN compensation as well as third-party surveys about compensation that were circulated among the hospitals. The plaintiffs collected various emails, transcripts, and other documents that clearly showed how HR professionals exchanged wage information directly. Even though evidence of an overt conspiracy to depress prices was lacking, the Court concluded that the wage information sharing was conclusive enough to allow the plaintiffs to pursue their case on those grounds.

Since the information sharing was allegedly designed to decrease nurse compensation, it could be considered a violation of Section 1 of the Sherman Act. There was no doubt that this information could tip the scales and give the hospitals more leverage over nurse wages.

Of the five cases, only two, *Albany* and *Detroit*, settled for substantial sums.[26] Albany's plaintiffs received a total of $14 million from the five hospital defendants, while the RNs in Detroit received $90 million from the defendants.[27] The remaining three class action lawsuits were not certified, and the cases settled for small sums.

---

[25] *Fleischman v. Albany Medical Center*, No. 06-cv-0765 (N.D.N.Y. July 22, 2010). In addition to wages, some of the plaintiffs alleged that the information sharing agreements included signing bonuses, merit raises, certification bonuses, work schedules and the like. Information exchanges can be used to suppress competition among employers and thereby depress wages and other forms of compensation. A good example is *Todd v. Exxon Corp.*, 275 F.3d 191 (2d Cir. 2001). In that case, the major petroleum companies exchanged sensitive information regarding the compensation of certain specialized categories of workers.

[26] Most cases settle before they reach the trial stage. Settlements ensure that the plaintiffs recover some damages while reducing the costs to the defendants. At the same time, settlements reduce the need for lengthy trials and improve the efficacy of the Court system.

[27] For an examination of the deterrent role of antitrust damages in Section 1 cases, see Roger D. Blair and Anita Walsh, *Antitrust Damages, Fines, and Deterrence: Collusion in the Nurse Labor Market*, Competition Policy International, Antitrust Chronicle (2019).

6.5.2 Class Certification

When a large group of antitrust victims has suffered antitrust damages that are individually small, a class action, which combines all plaintiffs, may be the only feasible way for them to proceed. The court, however, must first certify the class. Class certification allows the class action lawsuit to proceed. Before certifying the proposed class, the court must be convinced that the small number of class representatives will adequately represent the interests of everyone in the class. The injury experienced by the class representatives must be the same as the injury suffered by the class members. If there is any conflict of interest, the class will not be certified.

It is also essential that common proof will be sufficient to prove both liability and the fact of injury. This means that proof for one is proof for all. Otherwise, the court might have to conduct a large number of mini-trials within the overall litigation. When it comes to individual damage awards, the court will be less concerned about common proof. In a class action, the damage award goes to the class. This sum must be distributed to the class members on some sort of formulaic basis, which may prove to be problematic. In most instances, however, the Court is not troubled by this at the class certification stage. The class actions for Chicago, Memphis, and San Antonio were not certified by the courts on the basis of common proof,[28] conflicts of interest,[29] and feasibility of the claim, respectively.[30]

6.5.3 Impact on Hospital Costs

Since there is widespread concern over burgeoning health care costs, one might suppose that the reduced wages would reduce the hospitals' costs and thereby benefit patients. This, however, is not the case. It is consistent with our intuition that the reduced wages will reduce the average cost of producing acute care hospital services. This average cost reduction improves hospital profits and thereby provides an incentive for collusion. But the

---

[28] In the Chicago case, the judge determined that the damages model was not accurate enough since it relied on averages which would have overcompensated some nurses and undercompensated others.

[29] The class representatives in the Memphis case were not considered appropriate for the class since one had ties to a nurse union and another was filing for bankruptcy. Their conflicts of interest would not have accurately portrayed the wishes of the wider class.

[30] In San Antonio, the class was denied since the Court determined that there was not enough evidence to conclude that the conspiracy would have resulted in wage depression.

effect of monopsony is to raise marginal cost.[31] Since marginal cost is what drives price and output decisions, the increase in marginal cost leads to a reduction in the hospitals' output and higher hospital charges.[32] In other words, since there are fewer nurses employed, fewer nursing services can be offered. A reduction in the quantity of services in the output market equates to an increase in price for patients. Thus, collusive monopsony has no redeeming virtues.

6.5.4 Empirical Evidence

For decades, the nurse labor market has been held up as a prime example of monopsony power and could therefore be a ripe environment for collusive monopsony. Indeed, several empirical studies that estimate labor supply elasticity conclude that nurses face substantial monopsony power from hospitals. For example, Daniel Sullivan estimated supply elasticities of 0.79 in the short run and 0.26 in the long run.[33] Staiger and colleagues estimated a supply elasticity of 0.1 for nurses,[34] while Hirsch and Schumacher similarly found evidence of monopsony in the nurse labor market, identified by comparing nurse wages to hospital concentration.[35] Later studies by DePasquale,[36] and Prager and Schmitt showed that mergers that increase concentration in nurse labor markets tended to decrease wages after consummation.[37]

The empirical literature largely corroborates the existence of monopsony power in the nurse labor market, with effects on wages at least in the short run. The presence of monopsony power indicates that collusive monopsony may be profitable. We argue that collusive monopsonistic

---

[31] This is reviewed in Chapter 2.

[32] For further analytical details, see Roger D. Blair and Christine Piette Durrance, Licensing Health Care Professionals, State Action and Antitrust Policy, 100 *Iowa Law Review* 1943 (2014).

[33] Daniel Sullivan, Monopsony Power in the Market for Nurses, 32 *Journal of Law and Economics* S135 (1989). For a discussion of the Lerner Index of Monopsony, see Chapter 2.

[34] Douglas O. Staiger, Joanne Spetz, and Ciaran S. Phibbs, Is There Monopsony in the Labor Market? Evidence from a Natural Experiment, 28 *Journal of Labor Economics* 211 (2010).

[35] Barry T. Hirsch and Edward J. Schumacher, Classic or New Monopsony? Searching for Evidence in Nursing Labor Markets, 24 *Journal of Health Economics* 969 (2005). Although the authors found evidence of monopsony power in the short run, they did not necessarily find monopsony power in the long run.

[36] Christina DePasquale, *Hospital Consolidation and the Nurse Labor Market*, unpublished (2018).

[37] Elena Prager and Matt Schmitt, Employer Consolidation and Wages: Evidence from Hospitals, 111 *American Economic Review* 397 (2021).

behavior among hospitals, at least in part, can explain some of the shortage in the nurse labor market.

6.6 Monopsony in the Broiler Chicken Market

Recently, there have been many claims of collusion and suppression of wages in the market for broiler chickens.[38] More specifically, there have been concerns related to information exchanges between major chicken processors to depress compensation for workers in their processing plants. In addition, there are competitive concerns with the tournament system of compensating growers.

On July 25, 2022, the DOJ filed a civil antitrust case against three major poultry producers – Cargill, Inc., Sanderson Farms, Inc., and Wayne Farms LLC – as well as the data consulting firm Webber, Meng, Sahl, and Company (WMS) and its president.[39] This suit alleged that these producers were exploiting their use of WMS for decades to share information on plant workers' wages. By monitoring each other's wages, they could maintain suppressed levels of compensation for workers.[40]

Simultaneously, the DOJ released a consent decree calling for the three accused firms to follow strict guidance enforced by the DOJ monitoring their business dealings and prohibiting the poultry producers from sharing competitively sensitive information about worker compensation.[41] In

---

[38] This is not the only livestock-based industry with allegations of wage suppression. According to a recent antitrust suit, dairy farmers in the southwest have suffered monopsonistic abuses at the hands of the Dairy Farmers of America. See https://news .bloomberglaw.com/antitrust/top-u-s-dairy-co-op-hit-with-antitrust-lawsuit-over-farmer-pay. Additionally, a Peruvian sheepherder, Cirilo Ucharima Alvarado, has alleged that members of the Western Range Association have depressed wages paid to sheepherders to create a shortage that would permit them to hire foreign workers on visas. The Association then allocates the visas to individual ranchers, sets wages at the legal limit, and prevents disgruntled workers from moving to another ranch. In addition to low wages, the Association members imposed poor working conditions on the sheepherders. See https://news.bloomberglaw.com/antitrust/sheepherder-sues-rancher-group-over-wage-antitrust-violations?context=search&index=0. Major meatpackers including JBS, Tyson, and Hormel Foods are also accused of suppressing wages of their workers at red meat processing plants through the use of no-poaching agreements, "highly regimented" wage schedules, and illegally exchanging data on compensation. See *Brown* v. *JBS USA Food Co.*, D. Colo., No. 22-cv-2946 (Nov. 11, 2022).

[39] See www.justice.gov/atr/case-document/file/1528331/download.

[40] This is not the first time such allegations have arisen. See https://news.bloomberglaw.com/ antitrust/tyson-perdue-to-face-expanded-antitrust-suit-on-immigrant-wages and https://news .bloomberglaw.com/esg/perdue-farms-set-to-settle-poultry-worker-wage-fixing-litigation.

[41] See www.justice.gov/atr/case-document/file/1528336/download.

addition to these sanctions, the firms would be required to pay an $84.8 million settlement to compensate the underpaid employees. Moreover, WMS would be prohibited from providing any services that could facilitate information sharing in this market.[42]

The same day that it was filed, Cargill, Sanderson, and Wayne Farms agreed to the terms of the consent decree.[43] In September of 2022, a judge tentatively signed off on the agreement which stipulated that Sanderson pay $38 million, Wayne Farms pay $31.5 million, and Cargill pay $15 million.[44]

In its filing, the DOJ also brought claims against Sanderson and Wayne Farms alleging violations of the Packers and Stockyards Act.[45] These companies were accused of exploiting farmers by forcing them to participate in what is referred to as a "tournament system," which can lead to suppressed compensation for farmers.[46] The tournament system rewards farmers with better quantity and quality of flock. Many commentators, including many antitrust scholars, argue that this system punishes farmers who are unable to afford to maintain the high costs of doing business in this industry, given that farmers who raise these chickens pay for all maintenance and facilities costs out-of-pocket.[47] In addition, farmers may receive reductions in their base pay because of less than satisfactory flock production.

In its July decree, the DOJ required that Sanderson and Wayne Farms eliminate this reduction in base pay, while maintaining the reward system imposed by the tournament system. Moreover, they prohibited retaliation against farmers who come forward regarding antitrust concerns in the future, and that the companies increase contract transparency.

---

[42] See www.justice.gov/atr/case-document/file/1528351/download.

[43] See https://news.bloomberglaw.com/antitrust/cargill-wayne-farms-sued-by-doj-for-sharing-wage-benefits-data.

[44] See https://news.bloomberglaw.com/antitrust/poultry-worker-wage-settlements-worth-85-million-get-first-nod. In May 2023, poultry producer George's, Inc. settled with the DOJ over its participation in a wage suppression scheme involving the major chicken processors. *U.S.* v. *Cargill Meat Solutions Corporation*, No. 1:22-cv-01821 (D. Md. May 17, 2023).

[45] See www.justice.gov/atr/case-document/file/1528331/download.

[46] Similar allegations have been made against other major poultry producers. See https://news.bloomberglaw.com/antitrust/pilgrims-pride-says-its-cooperating-with-doj-investigation?utm_source=rss&utm_medium=ATNW&utm_campaign=00000184-1a72-d6b7-a197-3a7acdb50001 and https://news.bloomberglaw.com/class-action/koch-foods-pays-15-5-million-to-exit-farmer-wage-fixing-case.

[47] For a more in-depth explanation of the broiler chicken industry, see Eduardo Pontual Ribeiro, Monopsony Power and Coordination in the Broiler Industry, 68 *Antitrust Bulletin* 24 (2023).

Sanderson, the third largest U.S. chicken producer, and Wayne Farms, the eighth, were attempting to merge before these allegations came to light. While the merger itself did not raise any red flags with the antitrust authorities, the allegations of abuse of the tournament system and subsequent call for settlement may have encouraged a quicker agreement with the DOJ than would have materialized otherwise. Some believe this merger will provide a new beginning for chicken farmers, since Wayne-Sanderson Farms will be the first major poultry producer to pay a guaranteed base rate to farmers.[48] While the true results of this merger remain to be seen, we can only hope that farmers and workers will receive the pay they deserve.

6.7 The NCAA Cartel

The star quarterback on the football team and the All-American forward on the men's basketball team receive no more than the athletes in the so-called non-revenue sports, such as fencing, golf, and tennis.

In hiring athletes to play an intercollegiate sport for a college or university, the athlete is paid in kind. In its Operations Manual, the NCAA specifies the payment to the athlete. Traditionally, the payment has been limited to room, board, tuition, books, and fees. Recently, the athletic programs have been permitted to add a limited amount of money, so that the athlete's scholarship amounts to the total cost of attendance.

Everyone on a "full ride" receives the same amount. In addition to controlling an athlete's compensation, the NCAA specifies the maximum number of athletes that can be employed in each sport.

If a college or university cheats by paying more than the allowed amount, the NCAA can impose sanctions. These sanctions may include the loss of bowl revenues. This is a serious financial blow since bowl revenues add millions of dollars to the budget. Another sanction is the loss of scholarships, which will impair the team's performance. This, in turn, will reduce attendance and donations.

The NCAA cartel agreement is not clandestine. Committees and subcommittees are charged with formulating proposals that are voted and ruled upon at a meeting of the full college and university membership. This very visible cartel has come under antitrust fire from time to time but has been able to survive due to the Supreme Court's misadventure in its *Board*

---

[48] See www.bloomberg.com/news/articles/2022-07-27/us-chicken-merger-spells-end-to-abusive-pay-system-for-farmers.

of Regents decision.[49] The Court pointed to a revered tradition of amateurism in college sports, which allowed the colleges and universities to limit compensation of athletes by agreement.[50] It should be noted that the Court cited no authority for the existence of the so-called "revered tradition."

The NCAA's control appears to be crumbling due to state legislation that permits the students to be paid for their "name, image, and likeness" (NIL). Now, schools compete in the recruiting process by facilitating NIL payments. As a result, the most prominent college athletes will be able to earn substantial sums of money. Note, however, that the colleges and universities can only facilitate these payments. The actual payment comes from a booster. The colleges and universities may not make the payments. This restriction may amount to the proverbial "distinction without a difference."

6.7.1 Restraints on Coaches

The NCAA also imposes limits on coaching staffs. For each sport, the NCAA has specified the maximum number of coaches. In general, the NCAA does not limit the salaries that can be paid. In fact, there are many head football coaches who earn multi-million-dollar salaries. There are two instances, however, in which the NCAA has restricted compensation.

Volunteer Coaches: In each sport, there is a provision for a volunteer coach that supplements the paid coach's staff. These volunteer coaches may not receive compensation in any form from the school.

An NCAA bylaw spells out the limitation on the number of baseball coaches that may be employed. This bylaw is under fire in *Smart* v. *National Athletic Association*.[51] The bylaw restricts the number of baseball coaches to one head coach, two assistant coaches, and one volunteer coach. A volunteer coach may not receive compensation in any form. The plaintiffs, who are volunteer coaches, allege that the bylaw restrains competition. In the absence of the bylaw, the schools would have competed for the coaching services of the volunteer coaches by paying them a salary.

---

[49] *NCAA* v. *Board of Regents of University of Oklahoma*, 468 U.S. 85 (1984).

[50] There is also a history of wage suppression in professional sports, including the National Basketball Association (NBA). For a review of the history of wage suppression in the NBA, see David Berri, Oscar Robertson, Antitrust, and the Fight Against Monopsony Power in the NBA, 66 *The Antitrust Bulletin* 328 (2021).

[51] *Smart* v. *National Collegiate Athletic Association*, No. 22-cv-2125 (E.D. Cal. Nov. 29, 2022). Also, see https://news.bloomberglaw.com/antitrust/ncaa-hit-with-antitrust-suit-over-baseball-coaching-restrictions.

Restricted Earnings Coaches: In the early 1990s, the NCAA imposed a rule placing caps on compensation for certain coaches in Division-I sports. This rule was coined the "Restricted Earnings Coach" rule. Three separate antitrust cases were filed on behalf of men's basketball coaches, baseball coaches, as well as coaches in other sports, but eventually these three cases were consolidated into one class-action suit, *Law* v. *NCAA*.[52]

This was not the first case of wage suppression in the history of Division-I sports. In *Hennessey* v. *National Collegiate Athletic Association*,[53] the NCAA decided to restrict the number of assistant football coaches to eight. This resulted in Lawrence H. "Dude" Hennessey being reduced from a full to part time position at the University of Alabama. The court held in favor of the NCAA, arguing that "[a] goal of the NCAA ... is to 'retain a clear line of demarcation be between college athletics and professional sports.'"[54]

In the case of *Law* v. *NCAA*, the restriction of compensation substantially reduced salaries of some coaches. There were coaches that had been earning $60,000 to $70,000 whose salaries were restricted to just $12,000 to $16,000. The court found that:

[b]ecause the Restricted Earnings Coach Rule specifically prohibits the free operation of a market responsive to demand and is thus inconsistent with the Sherman Act's mandates, it is not necessary for the Court to undertake an extensive market analysis to determine that the rule has had an anticompetitive effect on the market for coaching services.[55]

The jury awarded damages of over $22.0 million. After trebling, this would have amounted to $66.0 million plus costs and a reasonable attorneys fee. Following unsuccessful appeals by the NCAA, the parties settled for $55.0 million. Individual coaches received an average of some $12,000 per year.

6.8 Bidding for Elite Students

The most prestigious colleges and universities in the United States compete for the very best students. These elite students are often admitted to more than one of the elite schools. Interestingly, the elite schools have agreed among themselves to refrain from engaging in a bidding war over these

---

[52] *Law* v. *National Collegiate Athletic Association*, 5 F. Supp. 2d 921 (D. Kan. 1998).
[53] *Hennessey* v. *National Collegiate Athletic Association*, 564 F. 3d 1136 (5th Cir. 1977).
[54] *Ibid.*
[55] *Law* v. *National Collegiate Athletic Association*, 902 F. Supp. 1394 (D. Kan. 1995).

students. In most markets, such an agreement among ostensible competitors would run afoul of the antitrust laws. So, what is going on here?

In 1991, all Ivy League universities along with MIT were accused of colluding on financial aid decisions.[56] One can analyze this conduct as a buyer cartel. The academically elite schools compete for academically elite students. In effect, they buy these students by providing competitive offers of financial aid. The suit alleged that the schools agreed to offer financial aid packages to an elite student that made their net cost of attendance the same across the schools. The alleged purpose of the practice was to induce the students to choose the school that provides the best match for the student. But the result amounted to an agreement on price. It also eliminated competitive bidding for elite students. This case was resolved through settlements.

In the wake of this dispute, Congress provided an antitrust exemption for colleges and universities, provided that their admissions decisions are made on a totally "need blind" basis. The exemption permitted these schools to collaborate on their formulas for determining financial aid, but only if all admission decisions are completely "need blind."

In January of 2022, a class action suit was filed against the following elite schools: Brown, CalTech, Chicago, Columbia, Cornell, Dartmouth, Duke, Emory, Georgetown, MIT, Northwestern, Notre Dame, Rice, UPenn, Vanderbilt, and Yale.[57] That suit alleges that the schools did not qualify for the so-called 568 exemption to antitrust law because admissions decisions were, in fact, based on need to some extent.[58]

The result of the collaboration on need was lower prices paid for elite students or higher net prices paid by elite students. In either interpretation, one can readily see a *per se* violation of Section 1 of the Sherman Act.

According to the Complaint, the cartel agreed on a so-called "Consensus Methodology" for assessing the student's ability to contribute to his or her cost of attendance. All members agreed to use this formula for determining the extent of the applicant's financial need.[59]

---

[56] *U.S. v. Brown University*, 805 F. Supp. 288 (E.D. Pa. 1992). For an analysis, see Dennis W. Carlton, Gustavo E. Bamberger, and Roy J. Epstein, Antitrust and Higher Education: Was There a Conspiracy to Restrict Financial Aid?, 26 *RAND Journal of Economics* 131 (1995).

[57] See *Henry* v. *Brown University*, No. 1:22-cv-00125 (N.D. Ill. Jan. 9, 2022). It is interesting that Harvard, Princeton, and Stanford were not among the defendants.

[58] According to some estimates, more than 17,000 former undergraduates who received some form of financial aid in the past eighteen years could be eligible to join the suit.

[59] In *Mandeville Island Farms* v. *American Crystal Sugar*, 334 U.S. 219 (1948), the Supreme Court found that the collusive use of a formula that depressed the price paid was unlawful. In the elite student case, however, the formula would have been exempt if the schools had not included need in their decisions.

Allegedly, the implementation of the Consensus Methodology limited the financial aid for students and thereby increased the net prices that they paid. In effect, the purpose of the Consensus Methodology is to eliminate competition among the cartel members for recruiting the elite students. Put differently, the cartel agreement precluded the cartel members from getting in a bidding war with one another over the very best students.

This sounds like a classic cartel that usually receives a finding of *per se* illegality. But all the anticompetitive conduct is exempt from antitrust prosecution provided that the cartel members followed a need blind admissions procedure. Thus, the antitrust challenge is *not* because the agreement to employ the Consensus Methodology is anticompetitive, which it clearly is. Instead, it is based on the failure of some cartel members to adhere to a need blind admission procedure, which eliminated the antitrust exemption.

As with most antitrust litigation, defendants often find it economically sensible to settle with the plaintiffs rather than to go to trial. In this litigation, the University of Chicago was the first to buy its way out.[60]

6.9 Antitrust Damages

In most circumstances, an antitrust violation has many victims.[61] But only some of them are entitled to recover treble damages. Although Section 4 of the Clayton Act appears to confer a private right of action upon literally anyone who is an antitrust victim,[62] the Supreme Court has placed limits on those who have standing to pursue damages.[63]

First, a would-be plaintiff must have suffered *antitrust injury*.[64] This means that the injury must flow from the anticompetitive consequences of the antitrust violation. In the case of collusion in the labor market, the anticompetitive consequences are the depression of wages and/or salaries below the competitive level and the reduction in the number of workers employed. Since these consequences flow from the unlawful agreement, the employees would appear to have suffered antitrust injury.

---

[60] See www.bloomberglaw.com/login?target=https%3A%2F%2Fwww.bloomberglaw.com%2Fc itation%2FBNA%2520000001879f11d588afd79f3715b10001%3Fbna_news_filter%3Dantitrust.

[61] For an extensive discussion, see Chapter 5.

[62] Section 4 of the Clayton Act, 15 U.S.C. Section 15, provides that "any person who shall be injured in his business or property by reason of anything forbidden in the antitrust laws may sue therefore … and shall recover threefold the damages by him sustained."

[63] For an examination of private enforcement in antitrust cases involved in buyer cartels, see Roger D. Blair and Wenche Wang, Buyer Cartels and Private Enforcement, 38 *Managerial and Decision Economics* 1185 (2017).

[64] See *Brunswick Company* v. *Pueblo Bowl-O-Mat*, 429 U.S. 477 (1977).

Second, a plaintiff must have been injured *directly* by the unlawful conduct. This requirement is meant to avoid duplicative damages or the need for complex apportioning. In the case of collusion in the labor market, the employees must be the direct victims of the collusion, that is, those employees who are working at a reduced wage.

Third, the damage estimate may not be speculative. To avoid charges of speculation, the damages claimed must be based on a just and reasonable inference rather than mere guesswork.

6.9.1 The Measure of Damages

Assuming that the collusion among the employers is impermissible, the employees will have standing to sue for damages. The measure of damages is the underpayment suffered by the victims of the conspiracy – in this case, the employees. Consequently, the appropriate measure of damages (Δ) is the difference between the competitive wage, the wage but for the collusion (w_{bf}), and the actual wage (w_a), times the number of workers actually employed (L_a):

$$\Delta = \left(w_{bf} - w_a \right) L_a$$

In Figure 6.3, we can see that the damage will be equal to the difference between w_1, which is the but for wage, and w_2, which is the actual (collusive) wage, times L_2, which is the actual quantity of labor employed.

There are workers who would have been employed but for the collusion – in fact, there are ($L_1 - L_2$) of them. They have suffered antitrust injury because the competitive wage (w_1) exceeds their reservation wages. They are essentially priced out of the market by the collusion among the employers. These employees, however, cannot be part of the class since it would be difficult to prove that they would have worked at the competitive wage, since there is an incentive to misrepresent the willingness to participate. In addition, the damage for these employees would be the difference between the competitive wage and the reservation wage, which is the height of the supply curve. This gap narrows as one slides along the supply curve to the point e. Proving (or disproving) each employee's reservation wage along that segment of the supply is ordinarily not feasible.

Proving the amount of damages for those employees who are actually employed can be an econometric challenge because an estimate of antitrust damages requires a reliable estimate of the "but for" wage. To determine the "but for" wage, we must reliably estimate the supply of and demand for employees. These are typically difficult, but not impossible, to estimate. In

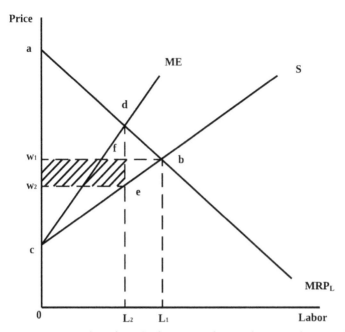

Figure 6.3 Damages resulting from the formation of an employer cartel are equal to $(w_1 - w_2)L_2$

the absence of reliable estimates, however, we are left with speculation and guesswork. These do not provide the necessary foundation for an admissible estimate of damages.

6.9.2 Standard of Precision

As a general proposition, the courts are demanding when it comes to proving the fact of injury but far less so when it comes to estimating the amount of the damage suffered. The logic is fairly straightforward. If an employee claims to have been injured, they will have to prove it. For a defendant to be liable, the preponderance of the evidence must support the plaintiff's allegation. Once the jury has found a defendant liable, however, the standard of precision in measuring the damages is relaxed. To estimate damages due to an employer cartel, the plaintiff must estimate the difference between the wage that would have been received if there had been no conspiracy and the actual wage that was received. While a plaintiff can be expected to present accurate evidence of the cartel wage, the "but for" wage is not observable because it did not actually occur, and therefore must be estimated. There is an unavoidable element of uncertainty surrounding such estimates due to data limitations. Consequently, the estimated under-payment may be imprecise.

In general terms, the U.S. Supreme Court explained that whenever damages are estimated, there is some unavoidable element of uncertainty involved. In the antitrust arena at least, we have learned to live with uncer-tainty. Once an antitrust plaintiff has proved the fact of injury with reason-able certainty, the burden of proof in estimating the amount of damages is somewhat relaxed. In *Story Parchment*,[65] the Supreme Court explained the different standards of proof for the fact of damage and the amount of the damage:

The rule which precludes the recovery of uncertain damages applies to such as are not the certain result of the wrong, not to those damages which are definitely attributable to the wrong and only uncertain in respect of their amount.[66]

Once a plaintiff proves the fact of the damage:

it will be enough if the evidence show[s] the extent of the damages as a matter of just and reasonable inference.[67]

While the jury can rely on reasonable inferences, there is a difference between drawing reasonable inferences and speculation or guesswork. Charges of speculation can be avoided by the proper use of modern econo-metrics that yield reasonable inferences. Using these methods, the impact of the cartel can be isolated once other factors that may influence wages are controlled for. The plaintiff should be able to provide a just and reasonable estimate of the damages that they suffered. Such estimates should not be deemed "speculative."

6.9.3 Estimating Antitrust Damages

Imprecision may remain even with relevant data and rigorous econometric examination. Nonetheless, the estimated wage differential is still the most reliable damage estimate that the plaintiff can produce.

One way to estimate the damages suffered by those that were actually employed is to estimate a reduced-form wage equation:

$$w = w\left(MRP_L, S_L, C\right),$$

[65] *Story Parchment Co. v. Paterson Parchment Paper Co.*, 282 U.S. 555 (1931).
[66] *Ibid.* at 562.
[67] *Ibid.* at 563.

where w is the employee's wage, MRP_L is a vector of demand variables, S_L is a vector of supply variables, and C is a dummy variable that takes a value of one for cartel period observations and zero otherwise.[68] Using panel data before, during, and after the cartel, the coefficient on C is a measure of $(w_{bf} - w_a)$. This estimated underpayment can be applied to the number of employees (L_a) to estimate the total underpayment.

6.9.4 Proving Damages on a Class-Wide Basis

In our stylized model, each employee is paid precisely the same amount. For example, when hospitals compete in the nurse labor market, each nurse is paid w_1. When the hospitals collude, each is paid w_2. In this simple model, a nurse's damage claim is relatively straightforward: the underpayment is the difference between the competitive wage (w_1) and the collusive wage (w_2). In most cases, however, antitrust damage estimation is far more complicated. For one thing, the successful plaintiff is only entitled to recover the underpayment that is attributable to the antitrust violation.[69] The damage methodology must control for all other factors that could contribute to a reduction in employment and the wage paid.

In most cases, the damage claim will span several years. Although there is a four-year statute of limitations on damage claims, by the time of trial the damage period may be six or seven years. During that time, much can happen that can influence nurse wages, including normal inflation, hospital mergers or acquisitions, changes in technology or protocols, shifts in demand, and so on.

The discussion above implicitly assumes that the nursing services are homogenous. In an actual hospital, compensation across nurses may vary due to factors including experience, tenure, specialization, educational achievement, shift differentials, and the like.

There is another complication: wages are not just the take-home pay. The actual compensation of a nurse includes benefits such as health and life insurance, retirement contributions, paid vacation and sick leave, and

---

[68] If the expert had data from only cartel members, then C would represent the time period of the cartel observations relative to a time period before and/or after the conspiracy. If, however, the expert had data from cartel and non-cartel members, C could represent the time period during the conspiracy for the cartel participants.

[69] In *Bigelow* v. *RKO Radio Pictures.* 327 U.S. 251, 264 (1946), the Supreme Court found that antitrust damages must be found "by comparison of profits, prices and values as affected by the [antitrust violation], with what they would have been in its absence under freely competitive conditions."

bonuses. These benefits vary across hospitals and over time. It is, however, necessary to account for non-wage benefits in the damage analysis.

The bottom line is that damage estimation for a single employee is complicated. Estimation for a class of employees is necessarily more complicated, but it is not impossible. Fortunately, most cases where class certification has been approved settle before a rigorous measure of damages is needed.

6.10 Concluding Remarks

In this chapter, we have considered the antitrust law and economics of collusion on compensation. Most of our exposition has been confined to agreements on wages, but that was for expositional convenience. Agreements among employers to depress any and all forms of compensation are unlawful. Collusion in the labor market exposes the employers to antitrust sanctions including fines of up to $100 million. For those individuals involved in the conspiracy, fines up to $1.0 million and/or prison sentences of up to 10 years may be imposed. Moreover, those employees who have been underpaid may recover three times the reduced compensation through private damage suits pursuant to Section 4 of the Clayton Act.

7

No-Poaching Agreements

7.1 Introduction

No-poaching agreements may be complicated in practice, but they have a common theme: employers agree not to compete for one another's employees. Although agreements to refrain from competing are usually unlawful *per se*, such agreements have been found in an assortment of labor markets.

Horizontal no-poaching agreements among employers have been found in the employment of hardware and software engineers,[1] digital animators,[2] medical school faculty,[3] staffing agencies,[4] and various professional sports leagues.[5]

In some franchise systems, no-poaching agreements have been imposed on the franchisees by the franchisor. In this case, the agreement is vertical rather than horizontal. The economic rationale for these vertical restrictions is a bit difficult to understand, but their use has been widespread. Notable examples include Arby's, Burger King, Carl's Jr., Dunkin' Donuts, Jimmy John's, Little Caesar's, McDonald's, and Pizza Hut.[6]

In this chapter, we provide an economic analysis of no-poaching agreements. We also examine specific examples – both horizontal and vertical – along with their legality under Section 1 of the Sherman Act.

In Section 7.2, we examine the economic effects of a no-poaching agreement among rival employers. Not surprisingly, we find that wages, salaries,

---

[1] *U.S. v. Adobe Systems, Inc.*, No. 1:10-cv-01629 (D.D.C. Sept. 24, 2010) and *In re High-Tech Antitrust Litigation*, No.11-CV-02509-LHK (N.D. Cal. Oct. 24, 2013).
[2] *U.S. v. Lucasfilm Ltd.*, No. 1:10-cv-02220-RBW (D.D.C. Dec. 21, 2010) and *In re Animation Workers Antitrust Litigation*, No. 5:14-cv-04062-LHK (N.D. Cal. Mar. 30, 2016).
[3] *Danielle Seaman v. Duke University*, No. 1:2015cv00462 (M.D.N.C. Feb. 1, 2018).
[4] *U.S. v. Hee*, No. 2:21-cr-00098-RFB-BNW (D. Nev. Feb. 8, 2022).
[5] See Section 7.5 for a review of the major sports leagues.
[6] Alan B. Krueger and Orley Ashenfelter, Theory and Evidence on Employer Collusion in the Franchise Sector, 57 *Journal of Human Resources* S324 (2022) at Appendix Table 1.

and other forms of compensation are depressed when the employers collude rather than compete. In Section 7.3 we examine some prominent examples of no-poaching agreements, as well as their disposition. In Section 7.4, we turn our attention to the antitampering restrictions in the four major professional sports leagues. These restraints do not violate Section 1 of the Sherman Act because they are the product of collective bargaining. In Section 7.5, our focus is on the widespread inclusion of no-poaching restraints in a substantial number of franchise contracts. We close with some concluding observations in Section 7.6.

7.2 The Economics of No-Poaching Agreements

In *Lucasfilm*,[7] the allegations involved a horizontal no-poaching agreement among employers of digital animators. The class action complaint accused Lucasfilm and Pixar of agreeing not to solicit one another's digital animators. The economic effect of such an agreement is to depress the demand for the services of those who are employed by one of the defendants. The demand for the creative services is their marginal revenue product (MRP_L). The impact of the no-poaching agreement is shown in Figure 7.1.

In the absence of a no-poaching agreement, the demand for talented digital animators is shown as MRP_1, which is equal to the supply at a wage of w_1 and an employment level of L_1. In this case, employee surplus is equal to the area w_1ac.

A no-poaching agreement artificially eliminates (or suppresses) some of the demand, so the perceived demand falls to MRP_2. This new demand is equal to the supply at a wage of w_2 and an employment level of L_2. However, because the true demand curve does not shift, redistribution to employers is based on the differences in the actual wages paid to the remaining employed workers, and is hence equal to the area $(w_1 - w_2)L_2$. This can be thought of as employer surplus or profit.

Market allocation is another way of characterizing a no-poaching scheme. Current employees are "allocated" to their current employers. The availability of attractive job opportunities for those digital animators is reduced. As a result, the employer can retain the employee at a lower wage than would be possible if there were no agreement not to compete. Moreover, the employer has less of an incentive to provide better working conditions because they know that the employee will have a greater difficulty switching jobs.[8]

---

[7] *U.S. v. Lucasfilm Ltd.*, No. 1:10-cv-02220-RBW (D.D.C. Dec. 21, 2010).

[8] Daniel Ferrés, Gaurav Kankanhalli, and Pradeep Muthukrishnan, *Anti-Poaching Agreements, Corporate Hiring, and Innovation: Evidence from the Technology Industry*, Working Paper (2022).

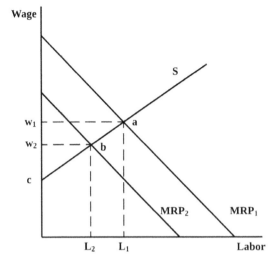

Figure 7.1 A no-poaching agreement depresses labor demand

7.3 Antitrust Treatment of No-Poaching Agreements

In October of 2016, the DOJ and FTC released their *Antitrust Guidance for Human Resource Professionals*,[9] which provides employers with advice on what firm behavior will trigger negative repercussions with the antitrust authorities. Regarding no-poaching agreements, the Agencies have established that:

An individual likely is breaking the antitrust laws if he or she … agrees with individual(s) at another company to refuse to solicit or hire that other company's employees (so-called "no poaching" agreements).[10]

No-poaching agreements are usually challenged as violations of Section 1 of the Sherman Act, which forbids agreements among competitors to refrain from competing with one another. In their *Guidance*, the Agencies take the position that no-poaching agreements are unlawful *per se*:

[N]o-poaching agreements among employers, whether entered into directly or through a third-party intermediary, are *per se* illegal under the antitrust laws.[11]

---

[9] See www.justice.gov/atr/file/903511/download.
[10] *Ibid.* at 3.
[11] *Ibid.* Not all scholars agree with this sentiment. Some argue that no-poaching agreements are not inherently anticompetitive. For an example, see https://laweconcenter.org/resources/brief-of-icle-and-law-economics-scholars-in-deslandes-v-mcdonalds/.

The federal antitrust authorities have warned that they will take action against employers who agree not to compete on terms of employment, including no-poaching agreements.[12] The Agencies have asserted that no-poaching agreements are *per se* violations of Section 1 of the Sherman Act. But this is only the opinion of the Agencies. They do not get to determine what the law is. Whether no-poaching agreements are unlawful *per se* or subject to the rule of reason is for the judiciary to decide.

Not everyone agrees that no-poaching agreements should be unlawful *per se*. Mutchnik, Johnson, and Fields offer a variety of circumstances in which employers enter into no-poaching agreements to avoid losing valuable employees.[13] But the benefits to the employers are at the expense of employees. The latter are denied the opportunity of a better paying position or more desirable work arrangements. In our view, the authors simply illustrate an assortment of circumstances in which employers benefit from not having to compete. One way to retain the most talented and highly valued employees is to pay them their marginal revenue product, so they cannot be induced to leave.

So far, DOJ's efforts to pursue criminal convictions for no-poaching agreements have been largely unsuccessful.[14] Their failures in criminal cases are interesting and deserve some investigation. One possible explanation is that there is no judicial development of a *per se* rule as can be found for price fixing. Another may be that the evidentiary requirements for a criminal conviction are much higher than for a civil conviction.[15]

U.S. v. Jindal:[16] In 2020, the DOJ filed its first criminal no-poaching case against Naraj Jindal and John Rodgers for allegedly violating Section 1 of the Sherman Act. Niraj Jindal was the owner of a physical therapist staffing company. In their indictment, the DOJ claims that these two defendants conspired with other staffing companies to fix wages for their employees in the Dallas-Fort Worth metropolitan area.

---

[12] For example, a group of truckers filed a class action antitrust suit against CRST International Inc. and other trucking companies for engaging in no-poaching agreements that suppressed their compensation. The DOJ has urged the court to treat no-poaching agreements as *per se* unlawful violations of Section 1 of the Sherman Act. See *Curtis Markson* v. *CRST International, Inc.*, No 5:17-cv-01262 (C.D. Cal. July 15, 2022).

[13] James H. Mutchnik, John H. Johnson IV, and Charles Fields, The Evolution of DOJ's Views on No-Poaching Litigation, 36 *Antitrust* 35 (2022).

[14] See https://news.bloomberglaw.com/daily-labor-report/lessons-from-the-first-criminal-no-poach-trial.

[15] Criminal liability requires proof beyond a reasonable doubt while civil liability relies on the preponderance of the evidence.

[16] *U.S. v. Jindal*, No. 4:20-cr-358 (E.D. Tex. Dec. 09, 2020).

In the end, Jindal and his co-defendant were acquitted on their counts of wage fixing and conspiracy. Jindal was, however, found guilty of obstruction.

U.S. v. DaVita:[17] The DOJ filed a criminal Section 1 case against DaVita and its CEO, Kent Thiry, for entering into a no-poaching agreement with Surgical Care Affiliates, LLC, Radiology Partners, and Hazel Health Inc. The DOJ characterized the agreement as a market allocation agreement, which is *per se* unlawful according to antitrust precedent.[18] The companies admitted that these agreements were in place, but claimed they would not be anticompetitive because there were many potential employers that were not privy to the agreement. Moreover, if an employee wanted to move to another employer within the group, they were required to notify their superior. This would allow the current employer to make competitive offers to retain desired employees. Just as in the Jindal case, a Colorado jury acquitted DaVita and its CEO.[19]

U.S. v. Hee:[20] When the Clark County school district wanted to hire school nurses for students with special needs, it turned to two staffing agencies. The nurse's duties would include constant care and performance of special medical procedures. The nurses were expected to accompany the students everywhere – in class, between classes, and during bus rides.

The two staffing agencies agreed between themselves to suppress the nurses' compensation by not bidding against one another. When one of the staffing agencies, VDA OC LLC, entered a guilty plea, the DOJ obtained its first victory in a criminal antitrust labor case.[21]

U.S. v. Manahe:[22] Four Portland residents, Faysal Kalayaf Manahe, Yaser Aali, Ammar Alkinani, and Quasim Saesah, each owned or managed home health care agencies. In 2022, the DOJ accused these four managers of colluding to fix wages of Personal Support Specialist workers, as well as refrain from hiring each other's workers during the first two month of the COVID-19 pandemic. Over a year later, the defendants were acquitted by a jury.

U.S. v. Patel:[23] Mahash Patel, a manager of Pratt and Whitney, individually directed firm suppliers of parts for jet engines to refrain from poaching

[17] *U.S.* v. *DaVita Inc.*, No. 1:21-cr-00229-RBJ (D. Colo. Mar. 25, 2022).
[18] See *U. S. v. Topco Associates, Inc.*, 405 U.S. 596 (1972), and *Palmer* v. *BRG of Georgia, Inc.*, 498 U.S. 46 (1990).
[19] Notably, this acquittal came one day after the *Jindal* decision.
[20] *U.S.* v. *Hee*, No. 2:21-cr-00098-RFB-BNW (D. Nev. Feb. 8, 2022).
[21] See www.bloomberglaw.com/bloomberglawnews/antitrust/XEH5QIVC000000?bna_news_filter=antitrust#jcite.
[22] *U.S.* v. *Manahe*, No. 2:22-cr-00013-JAW (D. Me. Jun. 10, 2022).
[23] *U.S.* v. *Patel*, No. 3:21-cr-00220 (D. Conn. Dec. 2, 2022).

one another's aerospace engineers. This so-called "hub and spoke" conspiracy involves vertical agreements between Mr. Patel and each of Pratt and Whitney's suppliers. The effect, however, is to constrain horizontal competition among the five input suppliers in the labor market for aerospace engineers.

Allegedly, the economic effect of the agreement is to depress the compensation of the engineer. Both the DOJ and the state of Connecticut filed suits against the participants in the conspiracy. At the end of the DOJ's case, the defendants asked for a judgment of acquittal. The trial court granted the defendants' motion, so the DOJ lost another no-poaching case.

7.4 No-Poaching in Action

No-poaching agreements among ostensible competitors have been found in a wide assortment of labor markets. These include hardware and software engineers, digital animators, medical school professionals, and many others. In this section, we examine a few of these high-profile cases along with their dispositions.

7.4.1 High Tech Employees

The DOJ filed suit against Adobe Systems, Apple, Google, Intel, Intuit, and Pixar for violations of Section 1 of the Sherman Act.[24] In particular, the defendants were charged with having entered into a series of bilateral agreements that restrained trade in the market for high-tech employees. These bilateral agreements have been termed no-poaching agreements: each party to a no-poaching agreement agrees to refrain from soliciting employees of the other firms.

In the absence of such agreements, Apple might identify a talented software engineer who was employed by Google and attempt to hire the employee away from Google. To retain that talented engineer, Google would have to start a bidding war with Apple. Irrespective of who ultimately wins the bidding war, the engineer ends up with a higher compensation package. No-poaching agreements prevent such bidding wars, to the benefit of the employer and the detriment of the employee.

Section 1 of the Sherman Act forbids agreements to not compete in the market. As no-poaching, or non-solicitation, agreements reduce

---

[24] *U.S. v. Adobe Systems, Inc.*, No. 1:10-cv-01629 (D.D.C. Sept. 24, 2010).

competition among major employers for the services of high-tech employees, such agreements disrupt the normal functioning of the labor market.

The DOJ found five separate agreements that involved "cold calls." If an employer calls an employee of another firm who has not applied to the caller, this is known as a "cold call." In some settings, cold calling someone else's employees is a very effective way of recruiting talented employees. Agreements to refrain from cold calling restrain competition in the labor market.

This suit was resolved without a trial in 2015. In the wake of this suit, a class action suit pursuing antitrust damages was filed on behalf of all employees covered by the non-solicitation agreements.[25] The suit was settled for some $415 million.[26]

7.4.2 Digital Animators

The antitrust litigation involving digital animators began with the DOJ's suit against Lucasfilm. According to the Complaint,[27] an effective way of filling vacancies for digital animators is to cold call employees of other firms. This can start a series of offers and counteroffers that increase the digital animator's compensation. In the end, the highest bidder ends up with the digital animator in question. In other words, the employee is looking for the "right" employer, that is, the one where the employee's value is the highest. This outcome is socially beneficial. The no-poaching agreement between Lucasfilm and Pixar interfered with the market mechanism by inhibiting the normal functions of the labor market.

According to the Complaint, Lucasfilm and Pixar agreed to the following: (1) to not cold call one another's digital animators, (2) Lucasfilm and Pixar would notify one another when making an offer to one of their employees, and (3) that the firm making the initial offer must not make a counter-offer above its initial offer. It seems clear that the purpose of this agreement was to prevent the compensation of talented digital animators from rising. The DOJ's suit was resolved without a trial.

A class action suit was filed in the wake of the DOJ suit to pursue antitrust damages.[28] At that time, the list of defendants expanded substantially

---

[25] *In re High-Tech Antitrust Litigation*, No.11-CV-02509-LHK (N.D. Cal. Oct. 24, 2013).

[26] See www.hightechemployeelawsuit.com.

[27] *U.S. v. Lucasfilm Ltd.*, No. 1:10-cv-02220-RBW (D.D.C. Dec. 21, 2010).

[28] *In re Animation Workers Antitrust Litigation*, No. 5:14-cv-04062-LHK (N.D. Cal. Mar. 30, 2016).

to include DreamWorks Animation, Walt Disney Company, Sony Pictures Animation, Blue Sky Pictures, and Image Movers, LLC.

The class action suit for antitrust damages was filed on behalf of creative animators, digital artists, and software engineers. The allegation was that the employers agreed among themselves to refrain from soliciting one another's employees.[29] The aim of the agreement was to depress the compensation of animators by avoiding bidding wars for these talented people.[30]

In addition to the anti-solicitation scheme, the defendants held annual meetings at which HR personnel discussed salary schedules for the industry. At these meetings, the defendants decided upon salary ranges for the following year.[31] Along with the annual meetings, some HR personnel were in constant contact with one another to ensure compliance with the basic goal of depressing compensation.

In its Complaint, the class sought to recover antitrust damages (Δ) equal to the difference between the compensation that they would have received but for the collusion (w_{bf}) and the cartel compensation received (w_a):

$$\Delta = \left(w_{bf} - w_a \right) L_a,$$

where L_a represents the actual number of labor services employed by the defendants. Business records of the defendants can be relied upon for the actual compensation paid (w_a) and the total employment (L_a). The compensation but for the collusion has to be estimated by an expert economist.

The plaintiffs alleged that antisolicitation agreements affect the compensation of all employees. The impact is not limited to those who would have gotten a call but for the agreement – it extends to everyone. This result was inevitable because the defendants apparently valued internal equity, which precludes significant differences across employees in a specific job category.[32]

---

[29] *Ibid.* at paragraph 2.

[30] This is not the only case we have seen where no-poaching agreements depress the compensation of the participating firm's employees. In *Hunter* v. *Booz Allen Hamilton Inc.*, 418 F. Supp. 3d 214 (S.D. Ohio 2019), the plaintiff alleged that Booz Allen, CACI, and Mission Essential had a no-poaching agreement that precluded an employee of one of them from seeking a better paying job at either of the other companies. The case settled on undisclosed terms.

[31] *In re Animation Workers Antitrust Litigation*, No. 5:14-cv-04062-LHK (N.D. Cal. Mar. 30, 2016) at paragraph 10–11.

[32] *Ibid.* at paragraph 9, 128–132

As with nearly all class action suits, the case on digital animators was settled. Collectively, the defendants paid $170 million to avoid a trial and exposure to treble damages.[33]

7.4.3 Medical School Personnel

No-poaching agreements have attracted antitrust scrutiny in health care settings.[34] In this section, we describe one particular high-profile case involving collusion between two prominent medical schools in North Carolina, as well as the effects of no-poaching agreements among staffing agencies.

Seaman v. Duke University:[35] The research triangle of North Carolina houses several major universities including Duke University, the University of North Carolina (UNC), and North Carolina State University, along with Research Triangle Park (RTP). RTP is home to hundreds of high-tech research and development firms. Both Duke and UNC have medical schools and are two of the largest academic medical systems in North Carolina, as well as two of the largest employers of physicians in the area.

Seaman was a private suit that arose because Dr. Danielle Seaman, a Duke faculty physician in radiology, was interested in an open position at the UNC School of Medicine. Despite being a "great fit," Dr. Seaman could not be considered because "lateral moves between Duke and UNC medical schools are not permitted."[36] Dr. Seaman filed suit on behalf of a class of similarly situated hospital faculty employees. The agreement was allegedly made between the Deans of the Medical Schools at their respective institutions and effectively prohibited the poaching of employees at the same rank.

---

[33] See www.cartoonbrew.com/artist-rights/animation-workers-set-to-receive-170-million-payout-from-wage-theft-lawsuit-161482.html: "The Walt Disney Company/Pixar/Lucasfilm/Imagemovers Digital, which settled for $100 million; Dreamworks Animation, which settled for $50 million; Sony Pictures, which settled for $13 million; and twenty-first Century Fox-owned Blue Sky Studios, which settled for $5.95 million."

[34] In 2021, the DOJ indicted Surgical Care Associates for no-poaching agreements with other health care companies. Several civil complaints have also been filed as a result of the DOJ allegations (e.g., *Roe v. Surgical Care Affiliates, LLC*, No. 1:21-cv-00305 (N.D. Cal. Jan. 19, 2021); *Spradling v. Surgical Care Affiliates*, No. 1:21-cv-01324 (E.D. Ill Mar. 9, 2021)).

[35] *Danielle Seaman v. Duke University*, No. 1:2015-cv-00462 (M.D.N.C. Feb. 1, 2018). The *Seaman* case has been resolved, but Duke and the University of North Carolina faced another challenge.

[36] *Ibid.*

Evidence presented in this case included an email communication, indicating that the recruiter "received confirmation today from the Dean's office that lateral moves of faculty between Duke and UNC are not permitted. There is an economic reason for this 'guideline' which was agreed upon between the deans of UNC and Duke a few years back." In later correspondence, UNC's Chief of Cardiothoracic Imaging admitted that "the 'guideline' was generated in response to an attempted recruitment by Duke a couple of years ago of the entire UNC bone marrow transplant team; UNC had to generate a large retention package to keep the team intact." It was further explained that "the only way [Duke and UNC] can hire each other's faculty is if there is an upward move, i.e., a promotion."[37]

The defendants argued that UNC, as a state institution, was immune from antitrust scrutiny under the state action doctrine.[38] A statement of interest in this case filed by the U.S. Attorney General took the position that UNC was not a state actor as articulated by the state action doctrine and clearly fails the two-part test that requires: (1) a clear state purpose, and (2) active supervision.[39] In this case, however, there was no state articulation of a policy for restraining hiring between employers, nor was there state supervision of this restraint of trade. The defendants also argued that the alleged agreement should be evaluated under the rule of reason rather than a *per se* standard since the agreement was ancillary to collaboration between UNC and Duke. There was no evidence, however, to support an ancillary restraint defense.

In February 2018, UNC settled its lawsuit and agreed to never again enter a no-hire agreement. In April 2019, Duke School of Medicine settled its case and Duke Health Systems agreed to pay $54.5 million. In 2020, new allegations emerged that this original conspiracy involved more than the medical schools. The new suit alleged that there were broad no-poaching agreements for forty-five years from 1978 to 2018.[40] In 2021, a settlement was reached in which Duke has agreed to pay $19 million to class members employed at either institution in any department between 2001 and 2018.[41]

---

[37] *Ibid.*
[38] *Parker* v. *Brown*, 317 U.S. 341 (1943).
[39] *Danielle Seaman* v. *Duke University*, No. 1:2015-cv-00462 (M.D.N.C. Feb. 1, 2018). Statement of Interest of the United States, 2019.
[40] *Binotti* v. *Duke University*, No. 1:20-cv-470 (M.D. N.C. Nov. 9, 2020).
[41] *Ibid.* For information on the Duke–UNC employee settlement, see https://dukeunc employeesettlement.com/.

7.4.4 Staffing Agencies

Some employers turn to staffing agencies for help on filling vacancies. In some cases, the employer wants to fill full-time permanent positions. In other cases, the employer is looking for temporary help to fill part-time vacancies. In either case, the employer is essentially outsourcing the search and recruiting effort.

The demand for a staffing agency's services is influenced by: (1) providing high quality personnel on a timely basis, (2) the wage that the employer must pay, and (3) the fee that the agency requires. Holding constant the experience and ability of the personnel supplied, the lower the wage, the more business the agency will obtain. One way to keep the wage down is to refrain from competitive bidding with other staffing agencies.

For example, the Illinois Attorney General Kwame Raoul, has alleged that six temporary staffing agencies established no-poaching agreements and utilized a common client, Vee Pak, to do so.[42] Attorney General Raoul claims that the use of these agreements is a *per se* violation of the Illinois Antitrust Act, and that the alleged collusion among these six staffing agencies has resulted in suppressed wages and other conditions of employment. According to the complaint:

[t]he Agency Defendants agreed with each other not to recruit, solicit, hire, or 'poach' temporary employees from one another at Vee Pak's Countryside and Hodgkins facilities.[43]

Moreover, if an employee attempted to switch employers and succeeded, they were allegedly returned to their original employer once the switch had been discovered.[44]

7.5 Antitampering Rules

The four major sports leagues in North America – Major League Baseball, the National Basketball Association, the National Football League, and the National Hockey League – all have antitampering rules that forbid the solicitation of another team's player or players.[45] In some instances,

---

[42] *The State of Illinois* v. *Alternative Staffing Inc.*, No. 2022-CH-05069 (Ill. Cir. Ct., Cook Cty. May 26, 2022).

[43] *Ibid.* at 2.

[44] Another example of a staffing agency case is *U.S.* v. *Hee*, No. 2:21-cr-00098-RFB-BNW (D. Nev. Feb. 8, 2022), which is discussed in Section 7.3.

[45] This section depends heavily on Roger D. Blair and John E. Lopatka, The Economic Effects of Anti-Tampering Rules in Professional Sports Leagues, 38 *Managerial and Decision Economics* 704 (2017).

the antitampering rules apply to coaches, scouts, and front office personnel. These rules are close cousins of no-poaching agreements. The specific terms of the antitampering rules vary to some extent across leagues. The vigor of enforcement and the penalties for violation also vary. But at the core, they all prevent a team from informing other teams' players that it is interested in hiring that player when the player's current contract ends. The economic effect of inhibiting this flow of information is to depress the player's compensation.

7.5.1 National Football League

We begin with the NFL because their antitampering rule is quite detailed and comprehensive. The NFL antitampering rules are by far the most elaborate among the leagues.' The NFL Constitution and Bylaws prohibit certain conduct by a "member" and a member's "stockholder, director, officer, partner, or employee."[46] The scope of the conduct forbidden by the rule is expansive, covering employment overtures to all employees of a member. An actor subject to the rule may not "[t]amper with a player or coaches or other employee under contract to or the property of another member club."[47] A separate explanatory document, the Anti-Tampering Policy, defines "tampering" as "any interference by a member club with the employer-employee relationship of another club or any attempt by a club to impermissibly induce a person to seek employment with that club or with the NFL."[48]

The league interprets "tampering" expansively, and it contemplates tampering through intermediaries. The Policy provides an example of tampering with a player in which a "club's representative, or a third-party intermediary of that club (Club A), is involved in a private meeting or conversation with a player (or his representative) who is under contract to, or whose negotiating rights are held by, another club (Club B)." If contract problems then arise between the player and Club B, Club A will conclusively be found to have tampered, even if Club A establishes that its private contact with the player "did not involve any expression of interest in the player or was not related in any way to the player's subsequent contract problem with his club."[49] Further, tampering occurs when a club's

---

[46] NFL Constitution and Bylaws, Article IX. Section 9.1(C). The rule also restrains the conduct of "any officer or employee of the League." *Ibid.*

[47] *Ibid.* Section 9.1(C)(11).

[48] NFL Anti-Tampering Policy (2009) (hereinafter "NFL Anti-Tampering Policy") at 1.

[49] *Ibid.* at 2.

representative makes a statement of interest in another club's player "to a member of the news media." Thus, the comment, "He's an excellent player, and we'd very much like to have him if he were available, but another club holds his rights," is prohibited.[50]

Conduct that would constitute tampering with players is not always prohibited. The Policy contemplates a free agency system, as established in a collective bargaining agreement (CBA). As its name implies, the free agency system releases players who satisfy specified conditions from any obligation to the club that had contracted with the player in the immediately preceding period. A club that signs an unrestricted free agent incurs no penalty, such as the forfeiture of a draft choice.[51] During certain periods, but not others, the league permits contact with a free agent that would otherwise constitute tampering. A player with four or more years of experience in the league becomes an unrestricted free agent at the expiration of his contract, which occurs in March. From that day until roughly the beginning of training camp in late July, any club may contact the free agent, and he may sign with any club. The antitampering rule does not prohibit conduct during this period. From late July until mid-November, after the tenth week of the season, the player may sign only with his prior club, and solicitation is banned during this period. If a player does not sign by mid-November, the player is barred from playing for the rest of the season, and he becomes free again to sign with any club in March. Solicitation restrictions do not apply beginning in March, though it is not clear whether they apply between mid-November and March.

As to non-player employees, the Policy provides that "[n]o club … is permitted to tamper with" such an employee of another club.[52] In general, "whenever a club wishes to contact a non-player employee of another club about possible employment, such inquiring club must first notify the owner or operating head of the employer club to express interest."[53] The league distinguishes among head coaches, assistant coaches, high-level executives,

---

[50] *Ibid.* at 3.

[51] The NFL CBA provides for "restricted free agents," who are players that have played for three but less than four years. Clubs can extend contract offers that impede the ability of these players to sign contracts with other clubs. For example, if a club makes a "qualifying offer," it may be entitled to a draft choice if the player signs with another club. The period of uninhibited solicitation is agreed upon annually by the league and the players' union, but it may not be less than 35 days, and it may end no later than five days before the draft. *See* NFL Collective Bargaining Agreement with the NFL Players Association Section 2.

[52] NFL Anti-Tampering Policy at 5.

[53] *Ibid.* at 4.

and other employees. In general, a club may not solicit any non-player employee during the playing season. Thus, with limited exceptions, a club may not "request permission to discuss employment with a non-player, non-coach employee of another club, whether or not that employee is under contract, during the employer's playing season."[54] Head coaches must be under contract while performing coaching duties, and during the playing season neither an active head coach nor an assistant coach may "discuss or accept employment for the current or a future season with another club."

In the offseason, a head coach is prohibited from discussing employment opportunities with another club unless his contract has expired or has been terminated or his club has granted permission to discuss them.[55] If an assistant coach is under contract for the succeeding season or seasons, a club must permit the coach the opportunity to discuss and accept an offer to become head coach of another club between the end of a season and March 1. No club is required to grant an assistant coach under contract to it permission to discuss a lateral move to another club between the end of a season and the opening of training camp; once training camp begins, a club is not even free to grant permission. If an assistant coach's contract expires at the end of a season, the employer club retains the exclusive right to re-sign the coach as an assistant coach for roughly a week after his club's final game.[56] A club may not solicit an assistant coach during his club's exclusivity period.[57]

A club may deny another club permission to discuss employment with a "high-level employee" under contract to the first team.[58] A team may not deny permission if the employee is not under contract.[59] In general, a club need not grant another club permission to conduct off-season discussions with low-level employees under contract to it, unless the second team is prepared to offer a high-level position. A club generally may not deny permission to conduct discussions with a low-level employee whose contract is expiring if the discussions occur after completion of the season.[60]

[54] *Ibid.* at 4.
[55] *Ibid.* at 6 (head coach), at 7 (assistant coach).
[56] *Ibid.* at 9.
[57] *See* NFL Constitution and Bylaws, Article IX. Section 9.1(C)(11) (prohibiting tampering while an employee is "the property of another member club").
[58] NFL Anti-Tampering Policy at 11. A "high-level employee" is defined as a "club president, general manager, and persons with equivalent responsibilities and authority." *Id.* at 10.
[59] *Ibid.* at 11.
[60] *Ibid.* at 11. The beginning of the period in which a club must permit discussions is extended if the "employee's primary responsibilities extend to recurring events beyond the playing season."

The sanctions for a violation of the antitampering rules are not specified but are characterized as "severe": "Any violation of this Anti-Tampering Policy will subject the involved club and/or person to severe disciplinary action by the Commissioner."[61] Sanctions in fact have been substantial. In one case, the league in 2008 stripped a club of its fifth-round draft pick and reversed the order of third-round picks to favor the aggrieved club.[62] The tampering allegedly took place by communication with the target player's agent. In another case, the league in 2015 fined the New York Jets $100,000 for tampering because the owner stated publicly that he "would love" for Darrelle Revis, who was at the time under contract to the New England Patriots, to return to the Jets.[63] In a third case, the league in 2011 forced the Detroit Lions to forfeit a seventh-round draft choice and swap fifth-round picks with the Kansas City Chiefs, moving down fourteen spots, as a sanction for an assistant coach's comments to a newspaper and contact with a player or agent.[64]

The Miami Dolphins club was found guilty of tampering when it made overtures to Tom Brady while he was under contract with the New England Patriots and later with the Tampa Bay Buccaneers. Apparently, Steve Ross, owner of the Dolphins, tried to hire Brady away from his current team by suggesting that partial ownership of the Dolphins might be in Brady's future. After a six-month investigation, the NFL Commissioner, Roger Goodell, concluded that Ross's conduct violated the NFL's antitampering rules. Goodell said that the investigation uncovered violations of "unprecedented scope and severity." Goodell went on to point out that he knew "of no prior instance in which ownership was so directly involved in the violations."

The punishment was substantial. First, the Dolphins lost their first-round draft pick in the 2023 draft and a third-round pick in the 2024 draft. The owner was suspended for a year and fined $1.5 million. In addition, another Dolphin executive, Bruce Beal was also fined $500,000 for his role in the affair.

---

[61] *Ibid.* at 13.

[62] The NFL stripped the San Francisco 49ers of a draft choice in 2008 for tampering with Lance Briggs, a linebacker under contract to the Chicago Bears, and reversed the order of third-round picks. See *NFL Strips 49ers of Fifth-Round Draft Pick for Tampering*, www.nfl .com/news/story/09000d5d807625f4/article/nfl-strips-49ers-of-fifthround-draft-pick-for-tampering.

[63] See *NFL Slaps Fine on Jets for Tampering in Darrelle Revis Case*, www.wsj.com/articles/ nfl-slaps-fine-on-jets-for-tampering-in-darrelle-revis-case-1430275094?alg=y.

[64] See *Lions' Jim Schwartz on tampering: NFL reached "wrong conclusion,"* http://content .usatoday.com/communities/thehuddle/post/2011/02/nfl-lions-tampering-chiefs-jim-schwartz/1#.Vkt2NNKrRpg.

7.5.2 Major League Baseball

Compared with the rules of the NFL, the rules of MLB are simple. MLB Rule 3(k) prohibits, absent permission of the current employer, "negotiations [and] dealings respecting employment, either present or prospective, between any player, coach or manager and any Major or Minor League Club other than the Club with which the player is under contract."[65] In one case, the league commissioner interpreted this rule and an antitampering rule in the collective bargaining agreement to prohibit a club owner from telling a co-owner of another club in the presence of the media in the off-season that "he would go as high as he had to" to sign a player whose contract with the second club was expiring.[66] The incident suggests that MLB interprets the term "dealings respecting employment" expansively to include an expression of interest in employing an individual.

Penalties are not set out specifically for violation of Rule 3(k), but the Commissioner is authorized to "take action consistent with the Commissioner's powers under the Major League Constitution" for a violation of any rule for which a particular penalty is not specified.[67] The Commissioner's disciplinary actions authorized by the Major League Constitution are extensive, including the "suspension or removal" of a club owner or employee, the imposition of a fine, and "such other actions as the Commissioner may deem appropriate."[68] In the case described above, the Commissioner suspended the owner from baseball for one year and took away the club's first-round draft choice for a year. In light of the relatively circumscribed authority the Commissioner had at that time, the court upheld the suspension but not the draft choice penalty.[69]

7.5.3 National Basketball Association

The NBA rules prohibit conduct in the nature of solicitation by players, other employees, and agents, or other representatives of a club or owner. The rules state that no specified actor other than a player may:

directly or indirectly, (i) entice, induce, persuade, or attempt to entice, induce or persuade, any [p]layer who is under contract to, or whose exclusive negotiating

---

[65] MLB Constitution and Bylaws, Major League Rule (MLR) 3(k) ("Tampering").
[66] *See Atlanta National League Baseball Club, Inc. v. Kuhn*, 432 F. Supp. 1213 (N.D. Ga. 1977). The relevant rule was at that time numbered "3(g)."
[67] MLB Rule 50(a).
[68] Major League Constitution, Art. II, Sec. 3(a).
[69] *See Atlanta National League Baseball Club*, 432 F. Supp. at 1223, 1226.

rights are held by, any other [m]ember of the Association to enter into negotiations for or relating to his services or negotiate or contract for such services or (ii) otherwise interfere with any such employer-employee relationship (or prospective employer–employee relationship in the case of a [p]layer subject to exclusive negotiating rights) of any other [m]ember of the Association.[70]

The act of enticing, inducing, persuading, or attempting to do so is described as "tampering."[71] With respect to actions directed at non-players, the rules prohibit the specified non-player actors from "tampering" with any "[c]oach, [t]rainer, [g]eneral [m]anager or any other person" under contract to a club.[72] The rules prohibit players on a club from tampering with other players and any other person under contract to another club. Notably, the rules prohibit a designated actor from attempting to induce any employee under contract to a club to enter into negotiations with another club.[73]

Potential sanctions are substantial. If a player violates the antitampering rule, the Commissioner has the authority to suspend him "for a definite or indefinite period, or to impose a fine not exceeding $50,000," or to impose both sanctions.[74] If a non-player violates the rules by soliciting either a non-player or player, the Commissioner's authority is even broader. The Commissioner "in his sole discretion" may suspend the offending person, prohibit the person's club from hiring the person solicited, order the forfeiture of draft picks by the offending club or the transfer of draft picks to the aggrieved club, and impose a fine of up to $5 million.[75]

7.5.4 National Hockey League

The NHL rules apply broadly to the conduct of "any officer, shareholder, partner, employee, agent or representative" of a club.[76] Except as to free agents, no identified individual may "directly or indirectly – tamper, negotiate with, make an offer to or discuss employment with any player, or his agent or representative, with respect to whom another [m]ember [c]lub has either the professional rights or the right to negotiate for said professional right without prior written consent of the [m]ember [c]lub." Eligible players become free agents on July 1, and while they are free agents they may be

---

[70] NBA Constitution and By-Laws, Article 35A(f).

[71] *Ibid.*, Article 35(e).

[72] *Ibid.*, Article 35A(e).

[73] *Ibid.*, Article 35(e).

[74] *Ibid.*, Article 35(e).

[75] *Ibid.*, Article 35A(e), (f).

[76] NHL By-Laws Section 15.1(a).

solicited by any club. No individual subject to the conduct restriction may engage in the tampering conduct described above toward "any non-playing employee of another [m]ember [c]lub, or his agent or representative, who is employed in the capacity of [g]eneral [m]anager, [c]oach, [s]upervisor of [s]couting, [s]cout or any other employee, including 'Assistants' to any of the above, whose primary function relates to scouting, drafting, procurement or coaching of playing personnel."[77] A restricted individual may discuss employment with a non-playing employee after the termination date of the employee's contract.[78] Forbidden tampering includes direct and indirect forms of communication: "The making or causing to be made, through any medium, public or private, any statement indicating an intention or desire of or interest in acquiring the services of any person" insulated from tampering may be deemed by the league commissioner to be a violation of the rules.[79] For a violation of the solicitation rules, the league commissioner may impose a fine of up to $5 million, prohibit the employment of the person who was subject of the tampering, order the deferment by the offending club of a draft choice, and if the tampering was of a non-player, award draft choices to the offended club.[80]

7.6 No-Poaching in Franchise Contracts

In a franchise license agreement, the franchisor grants a license to the franchisee to do business under the franchisor's trademark and trade dress. Ordinarily, as part of the franchise chain, the license agreement spells out the franchisee's obligation regarding location, hours of operation, staffing, menu items, food preparation, and many other aspects of the business.[81] In their survey of franchise contracts, Krueger and Ashenfelter found that no-poaching provisions appeared in over half of the survey.[82]

Krueger and Ashenfelter surveyed the franchise documents of the largest 156 franchises. Each chain had at least 500 units. No-poaching provisions were discovered in 58 percent of the franchise systems. Among those chains that imposed such restrictions were Applebee's Neighborhood Grill,

---

[77] *Ibid.*, Section 15.1(b).
[78] *Ibid.*, Section 15.1(b)(iii). Discussions may begin earlier if the player entry first occurs before the contract ends.
[79] *Ibid.*, Section 15.1(c).
[80] *Ibid.*, Section 15.2.
[81] For an extensive analysis, see Roger D. Blair and Francine Lafontaine, *The Economics of Franchising* (2005).
[82] Krueger and Ashenfelter, Theory and Evidence on Employer Collusion.

H&R Block, Holiday Inn, Jimmy John's, McDonald's, Sport Clips, and The UPS Store.[83]

Unlike the horizontal agreements examined above, these no-poaching restraints are vertical – the franchisor imposes the restraint on its franchisees. The specific language may vary from one franchise to another, but the economic effects are the same. One member of the system may not solicit an employee of another member of the chain. Thus, this amounts to an intra-chain restraint rather than an inter-chain restraint. Consequently, a McDonald's franchisee cannot hire another McDonald's franchisee's employee(s). This does not preclude a McDonald's franchisee from hiring a manager or other employee from Wendy's or Taco Bell.[84]

From Krueger and Ashenfelter's survey, it is clear to see that no-poaching provisions are empirically relevant. The next question is obvious – why are these provisions in franchise contracts in the first place?

One explanation for their presence that invokes antitrust concerns was explained by Krueger and Ashenfelter. Consider three Jiffy Lube franchisees in a labor market. If they all refrain from hiring one another's employees, the effect is to reduce the supply elasticity of attractive employees as alternative jobs do not exist without leaving the chain. Since the MRP_L – wage gap is:[85]

$$MRP_L - w = \frac{w}{\varepsilon_L},$$

where w is the wage and ε_L is the elasticity of labor supply, a reduction in ε_L widens the MRP_L – wage gap. This, of course, redounds to the employer's benefit.[86]

No-poaching provisions in franchise licenses have largely disappeared.[87] Following the publication of an early version of Krueger and Ashenfelter's work, the Attorney General of the State of Washington objected to the use of no-poaching restrictions by various franchise systems. He filed multiple

---

[83] *Ibid.* at Appendix Table 1.

[84] In some contracts, a former employee of a franchisee cannot be hired by another franchisee until some period of time has elapsed.

[85] Profit maximization by a monopsonist requires hiring labor to the point where $MRP_L = ME_L$. Since $ME_L = w + L\left(\dfrac{dw}{dL}\right)$, the marginal revenue product is equal to $\dfrac{w}{\varepsilon_L}$.

[86] Krueger and Ashenfelter examine the other theoretical explanations for the incentive to impose no-poaching restrictions. See Krueger and Ashenfelter, Theory and Evidence on Employer Collusion at S330–S335.

[87] Those that have not disappeared are continuing to be challenged. For example, see *Arrington* v. *Burger King Worldwide Inc.*, No. 20-13561 (11th Cir Aug 31, 2022).

discontinuances, and the response was quick – the restraint was removed from the licenses of seven major fast-food companies, including Arby's, Carl's Jr., Jimmy John's, and McDonald's in Washington.[88]

7.7 Concluding Remarks

When rival employers enter into a no-poaching agreement, they are agreeing to refrain from competing with one another in the labor market. Although one might suppose that such an agreement is illegal *per se* under Section 1 of the Sherman Act, that is not universally true. If such agreements were subject to collective bargaining, they would not violate Section 1. In addition, there are some circumstances in which no-poaching agreements have passed muster in Court. We need more experience with legal challenges to identify the antitrust boundaries.

---

[88] See www.atg.wa.gov/news/news-releases/ag-ferguson-announces-fast-food-chains-will-end-restrictions-low-wage-workers. Not all claims of no-poaching agreements among fast-food franchises have led to the removal of these restraints. For example, McDonald's faced a private suit in Illinois when two former employees argued the no-poaching agreement was unlawful under Section 1 of the Sherman Act. The judge, however, felt that "[w]ithout market power, defendants could not suppress plaintiffs' wages; another buyer would step in to pay plaintiffs more." *Deslandes* v. *McDonald's USA, LLC*, No. 1:17-cv-04857 (N.D. Ill June 28, 2022). Other cases have led to settlements. In *Fuentes* v. *Jiffy Lube International Inc.*, No. 18-cv-5174 (E.D. Pa. Nov 29, 2018), the parties settled for $2.0 million after private damage suits were filed alleging that employees suffered antitrust injury owing to a franchise requirement of no-poaching restraints.

8

Noncompete Agreements

8.1 Introduction

A noncompete agreement (NCA) is a vertical agreement between an employer and its employees. In the event that the employee leaves the employer, the employee can neither work for the former employer's rivals nor begin a business that competes with the former employer. There are many examples. An insurance executive at, say, Cigna may not be allowed to work for another health insurer for a specified period of time. A sales executive for an automobile manufacturer may not be permitted to take a similar position in a rival automobile firm. A physician may not be able to switch from one physician group to another in the same city.

NCAs result in monopsony power because they limit labor mobility. The elasticity of supply is restricted, that is, reduced, when labor mobility is limited. This, of course, allows employers to offer less generous compensation packages.

Since policymakers have become increasingly concerned about competition in the labor market, NCAs have attracted a good deal of attention. There are, however, pros and cons of NCAs and, therefore, reasonable people can disagree about their desirability. The Federal Trade Commission (FTC) has proposed a total ban on NCAs, which has raised the ire of the business community. Many commentators are dissatisfied with the FTC's extreme position, but members of affected groups – such as physicians and teachers – are in favor of being liberated by the FTC rule. In this chapter, we review the FTC's proposed rule and the cases for and against it.

In our next section, we provide a more in-depth description of NCAs and the economic rationale for their use. In Section 8.3, we focus on the costs and benefits of NCAs. In Section 8.4, we discuss the FTC's proposed ban on NCAs, as well as the dissenting view provided by former FTC

Commissioner Christine Wilson. In Section 8.5, we advocate for a balanced public policy regarding NCAs, and we close with some concluding remarks in Section 8.6.

8.2 Economic Rationale for Noncompetes

Noncompete agreements are often included in employment contracts. They are nearly always included in sales contracts involving a business. The economic rationales differ, as does the legal treatment.

8.2.1 NCAs in Employment Contracts

The thorny issue of NCAs in the labor market has been with us since the early 1400s. For the most part, they have not been treated kindly, but their appeal to employers persists.

The medieval guild system required an untrained worker to serve a seven-year apprenticeship. During that period, the apprentice would receive education, experience, and training in a craft under the guidance of a "master." The apprentice received minimal, if any, compensation but would provide labor services to his master. At the end of the apprenticeship, the former apprentice would become a "journeyman" until they established their own business and became a master craftsman.

Contrary to the customary guild rules, some unscrupulous masters insisted that the former apprentice could not practice their trade in competition with the master. Thus, the new journeyman was required to relocate to another town or city to earn a living. The purpose was obvious: the master did not want their former apprentice to provide competition in the local market. This imposed a nearly impossible burden on the newly minted journeymen, as geographic mobility was extraordinarily difficult. In the *Dyer* case,[1] the court rejected such restraints.

Having completed his apprenticeship, John Dyer was a journeymen who had promised to refrain from practicing his craft in competition with his former master for six months. His former master sued Dyer when a dispute arose as to whether Dyer had failed to sit out for the full six months. The Court observed that the restraint imposed on the former apprentice violated the common law and, therefore, was unenforceable.

As Harlan Blake pointed out over sixty years ago, the modern employer's interest in an NCA involves the cost of employer-sponsored training and

---

[1] *Y.B. Mich. 2 Hen. 5*, f. 5, pl. 26 (C.P. 1414).

the importance of protecting trade secrets and customer relationships.[2] From the employee's perspective, however, an NCA limits their job mobility and will depress their wages.

In most jobs, an experienced worker is more productive than an inexperienced worker. This is an example of learning-by-doing that increases an employee's marginal product. This, in turn, increases that employee's value in the labor market when the employee's improved job skills can be used by many other employers.

If the current job requires unique skills, the employee is worth more to the current employer than to all other employers, that is, the worker's market value will not rise. Now, let's examine the incentives of the employer and the employee.

In the case of enhanced marginal productivity, the worker's labor services are more valuable than they were originally. The current employer must pay the market wage, or the employee will switch employers. If the employee is subject to an NCA, however, the employer can underpay the employee, that is, pay less than the value of the employee's marginal product (VMP_L). It would be prudent to pay a bit above the wage of an untrained worker. Otherwise, the employee would be indifferent to the choice between leaving the current employer and staying with the current employer. The bottom line is that an NCA makes the worker worse off than they were before in the absence of the NCA.

In the case of idiosyncratic job skills, the worker is worth more to the current employer than to any other employer. Therefore, the employee has no better options than their current employment. Although the employer need not pay a premium for the employee's enhanced productivity, the employee is not better off with the current employer than they would be with other employers. In other words, the employee has no particular motive to stay with the current employer. An NCA protects the employer against the employee's departure. In its absence, the employer could keep the experienced employee by paying a bit above the market wage of an untrained worker.

8.2.2 NCAs in Sales Contracts

When an NCA is included in a contract involving the sale of a business, there is no coercion. The seller, who is bound by the NCA, wants to offer an NCA simply because their business is worth more to this

---

[2] Harlan M. Blake, Employer Agreements Not to Compete, 73 *Harvard Law Review* 625 (1960).

buyer with an NCA than without an NCA.[3] Consequently, the seller
willingly offers an NCA and receives a higher price. The buyer offers a
higher price with an NCA because the risk of having to compete with
the former owner is eliminated.

Until the decision in *Mitchel* v. *Reynolds*,[4] however, the *Dyer* ban on
NCAs appeared to forbid NCAs in sales contracts as well as apprentice-
ships. In the later case, the Court recognized that this was an error.

The NCA issue in *Mitchel* v. *Reynolds* involved the sale of a business.
Initially, a journeyman baker agreed to lease a bake shop from another
baker who promised to refrain from practicing baking in the local market.
The seller violated this condition of sale, which led the buyer to sue. The violating baker attempted to argue that this agreement acted as a restraint on
trade, but the Court recognized the utility of such agreements, claiming that

a man may, upon a valuable consideration, by his own consent, and for his own
profit, give over his trade, and part with it to another.[5]

Noncompetes involved with the sale of a business should be permissible. Both the buyer and the seller want to be able to enter into an NCA. An
NCA protects the buyer from the seller's competition; the seller wants this
because it permits the full capitalization of the profit stream.

For example, suppose that A owns and operates an extremely successful
business. The business generates annual profit of $200,000. The value of
the business is the discounted present value of the profit stream over five
years. If the discount rate is 10 percent, then the value of the business is:

$$PV(\pi) = \sum_{t=1}^{5} \frac{\$200,000}{(1.1)^t},$$

which is $758,157.35. To realize the full value, A must assure the buyer,
B, that A will not open a competing business following the sale to B.
Consequently, A agrees to refrain from opening a competing business for
six years within 100 miles of the original location.

This is an obvious agreement to *not* compete with B. But it is ancillary
to a legitimate transaction. If A cannot make this contractual obligation, B
will not pay the $758,157.35 for their business because B cannot be sure that
A will not turn around and compete with B, taking directly from B's profit.

---

[3]   An ancillary restraint is a restraint on trade that may seem objectionable on its face but is
      necessary to legitimize an economically desirable transaction.
[4]   *I P. Wms. i8i*, 24 Eng. Rep. 347 (Q.B. I7I1).
[5]   *Ibid.* at 186, 24 Eng. Rep. 349.

In effect, there will be incomplete capitalization of the valuation by A. It is clear *ex ante* that both A and B want to enter into an NCA since both benefit from it.

Notably, in the *Mitchel* v. *Reynolds* opinion, the Court noted that employment agreements may be subject to:

> great abuses … from masters, who are apt to give their apprentices much vexation on this account, and to use many indirect practices to procure such bonds from them, lest they should prejudice them in their custom, when they come up to set up for themselves.[6]

In this way, the Court acknowledged the complexities of determining the procompetitive and anticompetitive effects of NCAs. To determine the value of such an agreement to a firm, we must consider the intended effects of the implementation of an NCA.

8.3 Noncompete Agreements: Pros and Cons

Noncompete clauses in employment contracts are controversial. On the one hand, they encourage employer-sponsored training and the efficient exchange of information within the firm, which is clearly beneficial. On the other hand, they limit the worker's ability to search for a better paying job.

8.3.1 Employer-Sponsored Training

In many employment settings, the employer must decide how much to invest in the development of an employee's human capital. This is complicated because the incentives of the employer and the employee are not perfectly aligned.

A profit-maximizing employer will expand employment until the value of the marginal product of labor (VMP_L) is equal to the wage (w). Since the VMP_L is the product of the output price (P) and the employee's marginal product (MP_L):

$$P \cdot MP_L = w,$$

this can be rearranged algebraically:

$$P = \frac{w}{MP_L}.$$

---

[6] *Ibid.* at 190, 24 Eng. Rep. at 350.

If an employer hires an untrained worker, the wage will be, say, 75 percent of a trained worker's value. If the employer incurs the cost of training, the employee can command a higher market wage of w. To reduce the employee's incentive to switch employers, the current employer must increase the employee's wage to w.

If an employer hires an untrained worker and pays 0.75w and then provides training, the worker will be worth w in the market. The employee must be paid w, but the employer then receives no return on the investment in training. A positive return would come from paying a wage below w, but this will induce the employee to leave for a "better" job. An NCA can resolve this problem, but not indefinitely.

In many NCAs, an employee cannot work for a rival employer for two years. During that period, the employee will earn a reduced wage since the worker's improved marginal product cannot be exercised. Following the employee's training, the employer raises the wage from 0.75w to 0.9w. Even though the worker deserves a wage of w, the employer is using an NCA to protect the underpayment of 0.10w. If the employee remains with the current employer, the present value of the underpayment will be:

$$PV(U) = \sum_{t=1}^{2} \frac{0.1w}{(1+r)^t},$$

where t is the total years of service and r is the discount rate. If the employee leaves the current employer, their income will be reduced by 0.25w for two years. If the present value of this differential is less than the present value of the impairment of the employee's human capital and work life, then the employee will depart in spite of the NCA. That is, if:

$$\sum_{t=0}^{T} \frac{0.1w}{(1+r)^t} - \sum_{t=1}^{2} \frac{0.25w}{(1+r)^t} > 0,$$

the NCA will not be effective.

8.3.2 Protection of Trade Secrets

A trade secret is a form of intellectual property that may be protected legally. One of the most famous trade secrets is the recipe for the Coca-Cola syrup. If an employee becomes aware of the employer's trade secret, the employee may not divulge that information to another employer. Consequently, the employee is not worth more to a rival employer and, therefore, the employee has no incentive to leave the current employer. In this case, there appears to be no need for an NCA. But appearances may be deceiving. Once a former employee has divulged a trade secret, it cannot be reclaimed. Moreover, trade secret litigation is expensive, and the outcome is uncertain.

In some instances, company-specific information may be difficult to classify as a trade secret. As a result, an employee who switches to a rival employer may bring something of value to the new firm. Suppose, for example, that an employee of Firm A is earning a salary of $100,000 per year. During the employee's job tenure, they acquire information that is worth $50,000 to Firm B, which is a competitor of Firm A. Assuming that the employee is equally productive working for Firm A and Firm B, the employee appears to be more valuable to Firm B. Thus, Firm B would rationally offer the employee a $50,000 signing bonus and continue to pay an annual salary of $100,000. Alternatively, Firm A could "buy" protection from employee defection by paying the employee more than their value of the marginal product.

A noncompete clause in the employment contract will also work. The terms of the noncompete need not preclude relocating to a rival forever. In some cases, limiting relocation for a relatively short period of time will suffice when the value of the information is short-lived.

A recent example involved the departure of an executive from Cigna and subsequent employment by CVS. Prior to her resignation, Amy Bricker had served as the head of Cigna's Express Scripts pharmacy benefits unit.[7] Bricker's employment contract with Cigna contained a noncompete clause that forbade her from working with any rival company. Consequently, when Bricker joined CVS as its chief product officer, Cigna sued CVS and Bricker to enforce its NCA with Bricker.[8] Cigna alleged that Bricker's new role at CVS would inevitably lead her to use Cigna's confidential information and trade secrets. CVS disputed this claim.

It has been alleged that many employers include NCAs even when they would seem to be unnecessary. Cigna does not seem to have adopted this practice. In fact, Cigna has incorporated noncompete clauses in the employment contracts of only the most senior managers. In its entire 70,000 person workforce, only sixteen employees are subject to noncompetes.

---

[7] See https://news.bloomberglaw.com/daily-labor-report/cigna-gets-restraining-order-in-cvs-executive-noncompete-case and www.bloomberglaw.com/bloomberglawnews/daily-labor-report/BNA%2000000185f36fd75aa5e5f3ffc7b00001?bna_news_filter=daily-labor-report.
[8] The employer that hires a worker who is breaching an NCA can be liable for the original employer's legal fees. For example, in *Accounteks.Net Inc. v. CKR Law LLP*, 2023 BL 156710, N.J. Super. Ct. App. Div., No. A-1067-20 (May 9, 2023), the new employer found itself liable for $175,854 in legal fees incurred by the plaintiff.

8.3.3 Adverse Consequences of NCAs

From an employer's perspective, an NCA is useful in protecting employer-sponsored investments in the employees and protecting confidential information. There are, however, adverse effects of NCAs that fall on trained employees subject to NCAs.

As workers gain experience and training – both formal and on-the-job – their market value rises. If they are subject to an NCA, however, they will be unable to take advantage of better economic prospects. The NCA restricts their mobility, which alters their supply elasticity. This, in turn, increases the employer's ability to engage in monopsonistic exploitation.

The use of NCAs makes it more difficult for new entry and/or growth of incumbent firms because they cannot hire experienced workers. The result will be less output and higher prices for consumers. This adverse economic impact moved the FTC to condemn NCAs. For example, two glass container producers, O-I Glass and Ardagh, were ordered to release their employees from NCAs. The FTC explained that the industry is concentrated and that pervasive use of noncompetes makes entry by new firms more difficult because they have problems finding experienced workers.[9]

8.3.4 Empirical Results

About 20 percent of all employees are bound by noncompete clauses. In some sectors, the fraction is much higher. In the tech sector, it is about 35–45 percent. In health care, some 45 percent of primary care physicians are subject to noncompetes. Evan Starr examined the consequences of varying enforceability of NCAs. On the plus side, he found that employer-sponsored training programs appear to be 14.0 percent higher in states with average NCA enforceability relative to states with little or no enforceability. On the negative side, he found that wages are 4.0 percent lower than in states with little or no enforcement.[10]

One explanation for this finding is that workers are deprived of the opportunity to switch jobs for higher pay and better working conditions. This outcome has unfortunate consequences for employers and for

---

[9] See https://news.bloomberglaw.com/antitrust/ftc-finds-three-firms-engaged-in-illegal-noncompete-agreements.

[10] Evan P. Starr, Consider This: Training, Wages, and the Enforceability of Covenants Not to Compete, 72 *ILR Review* 783 (2019).

consumers.[11] Employers find it more difficult to hire experienced workers so they can expand their businesses. As for consumers, output will be lower, and, therefore, prices will be higher.

Another empirical study found similar economic effects. Hawaii recently banned the use of NCAs for employees in technology fields. The results were striking: wages for new hires rose by 4.0 percent while job mobility increased by 11.0 percent.[12]

Other studies, however, have found evidence suggesting that NCAs actually result in higher wages for workers. Whereas the first study had to do with the enforceability of NCAs, another study which focused on the signing of NCAs found that employees who are made aware of their NCAs before accepting a job have 9.7 percent higher earnings, while those who are made aware after signing experienced "no observable boost in wages or training."[13] This suggests that informing employees of NCAs before they sign their employment contracts has positive effects for employees.[14]

Another study found that, in the market for primary care physicians, greater enforceability of NCAs is associated with higher, rather than lower, compensation. Lavetti, Simon, and White conducted a survey of primary care physicians across five states and collected panel data on the use of noncompetes and labor market outcomes, including earnings.[15] The authors found that "the annual rate of earnings growth increased by an average of 8 percentage points in each of the first 4 years of a job, with a cumulative effect of 35 percentage points after 10 years on the job."[16]

[11] Matt Marx found that workers who are subject to NCAs in technical fields will likely switch to another field when they want to change jobs. This means that employers in the same technical field will lose the potential to hire workers who have gained vital skills necessary to drive innovation. See Matt Marx, The Firm Strikes Back: Non-Compete Agreements and the Mobility of Technical Professionals, 76 *American Sociological Review* 695 (2011).

[12] Natarajan Balasubramanian, Jin Woo Chang, Mariko Sakakibara, Jagadeesh Sivadasan, and Evan Starr, Locked In? The Enforceability of Covenants Not to Compete and the Careers of High-Tech Workers, 57 *Journal of Human Resources* S349 (2022).

[13] Evan P. Starr, James J. Prescott, and Norman D. Bishara, Noncompete Agreements in the U.S. Labor Force, 64 *Journal of Law and Economics.* 53 (2021). *Id.* at 75.

[14] Alan J. Meese, Don't Abolish Employee Noncompete Agreements, 57 *Wake Forest Law Review* 631 (2022) used this fact to advocate for the use of NCAs. Instead of abolishing their use altogether, Meese claimed that properly disclosing the use of NCAs could have positive wage effects on employees.

[15] Kurt Lavetti, Carol Simon, and William D. White, The Impacts of Restricting Mobility of Skilled Service Workers: Evidence from Physicians, 55 *Journal of Human Resources* 1025 (2020).

[16] *Ibid.*

These empirical findings suggest that some employers are paying their employees for agreeing to restrict their job mobility. As an employee, being informed is important.

The inconsistency of these empirical results raises difficult policy issues.[17] Some studies seem to suggest that NCAs are harmful to employees, while others suggest their usage benefits employees. The variability in empirical results makes it hard to distinguish what, on balance, is the net effect of NCAs.

8.3.5 Legal Status of NCAs

States across the country have varying bans on noncompetes (see Table 8.1). For example, California and Oklahoma have total bans on noncompetes, while Maryland and Virginia only ban NCAs for low-wage employees.[18]

Table 8.1 *Limitations on noncompete agreements*

Total Ban
California
District of Columbia
North Dakota
Oklahoma

Bans for Low Wage Employers
Illinois
Maine
Maryland
Massachusetts
New Hampshire
Nevada
Oregon
Rhode Island
Virginia
Washington

---

[17] A survey of additional empirical findings on NCAs can be found in the Comments of Scholars of Law & Economics and the International Center for Law & Economics. See https://laweconcenter.org/wp-content/uploads/2023/04/ICLE-Noncompete-NPRM-Comments-final.pdf.

[18] What constitutes a "low wage" employer varies considerably across these states. For example, the threshold in New Hampshire is $30,000, while the thresholds in Oregon, Washington state, and Colorado are $100,000 or more.

While many states have begun to take their own stances on banning NCAs, the FTC has decided to ban NCAs entirely.

8.4 Proposed FTC Rule

8.4.1 Unfair Method of Competition

The FTC has decided that non-compete provisions in employment contracts constitute an unfair method of competition. After defining a noncompete clause as:

a contractual term between an employer and a worker that prevents the worker from seeking or accepting employment with a person, or operating a business, after the conclusion of the worker's employment with the employer,[19]

the FTC proposed a ban on noncompete clauses. More specifically, the FTC's imposed rule is:

It is an unfair method of competition for an employer to enter into or attempt to enter into a non-compete clause with a worker; maintain with a worker a non-compete clause; or represent to a worker that the worker is subject to a non-compete clause where the employer has no good faith basis to believe that the worker is subject to an enforceable non-compete clause.[20]

The FTC also recognized that an employer may have terms in their employment contracts that are not technically noncompete clauses but are de facto noncompetes. These are also included in the prohibition:

The term non-compete clause includes a contractual term that is a *de facto* non-compete clause because it has the effect of prohibiting the worker from seeking or accepting employment with a person or operating a business after the conclusion of the worker's employment with the employer.[21]

A non-disclosure agreement (NDA) may be used instead of a non-compete to protect trade secrets, but the FTC condemns de facto

---

[19] See www.federalregister.gov/documents/2023/01/19/2023-00414/non-compete-clause-rule, Section 910.1 (b).

[20] See www.federalregister.gov/documents/2023/01/19/2023-00414/non-compete-clause-rule, Section 910.2 (a). If the FTC believes that an NCA is an "unfair method of competition," it must view a departing employee using trade secrets of an employer to benefit the employee as a *fair* method of competition.

[21] See www.federalregister.gov/documents/2023/01/19/2023-00414/non-compete-clause-rule, Section 910.1 (b).

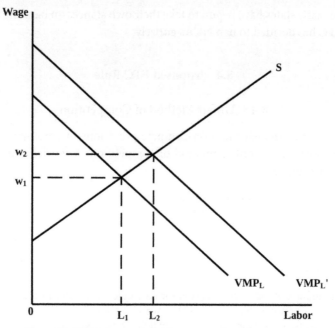

Figure 8.1 If MP_L increases, both wages and employment rise

noncompetes.[22] If an NDA is a de facto noncompete, it will violate the FTC rule.

The FTC has estimated that this ban could increase wages by $300 billion due to increased ability to change jobs and start businesses. They also allege that this increase will not be inflationary. The economic logic depends on increased productivity. Profit maximization leads employers to hire labor to the point where the value of the marginal product of labor equals the wage. We have already found this to be equivalent to:

$$P = \frac{w}{MP_L}.$$

If the increase in MP_L matches the increase in w, P will not change. But if the change in the wage exceeds the change in labor's marginal product, output prices will rise. This is clearly an empirical matter. (See Figure 8.1.)

---

[22] Natarajan Balasubramanian, Evan Starr, and Shotaro Yamaguchi, *Employment Restrictions on Resource Transferability and Value Appropriation from Employees*, Working Paper (2023) examined four contractual limitations on employees. In addition to NCAs, they studied non-disclosure agreements (NDAs), non-solicitation agreements (NSAs), and non-recruitment agreements (NRAs). Employees subject to all four restrictions earned

The FTC is not the only governmental agency to support a complete ban on NCAs. After the FTC released its plans for a total ban, the National Labor Relations Board (NLRB) General Counsel followed suit with an announcement condemning NCAs.[23] As a result, employers who include NCAs in their employment contracts may face challenges from the NLRB as well as the FTC.

8.4.2 A Dissenting View

During her time at the FTC, former Commissioner Christine Wilson strongly disagreed with the Democratic majority led by chair Lina Khan.[24] Wilson objected to the total ban on the use of NCAs in employment contracts, which is what the majority proposed. She pointed out that a total ban ignores legal precedents that span hundreds of years. Former Commissioner Wilson argued that NCAs should be banned only when they prove to be excessive in their scope or duration. This determination requires a fact-specific inquiry as the business justification for NCAs varies widely. Accordingly, a blanket ban is inappropriate.

Wilson also pointed out that the FTC has had extremely limited experience in evaluating the competitive impact of NCAs. In addition, she pointed out that the academic literature on the economic effects of NCAs is both limited and inconsistent.

When the FTC announced its proposed rule forbidding noncompete clauses in employment contracts, it asked for public comment. In response, the agency received nearly 27,000 public comments. Business groups, such as the U.S. Chamber of Commerce, opposed the FTC proposal, while labor groups supported it. For example, the American Hospital Association, which represents 5,000 hospitals and health care systems in the United States, is opposed to the FTC's proposed ban on NCAs. It argues that NCAs protect

---

5.4 percent less than employees with only an NDA. The authors pointed out that NDAs were far more common than NCAs, although NCAs have gotten far more attention. They also found that employers paid for imposing restrictions on their employees. In their study, Balasubramanian, Starr, and Yamaguchi found that the highest paid employees were those with NDAs in their contracts. Those with NCAs, NSAs, and NRAs earned some 3.0–7.0 percent less than those with NDAs. Employees with no restrictions earned the least.

[23] See www.nlrb.gov/news-outreach/news-story/nlrb-general-counsel-issues-memo-on-non-competes-violating-the-national.

[24] See www.ftc.gov/legal-library/browse/cases-proceedings/public-statements/dissenting-statement-commissioner-christine-s-wilson-concerning-notice-proposed-rulemaking-non.

a hospital's investment in training young physicians. In contrast, both the American Medical Association (AMA) and the American Nurses Association support the proposed ban. They argue that the ban will improve patient care and the continuity of care. As hospital concentration increases, NCAs make it difficult to find alternative employment according to the AMA.

The International Center for Law and Economics submitted a detailed analysis of the FTC's proposed rule. Their submission raised a number of talking points: (1) NCAs are not invariably anticompetitive and therefore do not warrant *per se* illegality, (2) there is no legal precedent for a *per se* prohibition, (3) the FTC has almost no experience in challenging NCAs and therefore may not recognize unintended consequences, and (4) the FTC lacks the appropriate resources to enforce its proposed rule.

In response to the FTC's proposal to ban all NCAs, some commentators have even argued that the FTC does not have the authority to issue such rules. For example, Rep. Victoria Spartz (R. Indiana) sits on the House Judiciary Committee and the Antitrust Subcommittee. She argues that the FTC's proposed rule should be subject to congressional approval. She does not feel that a blanket ban is appropriate. As a result, court challenges may follow a final issuance by the FTC.

8.5 A Balanced Public Policy

It is clear from the arguments spelled out in Section 8.3 that there are pros and cons associated with NCAs. Consequently, it seems inappropriate to implement a total ban on the use of NCAs. It also seems inappropriate to permit their unfettered use by employers. A balanced approach can prevent NCAs that are clearly anticompetitive while permitting those that are warranted. Herbert Hovenkamp has provided some guidance along these lines, and we will review his suggestions here.[25]

The FTC's proposal is essentially a total ban on the use of NCAs in employment contracts. The alternative is a nuanced approach that permits some NCAs while disallowing others. There is no doubt that a nuanced approach is more difficult to implement than an outright ban on all NCAs. It is possible, however, to identify some NCAs that are presumptively anticompetitive and should be banned.

There are many occupations that do not require much – if any – investment in the employee's human capital. Examples include clerical staff,

---

[25] This discussion is derived from Herbert Hovenkamp, Noncompete Agreements and Antitrust's Rule of Reason, *The Regulatory Review* (January 16, 2023).

fast food workers, grocery store clerks, janitorial staff, lawn maintenance workers, and many others. These employees do not receive any specialized training from their employers. In such situations, Hovenkamp found NCAs to be an anticompetitive means of attaining monopsony power. They prevented workers from moving to better paying jobs while having no procompetitive benefits. In these cases, NCAs should be presumed to be unreasonable restraints in the labor market and therefore impermissible.

This presumption does not hold for all employees. Some employees receive training that improves the employee's marginal productivity and therefore makes the employee more valuable to the firm. If the employee's improved job skills are useful to rival employers, the employee may seek a higher paying job elsewhere. In addition, the newly trained worker may be interested in a job that offers better working conditions. The problem is that the original employer has incurred the cost of training the employee but will not realize any benefit for having done so.[26] In this circumstance, an NCA may be appropriate.[27]

There are some employees who are privy to the employer's trade secrets or other proprietary information such as business plans for new product introductions, marketing plans, plant expansion plans, and so on. Taking the information to a rival employer would competitively disadvantage the original employer. In such cases, an NCA may be used to protect the legitimate interests of the employer. Hovenkamp suggests that the NCA should not be overly broad in scope or duration. Precisely where to draw the line, however, is far from clear. Finding the correct balance requires the fact-specific inquiry that former Commissioner Wilson found to be necessary.

Moreover, the effects that some studies have found at the state level are not necessarily applicable at the national level. While we have seen varying bans in states such as California and Oregon, drawing conclusions about the effects of a national ban from these state-specific bans could lead to unfortunate outcomes for both employers and employees. It is clear that

---

[26] For example, Prudential Security required its security guards to accept a noncompete as a condition of employment. They agreed not to work for a competitor within 100 miles of their former job site for two years after leaving Prudential. It is not obvious that the security guards had employer-sponsored training, nor is it obvious that they would have been privy to Prudential's trade secrets. See https://news.bloomberglaw.com/antitrust/ftc-finds-three-firms-engaged-in-illegal-noncompete-agreements.

[27] As a condition of employment in some employment contracts, the employee is required to pay the employer for the training if the employee resigns prematurely. In some instances, the reacquired payback is much larger than the actual training cost. FTC Chair Lina Khan maintains that the payback provision acts like an NCA. She wants to forbid such contract terms.

local labor markets differ, so an all-out ban on NCAs could have varying effects in local labor markets across the country. While this ban may be beneficial to some, it could be detrimental to others. This lack of clarity, once again, highlights the importance of emphasizing a balanced public policy on NCAs.

8.6 Concluding Remarks

An NCA clause in an employment contract limits the job prospects of a departing employee. This limitation reduces the employee's supply elasticity and thereby permits a certain degree of monopsonistic exploitation by the employer. In some cases, however, NCAs may be motivated by legitimate business concerns. For one thing, employer-sponsored educational and training programs are investments that an employer expects to generate returns. An NCA may be necessary to protect that investment. In addition, some employees become aware of confidential information and trade secrets that a departing employee could use to their former employer's disadvantage. An NCA can provide the protection that is needed.

There are alternatives to NCAs that may be less restrictive. For example, a non-disclosure agreement will prevent a departing employee from disclosing confidential information or trade secrets to any other firm. A nonsolicitation agreement prevents a departing employee from taking clients or customers to their new job. NSAs do not, however, preclude clients or customers from following the departing employee.

In many cases, NSAs have been imposed on employees who receive little, if any, training and who are not privy to confidential information or trade secrets. There seems to be no sound business rationale for requiring such employees to be bound by an NCA.

California, North Dakota, and Oklahoma already ban noncompetes. Massachusetts and some others have less restrictive bans than the FTC's proposed ban. If the FTC's proposal is implemented, it will replace all state laws. The problem then becomes one of enforcement. Noncompetes are everywhere, but the FTC cannot sue everyone. It may have to choose between challenging a merger and suing an employer.

9

Unions and Collective Bargaining

9.1 Introduction

In response to monopsony power enjoyed by dominant employers, employees have formed unions to level the playing field. Put differently, unionization creates countervailing power to offset the employer's monopsony power in the labor market. Between the passage of the Sherman Act in 1890 and passage of the Clayton Act in 1914, labor unions were targeted as unlawful cartels. Dissatisfied with this turn of events, Congress exempted labor unions from antitrust prosecution in Section 6 of the Clayton Act. In effect, the language of Section 6 excludes antitrust challenges to the formation of labor unions on jurisdictional grounds. As we will see, the effort was not entirely successful.

In this chapter, we begin with a brief review of the legislation that provides a limited antitrust exemption for the formation of employee unions and their conduct in the labor market. In Section 9.3, we turn our attention to the objective function of labor unions. In Section 9.4, we provide an economic analysis of the bargaining solution that results from the formation and implementation of countervailing power. We treat the union as a labor monopolist in Section 9.5. In Section 9.6, we provide some examples before turning our attention to the plight of independent contractors who are not employees and therefore may not unionize in Section 9.7. In Section 9.8, we provide some closing observations.

9.2 Labor Legislation

When Congress passed the Sherman Act in 1890, it prohibited every conspiracy that restrained trade or commerce.[1] Since labor unions certainly resemble a

---

[1] 15 U.S.C. Section 1 holds that "[e]very contract, combination in the form of trust or otherwise, or conspiracy, in restraint of trade or commerce among the several States, or with

labor conspiracy, Section 1 of the Sherman Act appears to outlaw labor unions. The results were a series of antitrust challenges to labor unions. Dissatisfied with this harsh treatment, Congress included Section 6 in the Clayton Act:[2]

the labor of a human being is not a commodity or article of commerce. Nothing contained in the antitrust laws shall be construed to forbid the existence and operation of labor, agricultural, or horticultural organizations, instituted for the purposes of mutual help, and not having capital stock or conducted for profit, or to forbid or restrain individual members of such organizations from lawfully carrying out the legitimate objects thereof; nor shall such organizations, or the members thereof, be held or construed to be illegal combinations or conspiracies in restraint of trade, under the antitrust laws.

The language of Section 6 is inconsistent. The first sentence appears to remove the labor market from antitrust jurisdiction, which would seem to immunize colluding employers. It is unclear how Section 1 of the Sherman Act could apply to the labor market given the statutory language in the first sentence of Section 6 of the Clayton Act. But the rest of Section 6 seems to clarify Congress's intent. The purpose of Section 6 was to protect unions from antitrust prosecution.

This should have put antitrust prosecution on the shelf on jurisdictional grounds, but litigation against unions continued and the Supreme Court failed to recognize Congress's message regarding labor unions. Since it did not get its message across in the Clayton Act, Congress passed the Norris-La Guardia Act of 1932.[3] The Norris-La Guardia Act provides protection from antitrust prosecution:

No court of the United States shall have jurisdiction to issue any restraining order or temporary or permanent injunction in any case involving or growing out of any labor dispute to prohibit any person or persons participating or interested in such dispute (as these terms are herein defined) from ... [b]ecoming or remaining a member of any labor organization or of any employer organization.[4]

As long as a union pursues the legitimate goals of improving wages, hours, and working conditions of its members, the union should be free of antitrust attack.

foreign nations, is declared to be illegal. Every person who shall make any contract or engage in any combination or conspiracy hereby declared to be illegal shall be deemed guilty of a felony, and, on conviction thereof, shall be punished by a fine not exceeding $100,000,000 if a corporation, or, if any other person, $1,000,000, or by imprisonment not exceeding 10 years, or by both said punishments, in the discretion of the court."
[2] 15 U.S.C. Section 16.
[3] 29 U.S.C. Section 104.
[4] *Ibid.* at (b).

9.2.1 Non-Statutory Labor Exemption

Section 6 of the Clayton Act and the Norris-La Guardia Act protect labor unions from Section 1's prohibition of agreements not to compete. Since union members also agree on the terms of employment that they will accept, they would appear to be vulnerable without the exemption. What is not covered is an agreement between the union and an employer or group of employers. For this, we have the non-statutory labor exemption.

The non-statutory labor exemption emanates from judicial interpretations of the vague language of Section 6 of the Clayton Act and the Norris-La Guardia Act. It developed over time as disputes arose over the boundaries of the statutory labor exemption.

As long as the union negotiates with employers over wages, hours, and working conditions, it is safe from antitrust attack. A union gets in trouble when it agrees with one employer to put a rival employer at a competitive disadvantage. Such conduct is vulnerable to antitrust prosecution.

9.3 The Union's Objective Function

A union is an organization of workers who have agreed to cooperate instead of compete in the labor market. We can think of this as an employee cartel or a labor monopoly. For the usual cartel (or monopoly), it is safe to assume that the goal is profit maximization. For unions, however, profit maximization seems to be an inappropriate target since it would involve the unemployment of workers who would be willing to work at the competitive wage. This realization raises an obvious question: What is the union's objective function? In the labor economics literature, the major competitors appear to be profit maximization and efficient bargaining.[5]

9.3.1 Monopoly Model

In the so-called monopoly model, the union sets the employee's wage and the firm selects the employment level. This conduct is consistent with profit maximization – set the wage at the level that equates marginal revenue and the reservation wage of the last worker hired. In comparison

---

[5] A major contribution to the labor literature examining unions was provided by Richard B. Freeman and James L. Medoff, *What Do Unions Do?* (1984). Following their publication, a review symposium on the book was published in the *ILR Review*. See *ILR Review* 38 (1985).

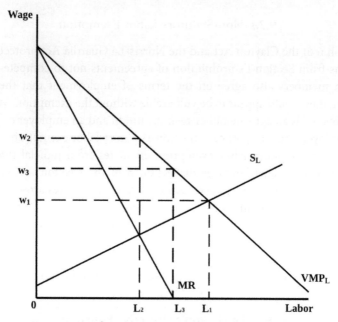

Figure 9.1 Profit maximization and wage bill maximization

with the competitive solution, which involves the equality of the value of the marginal product of labor and the reservation wage, employment will be lower, and the wage will be higher. This would leave some – perhaps many – willing workers to face unemployment.

This result is displayed in Figure 9.1, where VMP_L is the demand for labor, MR is the corresponding marginal revenue, and S_L is the supply of labor. The competitive solution is found at the equality of demand and supply. In this example, the wage is w_1 and the employment level is L_1. If the union behaved as a profit maximizer, it would operate where the reservation wage of the last worker employed was equal to the employer's marginal revenue. Thus, the monopoly wage would rise to w_2 and the employment level would fall to L_2.

Those workers who remain employed are better off as their wage is w_2 rather than w_1. Unfortunately, there are $(L_1 - L_2)$ workers who are willing to work at a wage of w_1 but are now unemployed. This can lead to defection from the union and provide a source of non-union competition. This potential for instability will prove to be most troublesome in "right-to-work" states where union membership cannot be compelled.

The trade unions representing carpenters, electricians, plumbers, and other skilled workers dealt with the excess supply problem by limiting membership. Union members were more or less guaranteed to be employed in "closed shop" states in which only union workers could be employed. In right-to-work states, however, this strategy was ineffective.

The monopoly union need not set the wage at the profit maximizing level. Instead, it could set the wage at a lower level with the goal of maximizing the total expenditure on labor. In this event, the union would set the wage at the level that equates marginal revenue to zero. The resulting wage and employment level will maximize the employer's wage bill. This solution still leaves some willing workers unemployed, which may induce union instability, but it is a bit more appealing than simple profit maximization.

This solution is also shown in Figure 9.1. Again, the competitive solution is a wage of w_1 and an employment level of L_1. If the union restricts employment to L_3, the wage will rise to w_3, which is lower than w_2, but higher than w_1. Employment, however, will be higher – L_3 exceeds L_2. Consequently, the number of unemployed workers willing to work at w_1 shrinks from $(L_1 - L_2)$ to $(L_1 - L_3)$.

9.3.2 Efficient Bargaining

In the efficient bargaining conception of union conduct, the union employs its power as a monopolist supplier of labor to push the employer off its derived demand (VMP_L) for labor. In this way, the union obtains more of the surplus for its workers. The outcome depends on the market structure on the employer's side of the market. It may be the case that the union is dealing with a single employer, that is, the monopoly union confronts a monopsony employer. In that event, the solution involves a determinate employment level, but an indeterminate wage level that is subject to bargaining.

If the monopoly union confronts many employers that have no market power in the labor market, the union may pursue an all-or-nothing strategy that extracts some – or even all – of the employer surplus.

At the end of the day, the goal of a monopoly union is to maximize total labor and management surplus. In doing so, it maximizes the size of the pie. The union then bargains with the employer to extract as large a piece of the pie as it can for its members. Hendricks and Khan find that a union will actively balance the negative effects of wages on employment with the positive effects of wages on the utility of employees and the probability of escaping discharge.[6]

---

[6] Wallace E. Hendricks and Lawrence M. Khan, Efficiency Wages, Monopoly Unions and Efficient Bargaining, 101 *The Economic Journal* 1149 (1991). For additional discussions of efficient bargaining and union organization, see Andrew J. Oswald, The Microeconomic

9.4 Unions and Bilateral Monopoly

When a powerful employer confronts a powerful labor union, the economic results are indeterminate because they are the product of bargaining. As we will see, the employment level should be determinate, but the wage will fall within a wage range. The precise location in that range is indeterminate.

We begin with a labor market in which there is monopsony power in the hands of the employer. The supply of labor is competitively structured. Under these circumstances, profit maximization by the employer will have unfortunate economic effects for the firm's employees and for consumers. There will be an incentive for the employees to unionize to level the playing field. Following unionization, both wages and employment will rise, output prices will fall, and both consumer welfare and social welfare will increase.

A producer with no market power in its output market may enjoy monopsony power in the labor market. The firm's profit function (Π) is:

$$\Pi = PQ(L,K) - w(L)L - rk,$$

where P is the market-determined price of the output, $Q(L,K)$ is the production function, $w(L)$ is the supply of labor (L), and r is the price of capital (K). For simplicity, assume that capital is fixed. As a result, the employer will maximize its profit by hiring the quantity of labor where the value of labor's marginal product equals the marginal expenditure on labor:

$$\frac{\partial \Pi}{\partial L} = P\frac{\partial Q}{\partial L} - \left[w + L\frac{dw}{\partial L}\right] = 0.$$

The first term, $P\dfrac{\partial Q}{\partial L}$, is the value of the marginal product of labor (VMP_L), while the second term, $w + L\dfrac{dw}{\partial L}$, is the marginal expenditure on labor (ME_L). To maximize its profit, the employer should expand the employment of labor until the VMP_L equals the ME_L. The employment level of L_2 and the corresponding wage of w_2 are displayed in Figure 9.2.

Theory of the Trade Union, 92 *Economic Journal* 576 (1982); Thomas E. MaCurdy and John H. Pencavel, Testing Between Competing Models of Wage and Employment Determination in Unionized Markets, 94 *Journal of Political Economy* S3 (1986); James N. Brown and Orley Ashenfelter, Testing the Efficiency of Employment Contracts, 94 *Journal of Political Economy* S40 (1986); Henry S. Farber, *The Analysis of Union Behavior* in *Handbook of Labor Economics*, Vol. II, Orley C. Ashenfelter and Richard Layard eds. (1986). Notably, some studies have found the presence of unions to have negligible effects on wages. See John DiNardo and David S. Lee, Economic Impacts of New Unionization on Private Sector Employers: 1984–2001, 119 *Quarterly Journal of Economics* 1383 (2004).

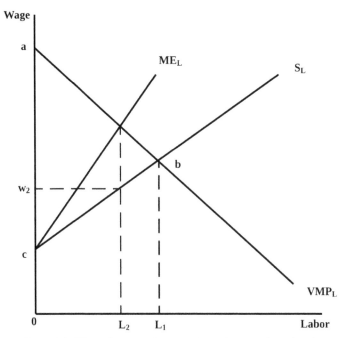

Figure 9.2 Bilateral monopoly expands employment from l_1 to l_2

At an employment level of L_2, there is a gap between the VMP_L and the wage paid. This is "monopsonistic exploitation" in the sense that labor is paid less than their contribution to the firm's profit. In terms of social welfare, too few units of labor services are being employed, which is obvious in Figure 9.2. From a social perspective, the employment of labor should expand to L_1. But it is privately optimal, that is, profit maximizing, to restrict employment to L_2.

If the employees form a labor union, the employer will have to bargain with the union on the terms of employment. The market structure has changed to one of bilateral monopoly: a single supplier of labor services and a single employer of these services. A formal treatment of bilateral monopoly was introduced by Bowley.[7] For more accessible treatments, see Machlup and Taber,[8] and Blair, Kaserman, and Romano.[9]

---

[7] A. L. Bowley, Bilateral Monopoly, 38 *Economic Journal* 651 (1928).

[8] Fritz Machlup and Martha Taber, Bilateral Monopoly, Successive Monopoly, and Vertical Integration, 27 *Economica* 101 (1960).

[9] Roger D. Blair, David L. Kaserman, and Richard E. Romano, A Pedagogical Treatment of Bilateral Monopoly, 55 *Southern Economic Journal* 831 (1989). See also Roger D. Blair and

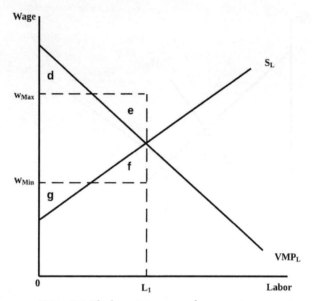

Figure 9.3 The bargaining range from w_{min} to w_{max}

The union cannot restrict the availability of labor services to increase wages. The employer cannot restrict employment to depress wages. In a bilateral monopoly, the usual optimizing calculus fails us. The union and the employer should cooperate to maximize the surplus that the supply and demand conditions will permit and then bargain over the shares of that surplus.

It is clear in Figure 9.2 that labor should be employed at L_1. This employment level will maximize the sum of the employer surplus and employee surplus, which is area abc. Once the quantity of labor services has been agreed upon, then bargaining over the wage begins. Since the quantity of labor has been determined, the wage is no longer a rationing device, that is, the wage has no effect on the quantity employed. Now, the wage serves as a means of dividing the surplus.

Since the wage that will actually be paid is the product of bargaining, it is indeterminate. We can, however, identify the range within which the wage paid will be found. In Figure 9.3, we have reproduced the derived demand for labor, VMP_L, and the supply of labor, S_L. The surplus maximizing employment level is L_1. The agreed upon wage will be on the vertical line

Christina DePasquale, *Bilateral Monopoly and Antitrust Policy in Oxford Handbook on International Antitrust Economics*, Roger D. Blair and D. Daniel Sokol eds. (2014).

at L_1. The upper bound on the wage is w_{Max} and the lower bound is w_{Min}. At the upper bound, there is no employer surplus. The employer has been pushed off its derived demand. Triangle d equals the employer surplus, but the corresponding triangle e represents negative surplus. Both triangles are equal at w_{Max} and L_1, so there is no employer surplus.

Similarly, at w_{Min}, there is no employee surplus. At L_1, the employees have been pushed off the supply curve. Triangle g represents surplus, but triangle f is negative surplus. Since these triangles are of equal size, there is no employee surplus at w_{Min} and L_1.

The competitive wage is within the bargaining range, but there is no reason to suppose that the employer and the union will agree on that value. The employer continues to have a profit incentive to bargain for lower wages while the union has an incentive to bargain for higher wages. Although strikes occur when the sides cannot agree on a wage, this should not occur as both sides lose.

9.5 Unions and All-or-Nothing Offers

If the union faces unorganized employers, this looks like the usual monopoly profit maximization problem. The union sets the wage rate and firms determine the employment level as price takers.

The problem with this concept is that workers are human beings with bills to pay and families to feed. Labor services are not widgets. An alternative objective would be to set the wage that maximizes the employee surplus. This can be done with an all-or-nothing offer to supply labor services.

9.5.1 The All-or-Nothing Approach

When workers form or join a union, they do so to obtain better wages, hours, and working conditions. The union may be able to offer these benefits without sacrificing employment through an all-or-nothing offer to the employers.

This approach is illustrated in Figure 9.4. The demand for labor services is the value of the marginal product of labor (VMP_L) while the supply is S_L. Ideally, the firm would like to hire L_1 units of labor services and pay a wage of w_1. At this solution, the employers enjoy employer surplus equal to area acw_1 while the workers experience employee surplus of w_1cd. By making an all-or-nothing offer, the union can convert some of the employer surplus to employee surplus.[10]

---

[10] In theory, the union could extract all the employer surplus.

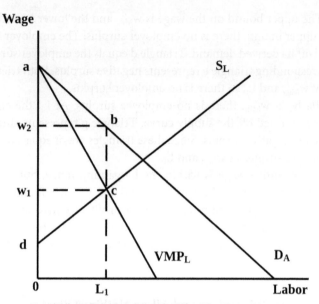

Figure 9.4 The "all-or-nothing" offer of a monopoly union

In an all-or-nothing offer, the union agrees to provide L_1 units of labor services, but it demands a higher wage than w_1. Ordinarily, if the union wage is above w_1, fewer labor services will be employed. But in an all-or-nothing offer, there are two options: (1) the employer gets L_1 and pays a wage above w_1, or (2) the employer gets no labor services at all. If the wage leaves some employer surplus, the employer is better off accepting the offer rather than having no surplus at all. In the limit, the union could extract all the employer surplus. This is shown in Figure 9.4 when the union wage is w_2 and the quantity of labor services is L_1.

At w_2, the employee surplus is equal to area w_2bcd while the employer surplus is reduced to area abw_2.

To gain a further understanding of the effects of all-or-nothing offers, we will refer back to the same numerical example we provided in Chapter 2.[11] Again, suppose that the labor supply curve is $w = 10 + 0.5L$, where L is the number of hours worked, and the demand for labor services is $w = 50 - 0.5L$. To induce this worker to provide forty hours of labor services per week, they must be paid $30 per hour. The employer surplus is calculated as $\frac{1}{2}(50 - 30)(40)$, which is $400.

[11] Note that in Chapter 2, we are talking about all-or-nothing offers by the employer, while this analysis focuses on all-or-nothing offers by the union.

Suppose the employee union requires that the employer pay $31 per hour but members will still work the required forty hours per week. If the employer does not agree to these terms, the members of the union will refuse to work. At $31 per hour, the employer would prefer that the employees work thirty-eight hours per week, but the union has established that this is not an option. If the employer accepts the offer, their employees will work forty hours and earn $1,240 per week. The employer's surplus will decline to $360.[12] Despite the extraction of some employer surplus by the employee union, the employer is still better off accepting the offer than not because some positive surplus is better than the alternative of realizing no surplus at all.

9.6 Real-World Examples

In the private sector, unions have been declining in importance for many years.[13] At present, only a bit over 6 percent of employees in the private sector are unionized. In the public sector, however, unions are more important. Unions of teachers, firefighters, and law enforcement officers have an important influence on the salaries, benefits, and job protection of their members. In this section, we examine a few cases of unions in the private sector.

9.6.1 Organizing an Amazon Union

In employment situations involving a large employer with substantial monopsony power and an unorganized workforce, a union can level the playing field. The result is a change in the market structure to one of bilateral monopoly. The determination of wages, hours, and working conditions is the product of bargaining. As we have seen, the economic results are positive on social welfare grounds. But this outcome is not likely to be beneficial to the employer which had been wielding monopsony power. Consequently, employers typically resist unionizing efforts.

Many workers do not support unionization for a variety of reasons, including fear of having to go on strike with no paycheck, expensive union

---

[12] Employer surplus after all-or-nothing offer: $\frac{1}{2}(50-31)(38)-\frac{1}{2}(31-30)(40-38)=\$360.$

[13] See Suresh Naidu, Is There Any Future for a US Labor Movement?, 36 *Journal of Economic Perspectives* 3 (2022) for an examination of unions in the more modern political climate.

dues, and mistrust of the union leaders. Amazon provides an excellent example.[14]

Until 2022, none of Amazon's U.S. locations were unionized. Following his dismissal from Amazon's JFK8 location in Staten Island, NY, Christian Smalls began organizing the Amazon Labor Union. Despite Amazon's efforts to defeat the union at the ballot box, Small's organizing efforts succeeded. The vote was 2,654 in favor of the union and 2,131 opposed.[15]

Both workers and union leaders found that winning the union election is only the first step in the arduous process of getting a contract. Amazon filed a number of objections to the union's election process. These have to be investigated and ruled upon by the National Labor Relations Board (NLRB). The union must also prepare a constitution that sets out the extent to which the union workers play a role in the operation of the union. Negotiating a contract and getting it ratified by the membership is a long process that can take years.

At JFK8, there is some disagreement within the union regarding strategy. Smalls appears to be spending a good deal of his time and attention on organizing other locations before finalizing the union effort at JFK8. He seems to be somewhat intolerant of organizers who disagree with his strategy. The bottom line is that not much progress has been made at JFK8 more than a year after the successful union vote.

There have been two recent defeats at Amazon locations in Bessemer, AL, and Albany, NY. Apparently, the votes were taken before the union had built up majority support among the workers for unionization. The vote was close in Alabama, but in Albany, the vote was two to one against unionization.

9.6.2 Unions in Professional Sports

The benefits of unionization for employees can be seen most dramatically in professional sports. In professional sports, the unions are referred to as player associations, but they are unions. In the days before unionization, player salaries were so low that the players had to get jobs in the off season. Some players sold insurance, and some had jobs in construction. No one arrived at spring training in good physical condition. Players had to pay

---

[14] The discussion in this section draws upon facts found in www.bbc.com/news/business-60944677 and www.nytimes.com/2023/03/21/business/amazon-labor-union.html.
[15] Although the vote was taken in April 2022, the union vote has not been certified by the NLRB.

Table 9.1 *Salaries in major league sports*

Leagues	Contract minimum[a]	Average salary[b]
Major League Baseball (MLB)	$563,500	$4.03 million
National Basketball Association (NBA)	$898,310	$8.32 million
National Football League (NFL)	$610,000	$3.26 million
National Hockey League (NHL)	$700,000	$2.69 million

[a] This reported salary is based on a player's rookie season, that is, zero years of experience. See https://the18.com/en/node/55251.

[b] Average salaries from 2019/20 are reported here. See www.statista.com/statistics/675120/average-sports-salaries-by-league/.

for their own medicine and their own equipment – shoes and gloves; travel was economy at best.

The formation of player unions and recognition by management did not come easily. Eventually, however, the owners realized that fighting with the unions was pointless and they began to bargain in good faith.

The unions have been extraordinarily successful in obtaining both pay and benefits for their members. In addition to the greatly increased salaries, their new employment packages include improved travel, a generous per diem while on the road, health benefits, and pension benefits. The precise terms vary from league to league, but they all involve vast improvements from the pre-union contracts.

In Table 9.1, we have set out the league minimum salary as well as the median salary for each league. In contrast to the median household income of $67,521 in 2020,[16] the league minimum salaries are exceptional. The minimum salary that a team could pay in 2020 was $563,500 in baseball, $898,310 in basketball, $610,000 in football, and $700,000 in hockey.[17] It is doubtful that any of this would have occurred in the absence of union bargaining.

The number of players that will be hired is determined through collective bargaining. Once the roster size has been settled, it is entirely up to the teams to decide which players they will hire. Obviously, each team wants to hire the very best players as that maximizes the chance of winning games and attracting fans. But each team has a budget constraint, which is also determined through collective bargaining. The maximum wage bill for each team is known as the salary cap.

[16] See www.census.gov/library/publications/2021/demo/p60-273.html.
[17] See www.nbcsportschicago.com/nhl/chicago-blackhawks/kane-toews-among-highest-paid-players-in-the-nhl-this-season/184487/.

The union has little to do with how a team spends its money. Each player bargains with their team for as big a piece of the salary cap as possible. In nearly all cases, the salary cap proves to be a binding constraint on the team. In fact, managing the salary cap is both a big responsibility and an art.

In MLB, however, the rules are quite different. There is no salary cap that limits a team's total wage bill. There is, however, a luxury tax that kicks in when the wage bill exceeds a specific threshold. This threshold is not usually binding on most teams. The vast majority are well below the threshold.

9.6.3 Unionization Efforts at Starbucks

The Starbucks chain of coffee shops has over 9,300 company-owned locations within the United States. Until recently, there was little union organizing effort. In part, this was because Starbucks paid decent wages, provided health insurance benefits to both full-time and part-time workers, and even paid college tuition for its employees. Not surprisingly, the Starbucks management has been resisting unionization efforts with mixed success. At this point, only a bit over 3 percent of Starbucks locations are unionized.

Recently, however, Workers United has been organizing barista unions around the country. The NLRB reported that it has certified unions at over 285 Starbucks stores. In fifty-eight locations, the union was defeated.

The baristas are turning to Workers United in an effort to obtain higher wages and better working conditions, which are the usual worker demands.

9.6.4 Are Strikes Always Irrational?

In a bilateral monopoly, the employers and employees should agree on an employment level that maximizes the surplus. The next step is to negotiate the compensation that will be paid since this will determine each party's share of the surplus. A failure to reach an agreement means that the employees will go on strike, or the employer will lock out the employees. When this occurs, the employees have no income, and the employers earn no profit. How can this make any sense?

We can examine this question in the context of the 2023 strike by the Writers Guild of America (WGA). The WGA represents about 11,500 writers employed by movie and television studios. Prior to the strike, they had been negotiating with the studios on a number of issues. For one thing, the writers wanted higher pay and longer guarantees of employment. They also wanted increased residuals, which are royalties earned on reruns.

The studios have been in a cost-cutting mood. Thousands of employees have been laid off due to pressure on profits. Consequently, the studios sound reluctant to acquiesce to the WGA's demands.[18]

Whether the strike ultimately makes economic sense depends on the present value calculation. Sacrifices are made on both sides during the strike. Benefits – if any – will be realized in the future. If the present value of the flow of costs and benefits is positive, the strike was rational. If the present value is negative, then the strike will prove to have been irrational.

9.7 The Plight of Independent Contractors

FTC Commissioner Alvaro Bedoya has argued that gig workers should be allowed to form bargaining groups that look like unions. If these workers are independent contractors as the employers claim, antitrust precedent forbids collective action. But if these workers do not satisfy the Internal Revenue Service (IRS) definition of "independent contractors," then the employees would be free to form a union.[19]

The distinction between being an independent contractor and an employee is multifaceted. The IRS has offered some advice, but the dividing line is far from clear. In essence, the distinction depends on the extent of control that can be exercised by the firm paying for the services provided. The IRS examines the extent of control in three general areas: (1) behavioral control, (2) financial control, and (3) the type of relationship between the parties.

Behavioral control refers to control provided by the firm on how the worker does the job or task they are hired to do. The IRS specifically observes the instructions provided by businesses to workers on how to perform the required task.[20] Even in cases where there is no instruction provided, the IRS

---

[18] Movie and television writers are not the only employees to go on strike recently. Newsroom employees of a dozen Gannett newspapers went on a brief strike to protest Gannett's cost-cutting measures, which included substantial layoffs. The employees are demanding far higher wages and more job security.

[19] See www.bloomberglaw.com/bloomberglawnews/exp/eyJpZCI6IjAwMDAwMTg3LTZjODEtZDgxMC1hYmU3LWVkZDVmMDcwMDAwMyIsImN0eHQiOiJBVE5XIiIwidXVpZCI6IjZ5TU1CXWXRQR09ndU9VaVlUSm5SMUU9PW9tbzFvaVK0paZWJSMTFJaU5TT0xsaVVE9PSIsInRpbWUiOiIxNjgxMjExNjAyNDEwIiwic2luIjoiZzJWUm93RVNycm1hhL2JiUThLYLYU9CY2FpRkgwpPSIsInYiOiIxIn0=?isAlert=false&item=headline&region=digest&source=newsletter&advType=Alert.

[20] For example, in *Hill* v. *Pepperidge Farm*, the plaintiff delivered Pepperidge Farm products to retailers. Hill was paid a commission based on the value of the deliveries on a consignment basis. As a consignee, Hill was treated as an independent contractor

acknowledges that a business can have instructional control over a worker if the business can control aspects of the worker's performance. The IRS also looks to see if the business has provided training to the worker.

The IRS has defined evidence of financial control to be "[f]acts that show whether the business has a right to control the business aspects of the worker's job," including (1) the extent to which the worker has unreimbursed business expenses in connection with their job performance for the firm, (2) the extent of the worker's investment, (3) the extent to which the worker makes their services available to the relevant market, (4) how the firm pays the worker, and (5) the extent to which the worker can realize profit, given that an independent contractor can incur profits or losses.

The final category of examination is the type of relationship between the parties. Here, the IRS looks for evidence of the potential length of the relationship between the parties and how important the worker's labor is in the regular performance of the firm. Workers whose relationships with firms seem to be indefinite are more likely to be considered employees, as are workers whose labor is a vital part of a firm's daily operations.

Unionization is confined to employees. The goal is to give employees some countervailing power in dealing with their employers.[21] If the individuals supplying labor services are independent contractors rather than employees, they will not be permitted to form a union. In most professions – including doctors, dentists, lawyers, and architects – the members are not employees. Interestingly, mixed martial arts (MMA) fighters, as well as Uber and Lyft drivers, are also independent contractors and therefore cannot unionize.

9.7.1 Physician Collective Bargaining

Since physicians are independent contractors, they cannot unionize to bargain with powerful health insurers over reimbursement rates. If they form a group solely for the purpose of bargaining with the insurers, they will

---

by Pepperidge Farm. Hill argues that he should be considered to be an employee and pointed to Pepperidge Farm's direction and control of his efforts as being consistent with an employer–employee relationship. See *Hill* v. *Pepperidge Farm, Inc.*, No. 3:22-cv-00097 (E.D. Va. Feb. 17, 2022).

[21] A. Douglas Melamed and Steven C. Salop have proposed a limited antitrust exemption for joint negotiating entities, which would provide countervailing power for independent contractors who cannot unionize. This would be a welcome development that would level the playing field. See A. Douglas Melamed and Steven C. Salop, *An Antitrust Exemption for Workers: And Why Worker Bargaining Power Benefits Consumers, Too*, Working Paper (2023).

violate Section 1 of the Sherman Act. In the past, some physicians have sought an antitrust exemption under the state action doctrine.[22] These efforts were successful in three states – Alaska, New Jersey, and Texas. These experiments did not prove to be fruitful, and the legislation has "sunset."

9.7.2 Uber's Drivers

The drivers for Uber and its major rival, Lyft, are not employees. Instead, they are independent contractors. For the companies, there are two major advantages to relying on independent contractors. First, and probably foremost, the drivers for Uber and Lyft may not unionize. Only employees are permitted to form a union. Since independent contractors are not employees, unionization is not an option. The drivers, therefore, have no market power in dealing with Uber and Lyft. Second, since the drivers are not employees, neither Uber nor Lyft incurs payroll taxes. In addition, the drivers must cover their own health insurance and retirement plans. The unorganized drivers, of course, are worse off on both counts.

Uber has long considered its drivers to be independent contractors and therefore not entitled to minimum wages, overtime pay, and employer-sponsored benefits. In 2019, Uber settled a class action lawsuit on behalf of 15,000 California and Massachusetts drivers for $20.0 million. It settled a second suit with 1,322 drivers for $8.4 million. The company still regards its drivers as independent contractors.[23]

9.7.3 Individual Sports

In individual sports – boxing, golf, MMA, and tennis – the athletes are independent contractors. Each athlete is on their own to bargain over compensation and working conditions. Some individuals – the big-name stars of the sport – will have more negotiating power than the younger performers and therefore can negotiate better terms. But this is not always the case.

---

[22] For a law and economics analysis, see Roger D. Blair and Jill Boylston Herndon, Physician Cooperative Bargaining Ventures: An Economic Analysis, 71 *Antitrust Law Journal* 853 (2004); and Roger D. Blair and Kristine L. Coffin, Physician Collective Bargaining: State Legislation and the State Action Doctrine, 26 *Cardozo Law Review* 101 (2005).

[23] The fact that Uber settled their litigation is not evidence that Uber is wrong about the status of their drivers. Settling a lawsuit is a business decision. If the expected value of litigating to the plaintiffs is less than the expected cost to the defendant, the case should settle.

In golf, for example, a tournament attracted more attention and greater attendance when Tiger Woods participated than when he was absent. Presumably, the tournament sponsors would have been willing to pay an appearance fee to Tiger Woods. But this was not permitted. The PGA Tour, which is the organizing body, forbids paying appearance fees. A golfer must win their money on the golf course.

In MMA, things are different. A young fighter, or one with limited experience and no celebrity status, may earn as little as $20,000 for a fight, while a celebrity may earn $500,000. Both fighters, however, are independent contractors.

9.7.4 Summary

There is a growing concern for gig workers who are independent contractors but are at the mercy of powerful "employers." Uber and Lyft drivers may be independent contractors, but they claim to be abused by their respective ride sharing firms. If these drivers could bargain collectively for better compensation, they would be more successful since no one driver has any bargaining power.

Some legal scholars have argued that the labor exemption in Section 6 of the Clayton Act is not limited to employees although it has been interpreted that way. There is a chink in the armor – at least in the First Circuit.

Jockeys in Puerto Rico are independent contractors. Dissatisfied with their compensation, they agreed to strike, that is, to withhold their services. This action was challenged as a Section 1 Sherman Act violation. In the First Circuit, the key question regarding the antitrust status of the collective action by the jockeys was not whether they were independent contractors. Instead, the issue is whether the conflict is over the compensation of the jockeys for their labor services. In *Confederación Hipica de Puerto Rico* v. *Confederación de Jinetes Puertorriqueños*, the First Circuit ruled that this collective action to obtain better pay was protected by the labor exemption.[24]

Areeda and Hovenkamp have suggested that the First Circuit's decision should apply to Uber drivers.[25] They provide labor services to Uber's customers. The only stumbling block involves the fact that they also provide the use of their own vehicles.

---

[24] *Confederación Hipica de Puerto Rico Inc.* v. *Confederación de Jinetes Puertorriqueños, Inc.*, 30 F.4th 306, 314 (1st Cir. 2022), *cert denied*, 143 S. Ct. 631 (2023).

[25] Phillip Areeda and Herbert Hovenkamp, *Antitrust Law*, 2023 Supplement, 255d (2023).

9.8 Concluding Remarks

The importance of unions in the labor market has been declining for decades. This is not because employees have acquired more power in the market. Rather, it is due in part to a change in the composition of the economy, and in part to some major employers taking steps to reduce the need for union bargaining. When an employer offers good wages and benefits, reasonable hours, and safe working conditions, that firm's employees are less likely to need the promises of union organizers.

Employers would prefer to avoid having their workforce unionized. This, of course, is understandable as unions enhance the economic power of the employees. Large employers such as Amazon and Starbucks have been resisting unionization with mixed success amid a certain amount of criticism.

10

Monopsony and Merger Policy

10.1 Introduction

Mergers – both horizontal and vertical – raise competitive issues due to the resulting change in market structure. In the United States, merger policy is governed by Section 7 of the Clayton Act and its judicial interpretation.[1] In most instances, the competitive concern is with possible increases in market power in the output market, which may result in higher prices, lower output, and reduced quality or fewer product choices. In this chapter, our concern is with the development or enhancement of monopsony power in the labor market.[2]

A merger of employers may increase the new firm's ability to depress compensation below the pre-merger level. In this event, employees are worse off, but so are consumers. Compensation is reduced by decreasing employment levels, which will reduce output and consequently lead to higher output prices. In other circumstances, an otherwise unobjectionable merger may have unintended consequences in the labor market, which may render it unlawful.

We begin our analysis with a review of Section 7 of the Clayton Act's language in Section 10.2. We also examine the role of the Hart-Scott-Rodino amendment that requires pre-merger notification. In Section 10.3, we argue that mergers to monopsony may not be entirely rational, that is, profit maximizing for all firms. In Section 10.4, we focus on the intended and unintended consequences of merger to monopsony. In Section 10.5, we turn our attention to a merger that may increase monopsony power but

---

[1] 15 U.S.C. Section 18.
[2] Firms can hire labor services but cannot own the laborers, in contrast to other input suppliers. Consequently, we center our attention on horizontal mergers.

also improves efficiency, which means that there will be a welfare trade-off. Section 10.6 discusses antitrust standing and damages for victims of merger to monopsony. In Section 10.7, we discuss some real-world examples, and we close with some concluding remarks in Section 10.8.

10.2 Mergers and Antitrust Policy

Historically, a proposed horizontal merger was evaluated by either the Department of Justice (DOJ) or the Federal Trade Commission (FTC) on the basis of its likely impact in the output market. Recently, however, mergers are being analyzed for their effects in the labor market.[3]

Section 7 of the Clayton Act is a prophylactic measure designed to prevent changes in market structure that may facilitate collusion or noncompetitive unilateral behavior. Specifically, Section 7 holds that:

No person engaged in commerce ... shall acquire, directly or indirectly, the whole or any part of the stock or ... the whole or any part of the assets of another person engaged also in any activity affecting commerce, where in any line of commerce ... in any section of the country, the effect of such acquisition may be substantially to lessen competition, or to tend to create a monopoly.[4]

There are some critical features of Section 7. First, a successful plaintiff must define the relevant product or service market and the relevant geographic market. Second, the plaintiff must offer evidence to support an inference of negative consequences for social welfare due to either coordinated or unilateral monopsonistic effects *before* they occur.

When the merger – either horizontal or vertical – involves buyers, the concern centers on mergers that may substantially lessen competition on the buying side or tend to create a monopsony. The potential welfare losses of monopsony are analogous to those of monopoly and therefore are the proper concern of Section 7.[5]

Given the prophylactic nature of Section 7, the assessment of competitive effect ordinarily takes place before a merger is consummated. The reason is simple: it is easier to intervene before the eggs have to be unscrambled.

---

[3] Angerhofer and Blair provide some suggestions for such analyses and identify some problems. See Tirza J. Angerhofer and Roger D. Blair, Considerations of Buyer Power in Merger Review, 10 *Journal of Antitrust Enforcement* 260 (2022).
[4] 15 U.S.C. Section 18.
[5] See, for example, Roger D. Blair and Jeffrey L. Harrison, Antitrust Policy and Monopsony, 76 *Cornell Law Review* 297 (1991).

The actual pre-merger market structure is compared to the anticipated post-merger market structure, and inferences are drawn regarding the probable economic effect. The language of Section 7 and the structural analysis usually employed in evaluating proposed mergers make it difficult to mount an efficiencies defense when there is a presumption that the merger under review is likely to be anticompetitive.

If a merger would result in a monopsony or a substantial increase in buyer concentration, the Clayton Act would appear to condemn such a merger irrespective of any efficiencies.[6] After all, Section 7 clearly forbids a merger that "may ... substantially ... lessen competition or ... tend to create a [monopsony]." In spite of Section 7's language, however, efficiency considerations have crept into antitrust merger analysis.[7] The possibility that an apparently objectionable merger may result in procompetitive efficiencies has been recognized *in principle*.[8] In practice, however, the efficiencies defense has been largely academic.[9]

10.2.1 The Hart-Scott-Rodino Act

For decades, the DOJ and the FTC found out about mergers after they were consummated. Following the consummation of a merger, the business activities of the entities would be integrated and one of the merging parties would lose its identity. This made it difficult to avoid a competitively objectionable merger.

In 1976, Congress passed the Hart-Scott-Rodino Act, which requires pre-merger notification of an impending merger for acquisitions that exceed the threshold announced by the FTC.[10] This threshold is often

---

[6] Scott Hemphill and Nancy L. Rose, Mergers that Harm Sellers, 127 *Yale Law Journal* 2078 (2018) argue that a merger that creates monopsony power violates Section 7 of the Clayton Act.

[7] The 2010 Guidelines address efficiency considerations in Section 10.

[8] Although the Supreme Court has not endorsed the efficiency defense, most lower courts recognize that efficiencies are important considerations in assessing the lawfulness of a proposed merger. See, for example, *Federal Trade Commission v. Staples, Inc.*, 970 F. Supp. 1066, 1087 (1997).

[9] See, for example, Joseph Farrell and Carl Shapiro, Horizontal Mergers: An Equilibrium Analysis, 80 *American Economic Review* 107 (1990); Joseph Farrell and Carl Shapiro, Scale Economies and Synergies in Horizontal Merger Analysis, 68 *Antitrust Law Journal* 685 (2001); Gregory J. Werden, Luke M. Froeb, and Steven Tschantz, The Effects of Merger Efficiencies on Consumers of Differentiated Products, 1 *European Competition Journal* 245 (2005); Gregory J. Werden, An Economic Analysis of Merger Efficiencies, 12 *Antitrust* 1 (2007).

[10] The official rules for pre-merger notification are as follows: "If the transaction is valued at $50 million (as adjusted) or less, no filing is required. If the transaction is valued at more

referred to as the "$50 million (as adjusted)" threshold because it started at $50 million and is now adjusted annually for inflation. In 2023, the threshold was announced to be $111.4 million.[11] This gave the DOJ or the FTC time to review the proposed merger before it could be consummated. If the agency reviewing the proposed merger found competitive concerns, it would advise the parties that the merger would be challenged.

In most cases, one of two things would happen. First, the parties might decide to abandon the merger. Second, the parties might reach an agreement with the DOJ or the FTC on how to reduce their competitive concerns. Since most proposed mergers go unchallenged, are abandoned, or proceed following negotiations with either the DOJ or the FTC, there is very little litigation. This means that there are few judicial opinions that could provide some guidance on which mergers are lawful and which are unlawful.

10.2.2 Horizontal Merger Guidelines

The most recent horizontal merger guidelines were issued jointly by the DOJ and the FTC in 2010.[12] They are being revised at the time of this writing. The agencies addressed the issue of monopsony in Section 12, which provides the following guidance:

Market power on the buying side of the market is not a significant concern if suppliers have numerous attractive outlets for their goods or services. However, when that is not the case, the Agencies may conclude that the merger of competing buyers is likely to lessen competition in a manner harmful to sellers.[13]

When evaluating the effect on competition, the agencies claimed that a short-run reduction in quantity purchased resulting from a merger is not the best indicator of the effects of the merger on market power. The DOJ and FTC instead claimed to look at the effects of the merger wholistically, rather than strictly focusing on the competitive effects on the downstream markets in which the merged firms sell.

---

than $200 million (as adjusted), and no exemption applies, an HSR filing must be made and parties must wait until the statutory waiting period has expired before closing the deal. If the transaction is valued in excess of $50 million (as adjusted) but is $200 million (as adjusted) or less, only those transactions that also meet the size of person test require a filing." See www.ftc.gov/enforcement/premerger-notification-program/hsr-resources/steps-determining-whether-hsr-filing.

[11] See www.ftc.gov/enforcement/competition-matters/2023/02/hsr-threshold-adjustments-reportability-2023.

[12] See www.justice.gov/atr/horizontal-merger-guidelines-08192010.

[13] *Ibid.* at Section 12.

In a monopsony case, defining the relevant antitrust market takes some care. The broader the market definition, the smaller any one firm's share will be. Conversely, the narrower the market definition, the higher will any individual firm's share be. Thus, market definition is crucial in evaluating the competitive effect of a merger among employers.

In a monopsony context, the focus shifts from adopting the employer's point of view to that of the employee's point of view. To determine the size of the relevant antitrust market, we must consider all potential other uses for the services being provided by the employee. If there are many alternative uses for the employee's labor services, the employees will just turn to other employers if there is a suppression of wages by an employer or a group of employers in one market.

For mergers of producers, the Horizontal Merger Guidelines employ the SSNIP test. If a hypothetical monopolist could impose a "small but significant non-transitory increase in price" without losing so many customers that the price increase is unprofitable, then the collection of products or the sources of supply would constitute a relevant antitrust market. Naidu and Posner adapted this logic to the case of monopsony.

The SSNRW test asks whether a monopsonist could impose a "small, but significant non-transitory reduction in wages" without losing so many employees that the wage decrease would be unprofitable. If so, that set of employees constitutes a relevant antitrust labor market. For example, suppose that a monopsonist who employs fast food workers at burger restaurants reduced the wage paid by a small amount. If that reduction resulted in so many resignations that the wage decrease was unprofitable, then that set of employees would not constitute a relevant labor market.

Ordinarily, "small, but significant" means 5 percent and "non-transitory" means one year. The SSNRW test sounds like a reasonable, practical accommodation for an extremely important part of the determination of the relevant antitrust market. But we should not lose sight of the fact that it is purely hypothetical. The inferences that are drawn may be based on experience and empirical observations in other markets, but they are not usually based on empirical evidence from the market under consideration.

10.2.3 Exemption

Some mergers may be exempt from antitrust policy under state laws. For example, hospital mergers may be protected from antitrust scrutiny if a state agency issues a Certificate of Public Advantage (COPA). The FTC has examined the consequences of mergers that are protected by COPAs and

found undesirable effects. Following the mergers, hospital charges tend to
rise while compensation for nurses, pharmacists, and other non-medically
skilled workers tends to fall. The economic results are undesirable for
patients and their insurers. Unfortunately, this is only one example of state
action that may be woefully misguided.

10.3 Merger to Monopsony

If all employers in a local labor market merge, the previously competitive
labor market will become one of monopsony.[14] The economic results will
be good for the newly merged employers, but undesirable for everyone else.
This is relatively easy to show.

In Figure 10.1, VMP_L is the sum of the value of the marginal product curves for the employers in the local labor market. Thus, the VMP_L
represents the demand for labor. The supply of labor in the market is

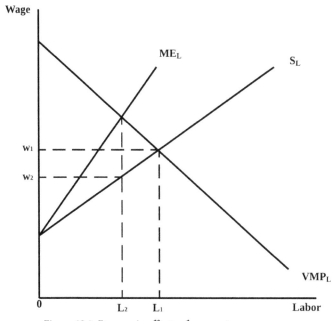

Figure 10.1 Economic effects of merger to monopsony

[14] This section builds on the insights of George J. Stigler, Monopoly and Oligopoly by
Merger, 40 *American Economic Review* 23 (1950). See also Roger D. Blair, Merger to
Monopsony: An Efficiencies Defense, 55 *Antitrust Bulletin* 689 (2010).

shown as S_L. Prior to the merger, the competitive wage was w_1 and the total employment was equal to L_1.

Once a firm is acquired, it is no longer an independent firm. Instead, it becomes a production site, and its operation is dictated by the management of the acquiring firm. Following the merger of the employers, the sole employer is a monopsonist. To maximize its profit, the employer will operate where the marginal expenditure on labor (ME_L) and VMP_L are equal.[15] At this equality, the employment level will fall from L_1 to L_2, which causes the wage to fall from w_1 to w_2. While the employer's profits rise, fewer workers are hired, those who are hired earn less, total output falls since fewer inputs are employed, and output prices must rise.

As a result of these undesirable economic consequences, the DOJ or the FTC may object to such a merger. Section 7 of the Clayton Act clearly forbids a horizontal merger that may substantially lessen competition in any line of commerce in any section of the country. A merger among employers that creates a monopsony obviously hinders competition in the local labor market and thereby violates Section 7.

If the merger has already been consummated, either the DOJ or the FTC can still challenge the legality of the merger. The problem is figuring out how to "unscramble the eggs." If the merger has not been consummated, it can be enjoined.

10.3.1 Feasibility of Merger to Monopsony

It will prove difficult to convince all the employers to join the merging firms. This can be seen in Figure 10.2, which depicts a single firm with its value of the marginal product of labor (vmp_L). At the competitive wage of w_1, the firm hires l_1 units of labor services. It enjoys employer surplus equal to area abw_1. If it merges with the other employers, employment will be curtailed, and the wage will fall to w_2. To make this lower wage stick, this employer and all the others will have to reduce employment to l_2. If the firm depicted in Figure 10.2 refuses to merge, profit maximization will lead this employer to expand its employment from l_1 to l_3 where its vmp_L equals the suppressed wage of w_2. At this employment level, the outsider's employer surplus soars to the area acw_2. In contrast, if the firm had merged, its employer surplus would have increased, but only to area $adew_2$, which is clearly smaller than area acw_2.

---

[15] See Chapter 2 for a more complete analysis of profit maximization by a monopsonist.

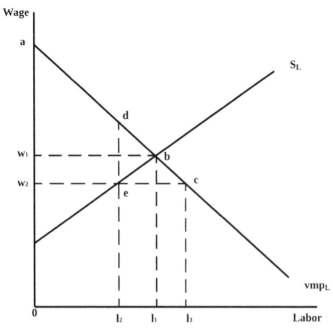

Figure 10.2 A firm earns more profit by not merging

10.4 Consequences of Merger to Monopsony

In some instances, employers merge to create monopsony power in the labor market.[16] If they are successful, the economic effects are predictable. Profit maximization will lead the merged firm to reduce employment below the sum of the pre-merger levels of the independent firms. If the labor supply function is positively sloped, the reduction in employment results in a wage reduction. The firm's profit rises while the quantity of output falls. Social welfare falls since the value of labor's marginal product exceeds the wage paid, that is, there is a misallocation of resources – too little labor is employed. There is also a redistribution of wealth – some employee surplus is converted into employer surplus.

These are the intended consequences of merger to monopsony in a labor market. There are, however, unintended consequences.

---

[16] For example, the University of Pittsburgh Medical Center (UPMC) employs over 90,000 workers in its sprawling 40-hospital network in western Pennsylvania. Allegedly, it has a 75 percent share in the relevant labor markets. UPMC is the product of a series of hospital mergers, which has given UPMC the power to suppress wages and impose noncompete agreements.

10.4.1 Consequences in the Output Market

Before the firms in the labor market merged, they operated where demand for labor services, VMP_L, was equal to the industry supply of labor, S_L, as shown in Figure 10.1. The resulting competitive wage and level of employment were w_1 and L_1, respectively.

Merger to monopsony in the labor market causes employment to fall to L_2 with a corresponding drop in the wage rate to w_2. The reduction in employment results in fewer units of output being produced. Since the demand for the output is negatively sloped, output price will rise when quantity falls.

Even though the merging firms may not have intended to influence price in the output market, restricting employment of labor did precisely that.

10.4.2 Consequences for Complementary Inputs

The exercise of monopsony power involves a reduction in the quantity of labor employed. This reduces the demands for all complementary inputs.[17]

To illustrate the effects in the output market, we had previously assumed that other input prices were constant, which is customary in partial equilibrium analysis. The monopsonist, however, would naturally decrease the quantity of other inputs used in response to the decrease in employees. In our model, we treat other inputs as complementary inputs, that is, the quantity demanded of other inputs is directly related to the number of employees.

This relationship operates through the employer's production function. Thus, a reduction in labor employed reduces the marginal productivity of all complementary inputs, which causes the cartel's demands for those inputs to fall, that is, shift to the left from D_1 to D_2 as is shown in Figure 10.3. If the supply curves of the complements, as denoted by MC_I, are positively sloped, the fall in demand will lead to reduced prices of those inputs. The consequences of this action are clear. The prices of complementary inputs are depressed and a social welfare loss, represented by area abc, is created. Some of the input suppliers' surplus, that is, area w_1dcw_2, is transferred to the employer as profit.

---

[17] Sugato Bhattacharyya and Amrita Nain, Horizontal Acquisitions and Buying Power: A Product Market Analysis, 99 *Journal of Financial Economics* 97 (2011) find evidence that consolidation has impacts further up the supply chain.

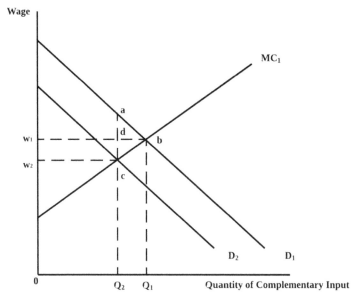

Figure 10.3 Reducing employment of labor causes the demand for complements to fall

The economic significance of the unintended consequence depends on the circumstances, that is, the amount of harm depends on the elasticity of the supply. If the newly merged firm's use of the complements is small in comparison with the entire market, the economic consequences will be minimal. For example, the merger may have a substantial impact on the local labor market but a negligible impact on the capital market, which is much broader.

If two hospitals merge and thereby acquire monopsony power in the nurse labor market, this will yield the results that we have described in Figure 10.3. This reduction in the employment of nurses will cause the demands for complementary inputs to be reduced. These demand shifts may have imperceivable effects in the market for hospital linens, plastic cups, and dressings. The effect on the local labor market for orderlies, however, may be far more pronounced.

Not all mergers have monopsonistic consequences, and some that do have adverse effects do not affect all categories of labor equally. An excellent empirical example is provided by Elena Prager and Matt Schmidt.[18] Prager and Schmidt examined the economic impact of hospital mergers

---

[18] Elena Prager and Matt Schmidt, Employer Consolidation and Wages: Evidence from Hospitals, 111 *American Economic Review* 397 (2021).

on the wages of three categories of workers: (1) those with general skills that could easily move to non-hospital settings, (2) those with specialized skills that are not unique to hospital settings, and (3) those with hospital-specific skills. Irrespective of employer concentration, those with general skills were unaffected by mergers. This makes economic sense since the newly merged hospital has no leverage over these workers. Their supply elasticity is very large. For those in the other categories, hospital mergers adversely affected their wages, but only when the post-merger employer concentration was substantial. As one would expect, the impact was most severe for those with hospital-specific skills.

10.5 Efficiency Considerations

Mergers among employers may raise competitive concerns when they result in monopsony power.[19] In some instances, the merging parties will experience efficiencies that cannot be realized by less restrictive means. These *merger-specific* efficiencies may offset the competitive concerns in some instances, but not in others. Here, we extend the welfare trade-off presented by Williamson to the case of monopsony.[20] In so doing, we clarify a possibly misunderstood aspect of the welfare analysis of cost savings.

When formerly competing employers merge, concentration on the employing side of the relevant market necessarily increases to some extent, which depends on the relative sizes of the merging firms. If the merger yields merger-specific efficiencies, one of three things is likely to happen.

First, if the market is unconcentrated before and after the merger, this sort of merger poses no antitrust concerns. Given the pre-merger and post-merger market structure, this merger would not attract much – if any – attention from the agencies.

Second, the merger could alter the market structure in such a way that noncompetitive pricing would occur, but the post-merger wages would still be above the pre-merger wages due to substantial efficiencies. In this case, the efficiencies cause the derived demand for labor to shift enough so that the post-merger monopsony compensation exceeds the pre-merger competitive wage. If these efficiencies are merger-specific, then this merger should still be applauded because employees benefit from higher wages

---

[19] This analysis applies equally to monopsony in markets for non-labor inputs.

[20] Oliver E. Williamson, Economies as an Antitrust Defense: The Welfare Tradeoffs, 58 *American Economic Review* 18 (1968). Williamson analyzed a horizontal merger that resulted in cost savings owing to productive efficiencies but also resulted in an output price increase. Thus, we see a trade-off between cost savings and allocative inefficiency.

and higher employment. The fact that wages are below the new competitive level is bothersome, but employees are still better off on balance. By hypothesis, the efficiencies are not obtainable without the merger, so we are better off with the merger than without it.

The third and most interesting possibility involves the Williamson trade-off as adapted to monopsony. In this case, merger-specific efficiencies reduce the transaction costs of the employers, but the increase in market concentration is sufficient to result in a wage and employment level of labor services below the pre-merger level.

More specifically, we are considering the situation in which the employers employ labor to provide a final good that is sold to consumers. The demand for labor is derived from the demand for the final good. If the cost of transforming the intermediate good into a final good falls, then the derived demand for labor will shift to the right, that is, the intermediate good becomes more valuable to the buyers of that input. In this case, transactional efficiencies lead to a shift in the derived demand for the labor services in question. The economic effects are illustrated in Figure 10.4.

The pre-merger wage (w_1) and quantity of labor services employed (L_1) are determined by the equality of the derived demand for labor (VMP_L) and supply (S_L). The efficiencies resulting from the merger of buyers lead to a shift in the derived demand for labor from VMP_L to VMP_L.' If the merger of formerly competing employers confers no monopsony power, then the quantity of labor services employed will expand to L_2 due to the increased value of the labor services. Due to the positively sloped supply, the wage rate rises from w_1 to w_2. In this case, everyone is a winner as employer surplus and employee surplus both increase. As a result, social welfare rises. Such mergers obviously should be permitted as they pose no competitive threats.

If, however, the efficiency-enhancing merger results in monopsony power, the quantity purchased will be determined by the equality of the marginal expenditure (ME_L) and the derived demand for labor (VMP_L'). In Figure 10.4, the profit maximizing quantity of labor services employed falls from L_1 to L_3 and the wage paid also falls from w_1 to w_3. As a result, there is a welfare loss due to allocative inefficiency as well as enhanced employer surplus that flows from the efficiency.[21] To be sure, there will be an increase in employer surplus that is simply a transfer from employees. But there is

---

[21] It is possible for the derived demand to shift enough for the post-merger quantity to increase despite the exercise of monopsony power. In this event, employee surplus would increase even though there would be some allocative inefficiency. This is the second possible outcome of a merger that was described earlier.

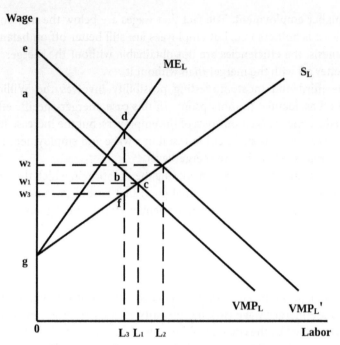

Figure 10.4 Efficiencies and changes in employment

additional employer surplus that results from the efficiency. It is only the latter that should be compared to the allocative inefficiency in evaluating the impact on social welfare.

If the lawfulness of this merger depends solely on its impact on the employees, then the merger would be unlawful due to the reduction in employee surplus from the pre-merger area w_1cg to the post-merger area w_3fg. On social welfare grounds, however, the allocative inefficiency captured by the triangular area bcf must be compared to the reduction in cost captured by the area between the two derived demand curves, that is, area abde. If the cost savings outweigh the allocative inefficiency, then the merger should be allowed; otherwise, it should not be allowed.

If the reduction in transaction costs outweighs the allocative inefficiency, the merger should not be barred. The merger is Kaldor-Hicks efficient because the winners (the employers) *could* compensate the losers (the employees) and still be better off.[22] But this need not always be

---

[22] For a discussion of Kaldor-Hicks efficiency, see Thomas J. Miceli, *The Economic Approach to Law 1–7* (2nd ed. 2009). For a more extensive treatment, see Richard E. Just, Darrel L. Hueth, and Andrew Schmitz, *The Welfare Economics of Public Policy* (2004) at 32.

the case. When the allocative inefficiency outweighs the cost saving, the merger reduces both employee welfare and social welfare. The merger is inefficient on the Kaldor-Hicks criterion because the winners cannot profitably compensate the losers. Such a merger should be forbidden. Since we cannot presume that the net effect of an efficiency-enhancing merger of rival employers will inevitably be positive or inevitably be negative, we need reliable estimates of the prospective cost savings as well as of the prospective allocative inefficiency. This is a particularly daunting requirement because both estimates are needed before the merger is actually consummated.[23] Mergers that have already been consummated can, of course, be challenged after the fact. In that event, proof of the cost saving will be possible – at least in principle – but estimating the allocative inefficiency will be no easy task.

From an economic perspective, social welfare is clearly the correct standard for evaluating economic effects. The Supreme Court, however, is not clear on this.[24] At times, the Court refers to social welfare, but it also refers to consumer welfare. In a monopsony context, however, the concern is with employee welfare rather than employer welfare. From the employee's perspective, the merger appears to be clearly undesirable. The wage paid falls, the quantity of labor services employed falls, and the employees do not appear to enjoy any benefits from the wage reduction.

10.5.1 The "Pass through" Requirement

The antitrust analysis of mergers is conducted in a partial equilibrium framework. Consequently, only the buyers and sellers in that relevant antitrust market receive any attention. In addition, the antitrust agencies focus on competitive concerns regarding price, quality, variety, and innovation. When examining mergers among sellers, the agencies have sought to protect consumers. One manifestation of this focus is the so-called "pass through" requirement in evaluating efficiencies.[25] If a merger

---

[23] This is even more complicated when the merger stops short of monopsony. In that event, the merged firm experiences cost savings while the rivals do not, but all employers realize wage decreases and higher profits. The other firms would appear to have an incentive to merge to realize similar cost savings. This could result in further decreases in wage and further antitrust enforcement issues. Moreover, if the merger turns out to be unlawful, the remedy may involve "unscrambling the eggs."

[24] See Roger D. Blair and D. Daniel Sokol, The Rule of Reason and the Goals of Antitrust: An Economic Approach, 78 *Antitrust Law Journal* 471 (2012) for a brief analysis.

[25] See www.justice.gov/atr/horizontal-merger-guidelines-08192010 at Section 10. See also Paul L. Yde and Michael G. Vita, Merger Efficiencies: Reconsidering the Passing-On

among competing sellers is presumptively anticompetitive based on the market structure, merger-specific efficiencies can only save the day if they will reduce marginal cost enough so that profit maximizing behavior of the merged firm will not result in a price increase above the pre-merger level. This, of course, means that there is no room for the Williamson welfare trade-off. In some cases, then, consumer welfare will be promoted at the expense of social welfare.

By analogy, we may infer that a similar "pass through" requirement will pertain to mergers among employers. In such cases, the efficiency must be sufficient so that profit maximization does not lead to lower quantities of labor services employed and lower wages paid. The merger illustrated in Figure 10.4 resulted in a post-merger wage (w_3) below the pre-merger wage (w_1). The "pass through" requirement was not met and, therefore, the merger would be challenged. The employees in Figure 10.4 will be protected at the sacrifice of social welfare.

10.6 Antitrust Damages

In general, the economic consequences of an antitrust violation ripple through the economy. Those who are injured in their business or property by reason of the violation have suffered antitrust injury according to the Supreme Court's ruling in *Brunswick*.[26]

This, however, is not sufficient to have antitrust standing to pursue antitrust damages under Section 4 of the Clayton Act. While the language of Section 4 is expansive as it applies to:

[a]ny person who shall be injured by reason of anything forbidden in the antitrust laws,[27]

the Supreme Court has narrowed the coverage to *direct* victims.[28] The direct victims of an unlawful merger may be the employees.

In some instances, a merger between the employers may go unchallenged by the DOJ and the FTC since the newly merged firm will have no appreciable power in the output market. Nonetheless, the merger may have significant adverse economic effects in the local labor market. Consequently, those employees who experience reduced compensation following the

---

Requirement, 64 *Antitrust Law Journal* 735 (1995); Paul L. Yde and Michael Vita, Merger Efficiencies: The Passing-On Fallacy, 20 *Antitrust* 59 (2005).

[26] *Brunswick Corp.* v. *Pueblo Bowl-O-Mat, Inc.*, 429 U.S. 477 (1977).

[27] 15 U.S.C. Section 15.

[28] *Illinois Brick Co.* v. *Illinois*, 431 U.S. 720 (1977).

merger may sue for the underpayment that they have suffered. The antitrust damages are measured by:

comparison of profits, prices and values as affected by the [antitrust violation], with what they would have been in its absence under freely competitive conditions.[29]

In more formal terms, antitrust damages (Δ) for the underpaid workers are given by:

$$\Delta = \left(w_{bf} - w_a \right) L_a,$$

where w_{bf} is the wage that would have been paid "but for" the unlawful merger, w_a is the wage actually paid, and L_a is the number of employees in the class. If this sum is proven at trial, the total award will be equal to three times that amount plus the costs of litigation including a reasonable attorney's fee.

Clearly, the intended victims of merger to monopsony have standing to redress their injuries. Sadly, this is not the case for the unintended victims. They are neither foreclosed employers nor underpaid employees. In other words, they are not one of the favored classes of antitrust plaintiffs.[30] A merger to monopsony in the labor market that reduces employment tends to reduce output, which in turn increases prices for consumers and decreases employment of other inputs. The overcharged consumers and other input suppliers who face suppressed compensation, however, do not have standing to pursue antitrust damages. Additionally, the now merged employers may keep some of their ill-gotten gains since they are not required to compensate the unintended victims.

Neither the overcharged consumers nor the underpaid suppliers of complementary inputs have standing to pursue antitrust damages. They are the victims of an antitrust violation even though it was not aimed at them. They are innocent bystanders and deserve protection. Additionally, the employers should be held to account for the full damages that they have imposed.

When employers merge, they reduce both the wage paid and the total employment. The now merged employers experience higher profits at the expense of their employees. Those intended consequences are vulnerable to private damage actions by the direct victims. The unintended victims,

---

[29] *Bigelow* v. *RKO Radio Pictures, Inc.*, 327 U.S. 251, 264 (1946).
[30] For a more complete analysis of the classes of victims of monopsony, see Brianna L. Alderman and Roger D. Blair, The Antitrust Victims of Monopsony, *Journal of Antitrust Enforcement* (2023); and Chapter 5.

that is, the overcharged consumers and underpaid suppliers of complementary inputs, do not currently have standing to sue. Antitrust standing should be granted to both the intended and unintended victims so that employers who acquire monopsony power by merging will be responsible for the entire cost of their illicit conduct.

10.7 Merger and Monopsony in Action

There are several examples of horizontal mergers that aroused concerns regarding the exercise of monopsony power. In this section, we examine two of those merger cases. First, we review the proposed merger between two health insurers, Anthem and Cigna. This merger was denied on competitive concerns in the insurance market but could have been denied on competitive concerns in purchasing services from health care providers. Second, we analyze the District Court decision in the Penguin Random House case. This decision barred the major publishing house from acquiring Simon & Schuster on monopsony concerns.

10.7.1 Anthem–Cigna Merger

Health insurers operate in geographic markets determined by state boundaries.[31] In 2015, two major insurance companies, Anthem Inc. and Cigna Corp., agreed to merge in a $54 billion deal. At the time, Anthem and Cigna were the second and third largest health insurers in the United States and competed on a regular basis.[32] Anthem was the largest of thirty-six insurers in the Blue Cross Blue Shield Association, owned an exclusive license in fourteen states to do business under the Blue Cross brand, and had about 39 million members. In certain local markets, Anthem's market share was even larger due to reduced competition. Although Cigna was the third largest health insurer, it was considerably smaller than Anthem, with some 13 million policyholders in the United States. It competed with Anthem, which leveraged its size to negotiate steep discounts with its in-network providers, through innovative health care plans and better customer service. Cigna's plans included value-based alternatives that would incentivize

---

[31] *U.S.* v. *Anthem, Inc., and Cigna Corporation*, No. 1:16-cv-01493 (D.D.C. July 21, 2016). Part of this section is derived from Chapter 18 of Tirza J. Angerhofer, Roger D. Blair, and Christine Piette Durrance, *Antitrust Policy in Healthcare Markets* (2022).

[32] At about the same time, Humana and Aetna, two other dominant health insurance companies, had also agreed to merge. If both of the mergers had been consummated, there would have been only three major health insurers rather than five.

hospitals and doctors to focus on good patient outcomes. Cigna's revenue grew on average by 13 percent in the six years before 2015. Anthem and Cigna competed for national and individual accounts as well as access to health care providers on the basis of price, customer service, care management, wellness programs, and reputation.

The proposed merger of Anthem and Cigna would have increased the newly merged firm's share of the covered lives in various local geographic markets. This consolidation necessarily would have increased the insurer's share of the total purchases of health care services from doctors and hospitals in those markets. The DOJ recognized the competitive problems that this would create, claiming that:

> Anthem's high market shares already give it significant bargaining leverage with doctors and hospitals. In the same 35 metropolitan areas referenced above, this merger would substantially increase Anthem's ability to dictate the reimbursement rates it pays providers, threatening the availability and quality of medical care. The merger also would deprive both providers and consumers of Cigna's innovative efforts to work cooperatively with providers and enter into "value-based" contracts that reward them for improving patient health and lowering cost.[33]

Anthem and Cigna compete with one another to attract doctors, hospitals, and other health care providers to their networks. The DOJ explained that:

> Anthem and Cigna, like other commercial health insurers, compete to sign up doctors, hospitals, and other healthcare providers for their networks. Competition in this market is the mirror image of competition in the markets discussed above. Insurers compete by offering healthcare providers access to greater numbers of patients, more generous reimbursement terms, better service, and more innovative collaborations. The proposed merger will eliminate this competition between Anthem and Cigna and likely lead to lower reimbursement rates, less access to medical care, reduced quality, and fewer value-based provider collaborations.[34]

The DOJ alleged that the proposed merger would have undesirable economic effects due to enhanced monopsony power. The DOJ alleged that Anthem already had substantial leveraging power with doctors and hospitals due to its large share of commercial patients. By merging with Cigna, the DOJ argued that the newly merged Anthem-Cigna:

> likely would reduce the rates that both types of providers earn by providing medical care to their patients. This reduction in reimbursement rates likely would lead to a reduction in consumers' access to medical care.[35]

---

[33] *Ibid.* at ¶8(d).
[34] *Ibid.* at ¶64.
[35] *Ibid.* at ¶71–72.

At trial, the Court's attention was centered on the anticipated economic effects on competition in the health insurance market. On this basis alone, the Court barred the Anthem–Cigna merger. Unfortunately, it did not address the monopsony allegation. In the Penguin case, however, the sole focus was on monopsony.

10.7.2 Monopsony in Book Publishing

There are five major book publishers that account for approximately 91.0 percent of the market for anticipated top-selling books, that is, books whose authors receive minimum advances of $250,000. Penguin Random House (PRH) is the largest book publisher in the United States. In 2020, Penguin offered to buy Simon & Schuster (S&S), the third largest publisher, for $2.18 billion. When PRH and S&S proposed merging, the DOJ objected and filed suit in Federal District Court. Interestingly, the DOJ did not object on the basis of concentration in book publishing. Instead, the DOJ challenged the proposed acquisition of S&S by PRH solely on monopsony grounds.

As in most merger challenges, the market definition was critical to the DOJ's success. The DOJ defined the "product" market to be the publishing rights to anticipated top-selling books. Although there are many books written for general audiences that consumers might view as perfect substitutes for anticipated top-sellers, publishing rights to those books were not included in the definition proposed by the DOJ.

The pre-merger market for trade books in the United States was dominated by the so-called Big Five: PRH, HarperCollins Publishers, S&S, Hachette Book Group, and Macmillan Publishers. If the merger had been consummated, the combined PRH and S&S would have had book sales of more than $3.26 billion while publishing about 3,000 new titles each year.

Book proposals, partial manuscripts, and completed drafts are offered to multiple publishers in an effort to generate contract offers from competing publishers. Several contract terms are important to the author, but the single most important term is the advance. In most cases, the advance is paid in four installments: (1) 25 percent upon signing, (2) 25 percent upon delivery and acceptance of the manuscript, (3) 25 percent upon publishing, and (4) 25 percent one year after publishing.

In many instances, the royalties earned on the sales of the book do not cover the advance. In that event, the author receives no further compensation, but the author is not required to return any of the advance.

There are other contract terms that are important to authors. These include the royalty rate, audio rights, and the number and timing of the

Table 10.1 *Examples of competitive bidding*

Beginning (High) bid	Winning bid	Number of rounds
$375,000	$550,000	1
$250,000	$750,000	4
$300,000	$1.5 million	7
$400,000	$1.1 million	5
$550,000	$825,000	8
$500,000	$600,000	2
$250,000	$700,000	3
$750,000	$1.1 million	X
$750,000	$1.05 million	3
$800,000	$1.5 million	1
$750,000	$1.1 million	X

Source: U.S. v. Bertelsmann SE & CO. KGAA, No. 1:21-cv-02886 (D.D.C. Dec. 31, 2022) at 12.

installments for the advance. The size of the advance remains the single most important term in the contract.

In some cases, the advance is determined through bilateral negotiation between a single editor and an author's agent. At trial, examples of auctions were introduced that illustrated the benefit of competition. Vigorous competition among publishers can lead to advances that exceed initial offers by hundreds of thousands of dollars (Table 10.1). Thus, for authors, competition is extremely important. Bestselling authors complained that the reduced competition among the major publishers would decrease the advances paid to these authors.

PRH and S&S argued that any adverse economic effects in the relevant antitrust market would be more than offset by the merger-specific efficiencies. Allegedly, the efficiencies would be so large that the newly merged firm could pay substantially higher advances to the authors of anticipated top-selling books.

In the Horizontal Merger Guidelines, the DOJ recognizes that efficiencies can save an otherwise objectionable merger. There are, however, significant caveats. First, the efficiencies must be merger specific. In other words, the efficiencies must be unattainable in the absence of the merger. Second, the efficiencies must be verifiable, that is, they may not be speculative.

Penguin argued that its superior supply chain would increase sales for the authors of these anticpated top-sellers and reduce expenses associated with returns of unsold books. In addition, Penguin claimed that operating costs would fall, and savings would be garnered by eliminating redundancies and consolidating workspace.

Michael Pietsch, CEO of the Hachette Book Group, testified that the PRH–S&S merger would reduce the advances to authors of anticipated top-selling books. He observed that there would be fewer rounds in an auction following the merger, which would result in lower winning bids.

Stephen King, the well-known author of horror fiction, also supported the DOJ's concerns. He testified that the merger would result in lower advances for authors. The ultimate result would be fewer books and less variety since reduced advances make it more difficult for authors to support themselves during the creative process.

Jonathan Karp, CEO of S&S, conceded at trial that the number of bidders can influence the winning bid in competitive situations.

In the end, the District Court rejected the claimed efficiencies and refused to permit the publisher's expert witness to present the efficiency defense at trial. Had the merger been permitted, the newly merged firm would have been as large as the next three publishers combined. But the merger was not allowed. The DOJ prevailed at trial, and the parties decided not to appeal the District Court's ruling. S&S's parent, Paramount Global, received a $200 million breakup fee due to the merger's failure.

10.8 Concluding Remarks

Merger policy in the United States, which is captured in Section 7 of the Clayton Act, is aimed at preventing the evolution of a noncompetitive market structure. The policy concern is that a merger or a series of mergers may permit coordinated conduct or unilateral conduct that reduces consumer welfare. Historically, the focus has been on the emergence of monopoly power. Recently, however, the DOJ and the FTC have recognized that competitive problems may surface on the buying side, that is, the development of monopsony power. We have illustrated these concerns with an examination of the Anthem–Cigna merger and with the proposed acquisition of Simon & Schuster by Penguin Random House.

In our view, it is important for the DOJ and the FTC to remain vigilant when it comes to horizontal mergers that may increase monopsony power. As we have shown, the exercise of monopsony power imposes losses on input suppliers as well as final goods consumers. There are no net benefits of monopsony, so the DOJ and the FTC should strive to preserve as much competition as possible.

11

Closing Thoughts

11.1 Economic Effects of Monopsony

If an employer is a monopsonist in the labor market, it faces no competition from other employers. By definition, there are no other employers, so competition cannot exist. Employees have only two choices: work for the sole employer or not work at all. As an empirical matter, pure monopsony is extremely rare.

The polar opposite of monopsony is perfect competition. In a perfectly competitive labor market, the labor supply function is infinitely elastic, which means that an employer can hire as much or as little labor as it pleases without affecting the wage. This market structure does not exist.

It is important to understand the models of pure monopsony and perfect competition for analyzing the structure of labor markets that we observe. In most empirically imperfect labor markets, there are elements of monopsony and the exercise of monopsony power.

If there is one lesson that should come through loud and clear, it is that there is nothing good about monopsony in the labor market. All the economic consequences of monopsony are negative. Aside from the monopsonist, there are no winners.

11.1.1 Compensation and Employment

A monopsonist is not an 800-pound gorilla. Its power results from the consequences of imperfect labor markets in which the labor supply functions are positively sloped. The wage and other forms of compensation that must be paid to the employees can be controlled to some extent through the firm's employment decisions.

In a competitive labor market, the employer hires the quantity of labor that equates labor's marginal contribution to the firm's profit to the wage.

If the employer has some degree of monopsony power, however, profit maximization will lead to a reduction in employment below the competitive level. In addition, the wage paid falls from the competitive level. Thus, the exercise of monopsony power results in fewer workers being employed and reduced compensation for those who are hired.

11.1.2 Allocative Inefficiency

In a competitive market, the worker's wage is equal to their marginal contribution to the firm's profit. Hence, resources are allocated efficiently. This requires that labor be hired to the point where labor's contribution (its VMP_L) is equal to its cost (its reservation wage). Profit maximization by a monopsonist results in a gap between labor's marginal contribution and its marginal cost to society. Too few units of labor services are employed. From a social welfare perspective, some surplus is lost. Thus, monopsony and the exercise of monopsony power harms society.

11.1.3 Redistribution of Wealth

In addition to the misallocation of resources, the exercise of monopsony power converts some employee surplus to employer surplus. As a transfer within society, economists usually treat this as a wash. To the extent that we are concerned with the welfare of the labor force, this redistribution should not be ignored.

11.1.4 Output Prices

Some observers have concluded that the depression of labor's compensation will reduce the monopsonist's costs and, consequently, result in lower output prices, which would benefit consumers. This is not correct. Reduced compensation of labor results from reduced employment. With fewer units of labor, the employer's output must fall. Since demand functions are negatively sloped, reduced output leads to higher – not lower – prices. Therefore, consumers are worse off.

11.2 Is Antitrust Enforcement the Answer?

Our main focus has been on the use of antitrust enforcement to attack the monopsony problem in U.S. labor markets. Historically, antitrust enforcement has been aimed at the "monopoly problem" in output markets.

Sections 1 and 2 of the Sherman Act have taken dead aim at collusion among sellers and unilateral monopolizing conduct in the output market. Section 7 of the Clayton Act has been employed to challenge mergers that may substantially lessen competition in any line of commerce. Again, the focus has largely been on the output market.

Until recently, very few antitrust cases have involved competitive concerns in the labor market. Now, however, collusion on wages and other forms of compensation, no-poaching agreements, and noncompete clauses in employment contracts are receiving much-needed scrutiny. In addition, the effects on the labor markets of proposed mergers have gained the attention of both the Department of Justice and the Federal Trade Commission.

Additionally, when a powerful employer confronts an unorganized workforce, it may possess some measure of monopsony power. If the workers form a union, they will have countervailing power. The market structure changes from monopsony to bilateral monopoly. The economic results will be positive since employment will expand, which increases output and thereby benefits consumers. Although the wage will be determined by bargaining and, therefore, is indeterminate, the wage is bound to rise.

When independent contractors are hired by powerful employers of their services, they are vulnerable to monopsonistic practices. There seems to be a growing sentiment that they should be entitled to the labor exemption. If their collective action is permitted, they will be free of antitrust challenges. Moreover, collective action will shift the market structure from an employer with monopsony power to one of bilateral monopoly. This change has positive economic effects and should be applauded.

It is clear that monopsony in the labor market is an unavoidable hurdle, which raises many questions regarding the appropriate policy measures to try and overcome its negative effects. Naidu and Posner argue that vigorous antitrust enforcement is essential to mitigating the monopsony problem, but that antitrust enforcement is not completely up to the task.[1]

To some extent, we agree with their assessment. They (and others) argue persuasively that labor markets are monopsonistically competitive. Labor

---

[1] See Suresh Naidu and Eric A. Posner, *Antitrust-Plus: Evaluating Additional Policies to Tackle Labor Monopsony*, Roosevelt Institute (May 2020). See https://rooseveltinstitute .org/wp-content/uploads/2020/07/RI_LaborMonopsonyandtheLimitsoftheLaw_ Report_202004.pdf.

supply functions are positively sloped for a variety of reasons. For one thing, the reservation wages of workers are apt to be different across workers due to age, gender, family responsibility, family income and wealth, proximity to the work site, and a host of other factors. As a result, some measure of monopsony power will often be present. The unilateral exercise of monopsony power is not unlawful. Unilateral conduct that is not competitively unreasonable does not violate the antitrust laws.

Naidu and Posner recommend some policies that will reduce labor market frictions and thereby reduce the exercise of monopsony power that is beyond the reach of the antitrust statutes.

The problem with monopsonistically competitive labor markets is that some degree of monopsony power can be exercised unilaterally. In that event, there is no antitrust remedy. This concern is not confined to labor markets. Moreover, the concern applies to monopolistic competition in output markets as well. There are unavoidable welfare losses in both cases.

Herbert Hovenkamp has provided a compact prescription for dealing with competitive problems in labor markets:

> The best antitrust policy for labour markets is one that simultaneously makes product markets as competitive as possible by minimising high costs and high markups, and that also makes labour markets as competitive as possible by eliminating undue labour market concentration and condemning restraints that unreasonably impair labour mobility.[2]

The public policy problem with Hovenkamp's advice resides in the practical problem of implementing it. Many output markets are oligopolistic or monopolistically competitive for reasons that do not offend the antitrust laws. Firms in competitively imperfect markets produce less than they would in perfectly competitive markets and, therefore, employ less labor. There is no antitrust remedy for this.

11.2.1 The Bottom Line

Labor markets are similarly imperfect. Even with the same occupation, one employer may not be the same as another. To the extent that an employer is preferred to another, the preferred employer can exercise some monopsony power. Moreover, workers have different reservation wages and, therefore,

---

[2] Herbert Hovenkamp, *Competition Policy for Labour Markets*, OECD Roundtable on *Competition Issues in Labour Market* (2019) at ¶52. See https://one.oecd.org/document/ DAF/COMP/WD(2019)67/en/pdf.

labor supply functions are positively sloped. Hence, any employer has some measure of monopsony power. These imperfections are beyond the remedy of the antitrust laws.

The best antitrust policy for labor markets is one that simultaneously makes product markets as competitive as possible by minimizing high costs and also makes labor markets as competitive as possible by eliminating labor market concentration and concerning restraints that unreasonably limit labor mobility.

Index

For EU product safety concerns, contact us at Calle de José Abascal, 56–1°,
28003 Madrid, Spain or eugpsr@cambridge.org.

www.ingramcontent.com/pod-product-compliance
Ingram Content Group UK Ltd.
Pitfield, Milton Keynes, MK11 3LW, UK
UKHW020351140625
459647UK00020B/2411

*9 7 8 1 0 0 9 4 6 5 2 5 0 *